CONTINUITY AND INNOVATION IN THE PUBLIC LIBRARY

THE DEVELOPMENT OF A SOCIAL INSTITUTION

CONTINUITY AND INNOVATION IN THE PUBLIC LIBRARY

THE DEVELOPMENT OF A SOCIAL INSTITUTION

Edited by
Margaret Kinnell
Department of Information and Library Studies,
Loughborough University

and

Paul Sturges
Department of Information and Library Studies,
Loughborough University

Library Association Publishing
London

© This compilation: the editors 1996
© The articles: the contributors 1996

Published by
Library Association Publishing
7 Ridgmount Street
London WC1E 7AE

First published 1996

British Library Cataloguing in Publication Data
A catalogue record for this book is available from the British Library

ISBN 1-85604-134-4

Typeset from authors' disks in 10/13pt Palermo by Library Association Publishing
Printed and made in Great Britain by Bookcraft (Bath) Ltd

❖ Contents

❖ Contributors

Alistair Black is Senior Lecturer in Information and Society in the School of Management, Leeds Metropolitan University and Chair of the Library History Group of The Library Association.

John C. Crawford is Library Research Officer, Glasgow Caledonian University. He completed an MA thesis in 1981 and a PhD in 1993 on the subject of 'Historical models of librarianship: the example of Scotland'. He has also written or co-authored a range of articles and contributions, including many on library history and is a Committee member of the Library History Group.

Michael Dewe has been a Lecturer in the Department of Information and Library Studies, University of Wales, Aberystwyth, since 1975. Previously, he worked in a number of London public library systems. He has been active in IFLA's Library Buildings and Equipment Section since 1981.

Alan C. Hasson is District Librarian, Cumbernauld and Kilsyth District Council and has research and professional interests in the fields of change management, marketing of services and services to young adults.

Peggy Heeks is a Research Fellow in the Department of Information and Library Studies, Loughborough University, and has had a long association with school libraries and their support services, first, as Senior Assistant County Librarian for Berkshire and, latterly, through research undertaken at Oxford and Loughborough Universities.

Margaret Kinnell Evans is Professor of Information Studies and Head of Department in the Department of Information and Library Studies, Loughborough University. She has extensive research experience in the fields of public sector management, marketing and library management, as well as practical experience as a public librarian.

Helen E. Meller is Reader in Social History, the Department of History, University of Nottingham. Her research interests are modern urban history, with current interests in European cities, the history of modern town planning and the role of women in cities.

Robert Snape is Head of Learning Resources and Student Services, Myerscough College. His research and professional work includes a doctorate in the social history of popular reading and the leisure uses of public libraries. He has 23 years' experience in public and academic libraries and is a Diploma Member of the Institute of Leisure and Amenity Management.

Paul Sturges is Senior Lecturer in Information and Library Studies at Loughborough University since 1988, and Associate Dean (Research) in the School of Education and Humanities since 1993. Originally a historian, he has written many articles on library history. Formerly, he was Chair of the LA Library History Group (1989–91); Secretary (1987–1991) and Chair (1991–1995) of the IFLA Round Table on Library History.

Bob Usherwood is Reader in Librarianship and Information Studies in the Department of Information Studies, University of Sheffield. Previously, he was Chief Librarian of Lambeth. His research interests include library management and public policy. He is also a member of the LA Council and many professional committees.

Introduction

❖ *Margaret Kinnell and Paul Sturges*

There are few social institutions in the Britain of the mid-1990s whose existence still goes largely unchallenged, and which receive support from all shades of political opinion. Amongst formally established institutions, the church or school might claim a recognition of this kind, but the roles of both institutionalized religion and education are increasingly questioned. In an increasingly multi-faith or no-faith society the churches' hold on the moral high ground is constantly challenged and they have less and less impact at local level. Buildings which once sat at the heart of communities, and where the essential rites of passage at baptism, marriage and death were performed, are marginalized with their tiny residual congregations. Many have become warehouses, office complexes, restaurants or apartment blocks. Schools, too, no longer command automatic respect; and since the advent of grant-maintained status, a significant number no longer put their contributions to local communities at the forefront of their concerns. So-called 'educational reforms' have removed many schools from the accountability at local authority level which distinguished the British education system from many in Europe. Local management of schools and grant-maintained status have made competitors out of schools which formerly cooperated as neighbours in service to their communities.

Only the public library, of all the institutions which came to prominence in the nineteenth century, retains its local roots and accountability and continues to be used and highly regarded by a wide cross-section of the public. It has a remit to serve all segments of society and to provide for every occupation or none, and its independence of political or other pressure groups is enshrined in the professional code of ethics of its managers.

The public library's contributions to neighbourhood survival and to social cohesion are unrivalled, even by those institutions not established in the same formal sense as church or school. Informal social institutions which offered a force for cohesiveness – the pub, corner shop, community hall – are long gone from many areas, along with the life-styles which once made for a sense of belonging: to street, neighbourhood or parish. Now, whole areas are almost devoid of life during the working day leaving only the old, sick or unemployed to while away time in isolation. 'Coronation Street' and other television soap operas owe much of their appeal to a nostalgia for the chummy neighbourliness engendered by a bustling, socially active community centred on the pub, shop or local club where people met and talked, and exchanged news and local information. In many places there are only two buildings left – the post office and the library – to fulfil the functions of a neighbourhood communications switchboard. Of these, the post office is now much more like a regular retail outlet than the dispenser of services it once was, when catching up with local news along with collecting benefits formed part of every community's social networking. The local library remains as the one place owned by the community at large where people from all backgrounds can use a range of materials and services, where collective memories are housed in local history collections and where current local and wider information sources can be accessed.

The public library as independent, neutral social space and community focus is only one of its functions. As the 1993 report by the organization Comedia once more highlighted, it may be one of the more significant aspects of its continuing contribution. The study by Comedia was undertaken directly as a result of interest in the role of public institutions and civic life:

> . . . the library appeared as a key institution of contemporary civic culture, perceived to be important because:

> It was used by a wider cross-section of the local population than almost any other public, commercial or retail institution in the town centres. It was an important resource for the elderly, both for book borrowing and newspaper reading; it was an entry point for many members of ethnic minority groups (often as students or language learners) into the wider civic society; it was a focal point for children and parents as well as for school use. This broad user profile cannot be emphasized too highly.[1]

The public library's role as a key information provider and local archive, as a safe environment in which people can socialize, browse and use materials, and as a meeting point for leisure, learning and entertainment makes it unique amongst institutions. No other public, or private, service offers so much to communities and individuals within towns, villages and neighbourhoods across the country. The recent Department of National Heritage review of the public library service undertook further research into the role of the public library now and into the future and found continuing public support for retaining this breadth of free provision.[2]

From perhaps the most extensive set of user surveys undertaken on a national scale, the findings of this work are still being assimilated. The extent to which it will influence government thinking on the public library's position as a free service has yet to be judged. Certainly, it has confirmed the high regard in which a core library service is held. Adequately defining what this should be for the next century has been more difficult. Populist ideas about libraries are difficult to disentangle from the present realities and future needs. A sense of the history of the public library is essential if these are to be truly representative of local communities' aspirations.

Generations of library work have placed understanding the needs of users as a high priority, so that now the perception of libraries and librarians is embedded in popular myth: media depictions of the public library are instantly recognizable even if they are outdated and stereotypical and perpetuate an image of libraries as mainly white, middle-class institutions which lend fiction. While users from the middle classes do predominate – as with other publicly funded organizations – and fiction is indeed still the main category of material to be issued, no other service can boast 33% of the population in regular, active use, with around another 25% using the service occasionally.[3] The range of services provided is also substantial and widely used: community information, children and young people's library services, business information, school library services, services also for prisoners, for the elderly and for the housebound. Indeed, such is the success of libraries in providing a diversity of services that it can be a major difficulty for libraries to focus on primary roles and identify their core services.[4]

The age profile of users is one of the significant factors in contributing to the strength of the library's positive social function. A high proportion of the elderly and children are regular users and services to these groups have become an increasingly important part of the overall portfolio of the public library, as have services to the disadvantaged. In *The libraries' choice*, a definitive statement of good practice issued by the then Department of Education and Science in 1978, which librarians still regard as having the highest relevance today, the needs of the housebound and handicapped, prisoners, ethnic minorities, adult illiterates, and deprived areas were seen to be of central importance.[5] Service philosophies were considerably shaped by this document and public libraries have taken up its recommendations by placing continuing emphasis on community needs and support for the education and information demands of the most vulnerable in society.[6] One of the most coherent recent sets of guidelines for public library services, the *Standards for the public library service in Scotland* issued by the Convention of Scottish Local Authorities, identified similar needs and noted the most important social changes which have had an impact on library provision:

Among these changes are the growing, and consistently maintained levels of unemployment; the greater amount of leisure time available to individual members of the community, whether on a voluntary or involuntary basis; the developments which are occurring in the new technologies, resulting in the readier accessibility of information of various kinds and in various formats; the growing need for and interest in adult and continuing education; the growing awareness of the needs of the physically and mentally handicapped and disabled; the growth of awareness of the needs of ethnic minorities and the growth in the numbers of such minorities . . . [7]

The adaptability of the public library service has been perhaps one of its greatest strengths and roles have developed in response to changes in society. Yet now, government has the structures of public libraries subject to revision, through local government restructuring and, additionally, the introduction of competitive tendering. The former offers to disrupt the very closeness to community which we have argued as a vital underpinning of services and the latter threatens to diminish much of the public service ethos that has inspired libraries.[8] The impact of the last round of local government reorganization in the 1970s, which changed the map of library authorities throughout the UK and helped to give them their present pattern of use, was profound. Small, neighbouring library authorities were brought together into larger units, collections were merged and common patterns of provision developed. New allegiances between libraries and other local services were forged and committee structures changed. Management styles as well as service structures were affected. The next round is moving in a radically different direction and will be even more fundamental in its effects: together with the more business-orientated approach to library service delivery, it is anticipated that it will redefine the nature of the service yet again. Education, arts and leisure functions have been the focus for library development during the 1980s and early 1990s, with public information networks and community information provision becoming ever more significant. Technological developments have been a driving force by making links to other information suppliers and outlets increasingly possible. There is now a justifiable fear that future roles will be defined as much by central government policies as by the impetus of information technology and social needs. The environment within which public libraries function is complex, threatening and challenging.

If the future for public libraries is to be influenced by political ideology as much as social imperatives, it is important to identify those common threads of motivation which have run through the history of the British public library movement. These continue to be important to our society but they need a restatement based on fresh analysis. The time is now ripe for such an analysis.

Public libraries, in common with so many other public services, are facing a reappraisal of their effectiveness and value which takes little or no cognisance of the past and the value of principles developed over time to match services to need. Funding priorities have to be established during a period of economic stringency like the present one, so debate on core objectives and future direction for library services is essential. Understanding the historical perspective and the contribution made by the public library service to the life of the nation should be one aspect of this debate, providing the necessary context for identifying desirable goals and aspirations: a vision for the future.

Certain elements have always been significant, despite their variable importance over time. Links to education have continued to figure strongly, with the broader social benefits of an educated workforce very much at the forefront of early and later advocacy for public libraries. There was a great deal of rather ritualistic promotion of public libraries as a way of improving the working classes intellectually and morally in the interests of potential competitiveness and the amelioration of living conditions. Thus, seeking to have the Public Libraries Acts adopted in Leeds, in 1861, for example, it was argued that:

> . . . a free library, where men of all grades might resort, and from which books of an instructive and elevating character could be circulated without charge, would greatly improve the social, moral and intellectual condition of the people of this populous and important borough.[9]

The reality was more complex. The relationship between schools and public libraries, for instance, has been particularly strong ever since early branch libraries were provided in the Board schools of some cities. School library services, those services to schools provided by public libraries acting as agents of the local education authority, became the successor to some of these early schemes. The 1988 Education Reform Act and the 1993 Education Act in effect reverse this enlightened policy, one which, as John Ballinger argued in 1899, has enabled there to be:

> . . . a library in every school department. The Education authority pays for the books, renewals, and book-binding, the library authority finds the service for organization and supervision, while the teachers take charge of the books in the school and do all the work of lending, advising, and guiding the reading of children.[10]

Since this time the school librarian, in cooperation with the school library service, has achieved even more. This type of partnership between educators and librarians has also been forged in the field of continuing education; the public library's role in adult education and adult literacy work, and in the wider development of cultural activities in communities can be traced back to the very origins of the public library system. Many of the Mechanics Institutes gave not only their buildings but their book stocks to the new municipal library services. The relationship was indeed so close that it has been argued that for a while it hindered the development of wider roles for the public library.

It can be strongly maintained that the public library achieved as much, or more, for adult education, broadly defined, through its provision of fiction and other recreational material as by its direct links to formal adult education. It is this provision of recreational reading material that has formed a constant theme of opposition to public libraries. The complaint of Colonel Sibthorp as the first Public Libraries Bill was set before the House, reads remarkably like another engine of free market philosophy, the Adam Smith Institute, which has argued equally strongly against the provision of recreational fiction through public funding:[11]

> ... he supposed they would be thinking of supplying the working classes with quoits, peg-tops, and foot-ball . . . He supposed that the hon. Member and his Friends would soon be thinking of introducing the performance of Punch for the amusement of the people. The Bill was wholly uncalled for . . . [12]

At the heart of the issues surrounding public libraries, from their inception up to the present day, has been an imprecise formal definition of role. Should they be a medium of education and instruction, an information source, a cultural focus for communities, or an addition to people's leisure pursuits through the lending of fiction? All or some of these have been argued as the library's principal purpose, with advocates for each and every nuance of service development and an increasing recognition of the interdependence of the various elements of public library services. Enhanced expectations of leisure in society, with recreational reading strongly retaining its popularity, despite the attractions of television, video and computer games,[13] has, for example, been seen as placing libraries firmly within the leisure and media industry. Public libraries are now significant players in the publishing field, with sales of hardback fiction dependent on librarians' buying power. Equally, the demand for information by business, individuals and community groups within society has intensified the need for libraries to respond with effective networking and cooperation with other information providers. Isolated communities rely heavily on the information sources provided throughout their local service point; public libraries are an essential element of the national information infrastructure. We would argue that this debate has been an indication of the essential richness of the public libraries' contribution and potential contribution even if it has made it harder to lobby on their behalf. There is so much that libraries do and so much that they could do. Balancing these various demands and needs with diminishing resources has become the main concern of most library managers. At the same time, local and central government politicians have had to grapple with the conflicting demands of the different constituencies for local funding and political support.

This volume explores these and other significant issues – including the political dimension of service development – which impinge on the direction which public libraries will take in the medium and longer term. Current concerns are related to the historical record, from the origins of public libraries in the mid nineteenth century through to the present day. The book is not intended to be another history of public libraries: Kelly's magnum opus is hard to replace and that task we leave to others. Rather, we and our contributors have traced the more pervasive arguments which have made British public library service a distinctive national institution, so as to consider the extent to which both continuity and innovation have been involved in the process.

We offer a group of essays which includes fresh new library history writing and openly polemical interpretations of the past of public libraries. Our contributors include well-known specialists in library history, but also representatives of thinking on a broader historical front, as well as on controversial issues in various aspects of librarianship. They are drawn from academic life, but also from library practice. Their approaches range from those internal to the library community to others which are very broadly contextual, and indeed the first chapter is a very wide-ranging study of the history of the leisure environment in which libraries exist. We are particularly pleased to be able to offer such an essay in this book precisely because discussion of library-related questions often lacks a sufficiently strong context, and can sometimes tend towards the inward-looking.

The essays draw on examples of a wide geographical variety from all over Britain, and some use a particular area to develop their argument. Similarly, the themes discussed vary from the broadest discussion of issues, through to specific examinations of aspects of services, such as home reading or services to schools. Naturally there is some discussion of common themes and reference by more than one contributor to particular events or situations, but such themes and events are approached from different viewpoints and for different purposes. No attempt has been made to restrict contributors on this, but the reader will find no simple duplication of information and ideas. The book as a whole is intended to provide a stimulating and multifaceted treatment of the past of public libraries with relevance to the present always in mind. Good history should always help us to think usefully about today and the editors believe that this book offers such opportunities.

REFERENCES
1 Comedia, *Borrowed time? The future of public libraries in the UK*, Bournes Green, Glos., Comedia, 1993, 1.
2 Aslib, *Review of the public library service in England and Wales for the Department of National Heritage*, London, Aslib, 1995.
3 MORI User survey 1992, *In*: Sumsion, J., *Practical performance indicators – 1992*, Loughborough, Loughborough University Library and Information Statistics Unit, 1993, Appendix 8.
4 Kinnell, M. and MacDougall, J., *Meeting the marketing challenge: strategies for libraries and leisure services*, London, Taylor Graham, 1994.
5 Department of Education and Science, *The libraries' choice*, London, HMSO, 1978.
6 Kinnell Evans, M., *All change? Public library management strategies for the 1990s*, London, Taylor Graham, 1991, Ch. 9.
7 Convention of Scottish Local Authorities, *Standards for the public library service in Scotland*, Edinburgh, COSLA, 1986, 10.
8 Ashcroft, M. and Wilson, A. (eds.), *Competitive tendering and libraries. Proceedings of a seminar held in Stamford, Lincs., Nov. 25–26 1992*, Stamford, CPI, 1993.
9 Kelly, T., *A history of public libraries in Great Britain 1845–1975*, 2nd edn, London, Library Association, 1977, 28.
10 *Ibid.*, 198
11 Adam Smith Institute, *Ex libris*, London, ASI, 1986.
12 Kelly, T., *A history of public libraries in Great Britain 1845–1975*, 2nd edn, London, Library Association, 1977, 14.
13 Policy Studies Institute, *Cultural trends No. 20: Employment in the cultural sector: books, libraries and reading*, London, PSI, 1994.

1   The leisure revolution

❖   *Helen E. Meller*

INTRODUCTION

Over the past two hundred years Britain has been the pioneer of industrialization and now, de-industrialization. There has been a shift from a society based on rural life and values to one that is urban. By the end of this century, technology applied to goods and services, transport and communications will have brought rural life within the framework of urban culture. A great cycle of social and cultural change has been completed. Many people now make the choice of where to live giving priority to their leisure pursuits rather than their work. What has happened could be described as a revolution in the role of leisure in modern society.[1] Yet both the terms 'leisure' and 'revolution' are slippery concepts to define. What is leisure? What gives people pleasure? What do they want? Contradictory elements such as excitement/routine, stimulation/relaxation, escape/emotional security, change and travel/stability and home comforts, solitude/communication are all components of the pursuit of leisure. Indeed, leisure need not necessarily even be pursued. Social ideologies of both the nineteenth and twentieth centuries have placed great emphasis on the importance of home and family life as a source of true pleasure and happiness. Over the past century, the 80% of the population whose homes were barely comfortable have sought a higher material standard of living, demonstrated by increasing comfort in home and family life. The moral code of the 'work ethic' has offered the carrot of more leisure and pleasure as reward for those who work hard. The shortcomings of this ideology were quickly evident if you happened to be a woman of any social class over the past century.[2] What leisure is and what it is for are thus, above all, cultural constructs.[3]

The concept of a leisure revolution is, therefore, an anomaly. What has happened over the past two hundred years is a shift in attitudes and aspirations which has been more evolutionary than revolutionary. The image of a leisure revolution is possibly as important as fact in developing the cultural construct and great changes have occurred which reinforce the image of revolution. The urbanization of the population did not simply change the context of people's lives, it changed their aspirations. Immigrants at the end of the eighteenth century, making their way in stages from hamlets to small villages, from villages to small towns, from county towns to major centres of manufacturing and commerce (or even the capital city), felt at each stage of this progress that they were seeing more of the world and could look forward to more excitements, more communication, more opportunities. Yet how did cities fulfil such ambitions? Scale by itself was not enough. What towns and cities offered were institutions and the means of communication which brought people in touch both with local and regional activities as well as bringing them within the mainstream of national culture. The most obvious examples of this were educational institutions and the local press. Yet there were many other formal and informal ways in which people in cities gained a sense of their own identity within a modernizing society and many of these were related to leisure. For example, the evolution of modern sport in its many forms was a most startling product of the first period of mass urbanization in the second half of the nineteenth century.[4]

The application of technology to leisure has had just as far-reaching effects in its impact on the image of change. It has been reinforced by the pressures of commercialization. The commercialization of leisure itself, though, was not a new phenomenon.[5] The enjoyment of luxury goods and their purchase, itself a form of leisure, has always been available in cities. Similarly, more sophisticated commodities such as the arts have also had a long history. The evolution of the modern theatre, for example, has antecedents stretching back for centuries. Thus the pursuit of leisure and its commercial provision is deeply embedded in the history, traditions and urban culture of the past. What the new technology achieved was to bring such commercialized leisure activities to a wider audience. The advent of cinema, radio and television, the current development of personal computers and the Internet, have all changed methods of communication. Broadly, what such technology has done is to break down the parochial limits of public imagination so that cultural parameters now include not only the local, regional and national but also the global. Increased personal mobility has also been similarly affected. Yet these developments do not totally eclipse other activities and forms of enjoyment that have had a longer history. In fact, in the following review of the leisure revolution over the past two hundred years it is hoped to show that leisure pursuits have evolved over a long period of time whatever the magnitude of current technological change. What has occurred in mature urban societies is the provision of increasingly sophisticated opportunities for leisure and pleasure which draw on a range of past and present experiences as well as future possibilities. The legacy of the past is both nurtured and recast by the demands of the present.

LEISURE AND SOCIAL CHANGE 1750–1850

Historians of leisure are always in a quandary when it comes to generalizations.[6] Not only is there the problem of defining leisure, there is also the difficulty of analysing the many social and cultural activities and institutions which fit, one way or another, into the framework of leisure. Obviously, the key parameters are resources, time and context, but that does not simplify the problem.[7] It merely makes the task of generalization overwhelmingly complex. The approach adopted here is to try to give some indication of social and cultural change in relation to leisure in the context of the city. What follows will be a view of the leisure revolution from an urban perspective. It is important, though, to get the process of urbanization itself into perspective.

Urbanization

It is often forgotten that Britain was one of the most urbanized nations long before the classic Industrial Revolution period. There was a network of county and market towns and cathedral cities, as there was in France, Britain's great rival at the end of the eighteenth century. Yet there were at least two significant differences in Britain. Scale and proximity made British towns more of a network with less extreme regional variations compared to France and, most importantly, London, for all its dominance, did not lay a heavy centralizing hand on the country as was the case with Paris. This meant that when industrialization took place, provincial cities such as Manchester, Birmingham and Leeds could feel that they were in the vanguard, that what happened there was a precursor of the new modern society.[8] It gave British provincial cities a vigour, vitality and a competitive spirit which enabled them to set about reconciling their past history and traditions with the challenge of modern industry and capitalism.

Perhaps this is one of the points which should be emphasized most in a review of the leisure revolution in cities. There were hardly any totally new settlements in the nineteenth century. The experience of urban growth, which was to alter the balance of the whole nation from country to city, was to take place around established towns and cities. All towns and cities had facilities for leisure and pleasure. All had institutions: religious, educational and social. There were even well-developed examples of cities based on the leisure industry which gave form to an ideal of sophisticated social life possible in provincial cities. The prime example of this was Bath. Peter Borsay's work on Bath has revealed the clever marketing strategies that were employed to make Bath a commercial success and how this depended on selling the idea of the salubriousness of the city, both physically and socially, to an ever-increasing number of possible customers.[9] What happened in the period before 1850, however, was a coming together of a number of factors: the speed of growth of the few industrial giants such as Manchester and Birmingham in the early nineteenth century, which was historically unprecedented and which contemporaries found shocking; the scale of the growth which meant that established ways of life and leisure were disrupted especially by physical changes such as the loss of open spaces and the shift of the population to residential suburbs; and, above all, the fact that the growth of towns and cities coincided with a religious Evangelical Revival which was to tear apart the framework of church and old established chapels and to make the salvation of the urban masses a key objective.[10]

Evangelicism

From the point of view of changing attitudes to leisure, the Evangelical Revival was the most important factor. In Britain, with the absence of centralized state administration, the Anglican Church provided the context for social life at every level.[11] Most towns had established groups of Nonconformists and, with industrialization, many of them rose to ever greater positions of influence in their local communities. Yet Old Dissent as much as the Anglican Church was challenged by the Evangelical Revival which inaugurated a cultural revolution. Evangelists were not only concerned about saving souls, they also wanted a transformation in social behaviour. In the context of the cities, this was to result in the repression of traditional and spontaneous leisure activities and the pursuit of what became known as rational recreation. Rational recreation was based on an educated understanding of liberal culture and its manifestations, especially classical music, art and literature and organized sports and pastimes which were so regulated as to eliminate violence.[12] The prophet of the Evangelical Revival in terms of the reform of social behaviour was a woman, Hannah More, and she used the most potent weapons then available to social reformers: the promotion of education and the written word. Her books on manners and morals became best-sellers and gave to the educated classes a clearly defined standard of behaviour which could be used to measure moral worth.[13] She was equally devoted to education, although she was only in favour of teaching people to read. They must be able to read the Bible and improving works but not to write. Writing might give them ideas above their station.

Her ideas were like the first swallows marking a new era in the history of leisure. Henceforth, in ever greater numbers, self-appointed social reformers, town councillors and magistrates up and down the land, in large cities and small, would begin the task of outlawing riotous and unseemly behaviour and, in the process, suppressing many traditional and established leisure pursuits. Josiah Strutt was to publish his study *The sports and pastimes of the people of England* in 1801 as the traditional leisure pursuits he outlined were fast disappearing.[14] It was a cultural revolution that has made both contemporary commentators and modern historians uneasy. Since Evangelists and social reformers were largely middle class and those who enjoyed popular pastimes were usually the poor, a strong class element had emerged in this cultural exchange. Given their access to local judicial and political power, it would seem that the reformers held all the trumps in an unequal struggle. It was enough to make the greatest commentators on the British class system, Marx and Engels, rage in fury at what they saw as the unconscionable crimes of one class against another. In the *Communist manifesto* of 1848, they wrote 'the economists, philanthropists, humanitarians, improvers of the condition of the working class, organizers of charity, members of societies for the prevention of cruelty to animals, temperance fanatics, hole and corner reformers of every imaginable kind . . . want all the advantages of modern social conditions without the struggles and dangers necessarily resulting therefrom.' The middle-class effort to control social behaviour and direct change can be 'summed up in the phrase: the bourgeois is a bourgeois for the benefit of the working class'.[15]

Evidence of the work of Evangelicals and the power of Marxist argument has influenced the writing of the history of leisure.[16] Yet research on British cities and specific social movements has revealed that what was happening owed as much to factors other than class and class domination. There are points in history when common activities suddenly become intolerable. These points are like signposts in the barometer of social change and they are connected to a wide range of emotions. A minor but obvious example of this is a change in the acceptable way of treating animals.[17] Bear- and bull-baiting were stamped out in Britain in the first half of the nineteenth century, though only reluctantly in places such as Bristol (a very large city in the early nineteenth century) and Stamford (a modest little market town). The urban British have always had a fondness for animals and the Society for the Prevention of Cruelty to Animals (founded in 1843) has usually done better than the other Victorian foundation, the Society for the Prevention of Cruelty to Children. This example does not offer proof against the domination of the middle classes in urban culture. It simply suggests that many people were ready to embrace a change in their social behaviour because they wanted to. It is true that the Evangelical mission in this respect was destined to win, as the new industrial employers wanted a sober, regular and reliable workforce. Yet the repression of popular pastimes could not have taken place without much tacit support.[18] Alternative forms of leisure were now required which would provide recreation and enable people to withstand the rigours of the regular and punishing routines of the new industrial processes.

Evangelicals, with their commitment to such a set of moral values that leisure pursuits were regarded with total suspicion, were not best placed to invent new forms of leisure. The promotion of rational recreation was built on the idea of educating the working classes in the merits of living decently. The methods initially applied were education and exhortation. What the Evangelicals had not fully appreciated, however, was that education is an open-ended process. Once people could read, they were subject to the communication of any printed word and the Evangelicals could not control that. If they wanted to influence behaviour, threats of hellfire were not enough. Much energy was expended not only proselytizing in the hope that conversion would alter behaviour but also in attacking accepted social evils which were seen to lead people astray. Prime amongst these was drink. The people who worked for the great nineteenth century Temperance Movement were pitting themselves against the established social culture of urban life.[19] The public house was the meeting point for news, company, political activity and all kinds of leisure pursuits.[20] What Temperance workers found was that to be credible they had to offer alternative forms of entertainment and places to meet. It was an experience which was to feed into the provision of leisure facilities in towns and cities on a private and public basis over the course of the century.

Gender roles and leisure

This triumph of rational recreation over the traditional pastimes and leisure pursuits has been emphasized to the exclusion of other consequences of the Evangelical revival which were to have far-reaching effects. Because of what they saw as the evils of drink and prostitution, Evangelical clergy and reformers worked to close down theatres, to forbid their wives and daughters from any form of public recreation and to ban dancing. They also worked to establish that other nineteenth century institution, the Sabbath, as a day of rest when organized leisure of any kind was banned. These actions were to have an extraordinary impact on women. In effect, the newly defined codes of social behaviour were to push gender roles to extremes in the pursuit of new forms of leisure. The work of Catherine Hall and Leonore Davidoff, *Family fortunes: men and women of the English middle class 1780–1850*,[21] has provided a detailed study of how women were excluded from public life and from the world of voluntary associations and leisure pursuits. The Evangelical revival had promoted the idea of the father as the patriarchal figure. The role of woman was to be the supportive wife and mother, concerning herself with the welfare of the home. As the home for the more affluent middle classes tended to be a detached villa in a leafy suburb and increased wealth was used to buy more domestic labour, middle-class women were left without a role. They were truly the leisure class of the mid-nineteenth century.[22] The historians of fashion have charted how the absurdity of Victorian female dress reached its apotheosis in the 1860s, when the tightest corsetting produced the smallest waists and the size of crinolines obstructed all but the most gentle and limited movement.[23] Middle-class women were to fight their way out of this nadir through demanding more education and leisure activities such as sport,[24] and finding a role for themselves in philanthropy and charitable work in cities.[25]

Ladies suffering the tortures of tight lacing and large crinolines, though, are a stereotype of Victorian womanhood. Studies of individual cities in the early nineteenth century have shown that it is a mistake to think in such terms. Urban society in Nottingham, Bristol, Sheffield and Cardiff was shaped by many factors – economic, social and cultural – and local studies reveal that it was rare to find a homogeneous urban middle class or working class.[26] The Evangelical Revival itself created great fissures in society, as sect did not communicate with sect. The result of this social fragmentation was that British cities lacked a universally accepted urban culture on the model of the great German or Italian cities. Prince Albert, a perceptive foreigner on English soil, was aware of this and in the reforming mode of the time tried to remedy it in a number of ways, including promoting the pursuit of classical music. The only major music festivals in provincial cities tended to be religious ones and, for the rest, there was a demand for new music and popular tunes. Albert, with his Antique Music Society which held Monday Concerts in the Crystal Palace at Sydenham Hill, wanted to introduce the British to a standard of music widely enjoyed in the major German state capitals. He employed German musicians, one of whom was the Westphalian, Charles Hallé, who went on to transform the musical life of Manchester. Hallé established the first professional orchestra and he was to use the special context of a large industrial city to mount an extremely successful commercial venture built on his ambition to create a public for classical music.[27] In fact, immigrants and ethnic minorities, especially the Jews (in places where they were well-established such as Manchester and Leeds), were to create a new musical life in British cities. At these concerts there were protocols of social behaviour, with conversation being banned and the only act of appreciation allowed being polite clapping at the very end of a piece. These concerts were an indication of the extent of the social revolution that had taken place over the past century. It was not an exclusively middle-class achievement. The Hallé concerts sought to attract working men who could travel to them on the new cheap public transport, the horsedrawn trams. Britain's towns and cities had been battered by the process of industrialization. French and German cities, on the whole, were still basking in their pre-industrial age.[28] Yet by the mid-nineteenth century, Britain's new giant cities, such as Manchester, Liverpool, Birmingham and Leeds, had a new self-consciousness of their importance.[29]

LEISURE AND THE CREATION OF URBAN CULTURE 1850–1914

In the glow of confidence brought by imperial and economic success, the British were to make an outstanding contribution in many fields to the development of modern leisure pursuits.[30] In the second half of the nineteenth century the British manufactured what they now defined and understood as urban civilization. It had many elements. At the centre were advances in education for nearly all groups in society, though worst served were the women and girls of the poorest classes. In the cities there was a revolution in local government. New duties, especially those relating to education and public health were to transform the sense of responsibility of local councils and to stimulate a new ideal of what local government could achieve. In the inner cities there was a transformation of philanthropic activity and much effort was expended on improving the quality of social life of the poor. This work was carried out largely by women and, through it, women were to find a way of contributing to fresh thinking about the need for provisions for leisure and recreation in the city. There was a new vitality and confidence amongst the urban working class which was beginning, at long last, to benefit from economic change. A fall in price of imported foods, from 1873 onwards, ushered in a century of cheap food. It was probably the single most important element in improving the real wages of the English working classes. With modest material resources and limitation of hours of work, the mass of British people were ready to contribute to the growth of organized leisure activities of every kind.[31] What was achieved was quite astonishing.

Organized sport

The strength of this development can be shown in the world of organized sport.[32] The evolution of organized sport was credited to the British public school system. The male youth of Britain, unlike their European counterparts, were sent away from the great cities where they lived to small semi-rural or small town settlements where enterprising headmasters established a network of boarding schools. Following Thomas Arnold of Rugby, with his mission to reform secondary education to inspire boys with the highest sense of moral duty to serve their country and the world, sport became the shibboleth of the new system. It kept boys occupied and bred team spirit. It became such a passion that by the end of the century the captain of cricket was idolized as the most charismatic figure in the school. Boys influenced by this were to go on to jobs administering the British Empire or working as clergy in the new parishes set up in British cities. They took their sport with them. Playing cricket was assumed to be one of the best ways of binding the nations of the Empire together or, equally, the social classes in cities. What happened to football, however, was to show that public-school patronage was irrelevant in the context of the city. The public schools may have decided to transform their football games according to the rules of the Football Association (FA) in 1863 and the Rugby Union of 1871 but their hold on the game could not last. The competition for the FA Cup was open to any team that played by the rules, and soon teams from towns and cities were competing with the teams of Old Boys drawn from the public schools. The moment of revolution was 1883. In that year Blackburn Olympic, a team supported by the mill workers, beat the Old Etonians in extra time. From that moment the urban working classes took the game for their own and it became one of the most dominating leisure pursuits in all cities. Supporting the football team became a part of civic identity.

Parks and open spaces
The reform of local government had generated an interest in civic identity from a different perspective. In the wake of the revelations of the reports from Royal Commissions and Select Committees, local councils began to feel a responsibility towards the health and well-being of all citizens. Concern for public health and education was to bring local councils towards a commitment to providing leisure facilities for all.[33] For the workers in Liverpool and Manchester there was no open space available to them in which they could play football, even if they wanted to. The loss of open spaces in cities had been the subject of reports of two Select Committees in 1833 and 1845. There was growing concern both for the loss of amenity for all citizens and for the destruction of areas of outstanding natural beauty which were often found adjacent to growing cities. Now, the Public Health Act of 1848 enabled local authorities to purchase and maintain parks and open spaces on the rates. Mostly, of course, this funding was totally inadequate for making substantial purchases of land. The acquisition of parks and open spaces by local authorities over the next half century was piecemeal and varied.[34] Sometimes there was a public subscription, as in Manchester; sometimes wealthy land owners with a vested interest, such as the Marquess of Bute in Cardiff, offered land.[35] Initially, the purchased land was left as open space.

Yet from the 1850s an interest in horticulture and the need for open space for ceremonial purposes, such as the Jubilee celebrations, encouraged local councils to think more clearly about the use of such space. The demands of sport were also a strong factor. Parks came to be seen as an important element of urban civilization. They were a visible sign that the quality of civic life was held to be more important than the mere commercial value of land. The introduction of plants and trees into an urban context was welcomed as a civilizing force, and the floral displays, arboretums and collections of plants fed what was to become a passion of the urban British – gardening. As a leisure pursuit it was one of the most universally enjoyed by those of all social classes with access to land.[36] A further development was the provision of bandstands in the park to provide music on summer evenings and there was a constant evolution of new facilities: boating lakes, clock golf, tennis courts and, of course, bowling greens. By the end of the century the provision of parks and open spaces within cities was held to be inadequate. Before the First World War, a number of town councils in large cities purchased country estates which townspeople could reach by new forms of public transport. By this time the role of the council in preserving the quality of the physical environment had become established and the achievements in this respect were to feed into the modern town-planning movement. A century later, 'greening the city' had become an important policy objective.[37]

Baths and washhouses

The pursuit of public health measures had encouraged local councils in another direction. Since the Baths and Washhouses Act of 1846, local councils had had the authority to provide baths and washhouses from the rates. Here, again, was another example of how the history of past institutions fed into the present and transformed them. Most cities had a variety of baths in private hands. Turkish baths, swimming baths, washrooms and laundries were commercially available, given that the supply of water often remained a serious problem until at least the third quarter of the century. The 1846 Act was directed towards getting local authorities to provide the facilities so that the poor could be encouraged to be clean. Yet swimming (as opposed to just washing) in the local river or the private swimming bath was already an established activity and, after all, the poor needed to be attracted to use new facilities. Town Councils began to build baths for the sport of swimming, and as they did so, they became more conscious of their role in making provision for the leisure of all citizens.[38] A local journalist in Bristol, writing in 1895, suggested that:

> The larger provincial towns are . . . laying out parks and playgrounds using, in fact, municipal funds to increase the pleasure and health of the community. It would be difficult to estimate the value of this development . . . the municipal evolution which is taking place is rendering local authorities more appreciative of the necessities of modern life and more anxious to adopt improvements that will add to the happiness of the communities they represent.[39]

Cultural institutions

The happiness of citizens was not the only objective which justified town councils in funding institutions which were ultimately to become, by the end of the century, institutions of leisure and pleasure. Cultural institutions, such as libraries, museums and art galleries, were to be found in most towns and cities by then. Yet the path which had led to such an achievement was extremely varied. What these institutions provided above all was a means for the inter-action of local, regional and national culture. They were ways of bringing towns within the mainstream. An example of this might be drawn not from the giant cities, where such contacts and interaction were more obvious, but in a little industrial town dependent on products which were subject to national and international fashions. In the modest town of Hanley in the Potteries, the sequence of development was as follows: the first important library in the town was formed for the Mechanics Institution (founded in 1826), and a museum – the North Staffordshire Museum – was added in 1851. In the 1840s, efforts were made to found an Art School and, with the help of the London School of Design, a school was established in 1847. In 1890 a North Staffordshire Technical and Art Museum was established in the Mechanics Institution building funded by the Staffordshire Chamber of Commerce. It was taken over by the Borough Council in the following year. Subsequently, the North Staffordshire Natural History Museum and Naturalists' Field Club were established in the same building in 1908.[40] It is a saga in which industry, local government and the pursuit of leisure activities all played a part. It was repeated in a variety of local patterns in towns and cities all over Britain.

Social progress and civilization
By the end of the century it had not only become acceptable for local councils to provide leisure facilities, it had also become an accepted measure of British civilization. By that time, the great days of British global domination, despite the continued existence of the Empire, were on the wane. Since 1890, both the German and American economies had become greater than the British econ-omy, and with economic power went cultural domination. The Americans and the Germans had developed large-scale industry and large-scale industrial combines – trusts and cartels – which were capitalist giants of a new order. One or two of the Americans, with Nonconformist backgrounds, felt the need to justify their unprecedented wealth by providing private funds for the future well-being of the world. Men like J. D. Rockefeller and Andrew Carnegie pio-neered a new kind of philanthropy, 'wholesale philanthropy' which cut across established philanthropic activities in Europe.[41] In wholesale philanthropy, philanthropic action was no longer a personal activity, in a local context and with limited objectives. Instead, huge sums of money were made available and experts were engaged professionally to seek out philanthropic objectives and to manage the dispensing of funds. Mr Carnegie himself was very clear about what he wanted to do. For him, the seven major objectives were those relating

to social progress and civilization:

(1) to found universities (if the philanthropist was rich enough);
(2) to establish free libraries and museums;
(3) to found and extend hospitals, medical colleges, laboratories and similar institutions;
(4) to provide public parks;
(5) to provide meeting and concert halls;
(6) to provide swimming baths;
(7) to provide churches.[42]

The munificence of Mr Carnegie supplied funds for many a branch library in British cities, amongst other institutions.

Mr Carnegie's first choice was the founding of a civic university. His priority was a recognition of the role universities could play in the cultural life of cities. Britain had witnessed a dramatic extension of university education beyond the confines of Oxford, Cambridge and London. University Colleges were established in the largest cities, funded by industrialists and leading citizens. Their original purpose was often related to local economic needs: for training engineers, designers and managers of industry. The need for technical and scientific education became urgent in view of the fact that Britain's secondary school system was dominated by the public schools. Yet, in town after town, plans for educational institutions devoted to science and technology were transformed into University Colleges. Matthew Arnold had caught the mood with his polemic *Culture and anarchy*, published in 1869. He cried out for 'sweetness and light' for Britain's cities and suggested that this could only be achieved by a group of dedicated members of the intelligentsia who would bring Liberal Culture to the Barbarians (the upper classes), the Philistines (the middle classes) and the Populace (the rest). Liberal Culture meant the pursuit of arts, literature and music.[43] Provincial University Colleges, living from hand to mouth on the meagre resources of private philanthropy, opened their doors to women, who were most likely to pursue the arts and to pay their fees.[44] In this way women were able to get some higher education and cities were to benefit from the foundation of an institution which would grow and develop according to the cultural demands of city and nation.

Apart from the pursuit of academic knowledge, university students were to play a significant part in the leisure revolution in British cities. They provided the manpower, and especially the womanpower, to sustain movements designed to provide for the leisure of the poor as a means of helping them combat the horrors of social life in an inner city suburb. The most famous of these was the University Settlement of Toynbee Hall in the East End of London. Canon Barnett, who founded the settlement in 1883, had the vision that sharing a common culture would bring together the Two Nations and heal the rift between the social classes. He was also deeply concerned that the very rich would become lost in a world of such luxury and ostentatious leisure pursuits that the new wealth would be like a poison in the body politic. He wrote

> simpler living and higher thinking would bring rich and poor nearer together; . . . Libraries, Art Galleries, good music, University teaching, must be as near to a West End as to an East End suburb. There can be no real unity so long as the people in different parts of a city are prevented from admiring the same things, from taking the same pride in their fathers' great deeds and from sharing the glory of possessing the same literature.[45]

In the Edwardian era, when plain living and high thinking seemed even less fashionable, Barnett actually wrote that he hoped there would always be slums in cities since they were necessary to rouse the social conscience. His own efforts in Whitechapel were very successful. There was an excellent Board School, an Art Gallery and a Settlement House for meetings, which also contained a Library, and there were many, mostly educational, activities organized by the young Oxford and Cambridge graduates who lived at Toynbee Hall. The Settlement Movement spread to the University Colleges in large towns.

The role of women
In cities such as Manchester and Bristol, the University Settlements built on the work of the earlier missions to the poor which had been established by different religious sects and denominations.[46] Many of the settlements were to be staffed and run by women.[47] Women always displayed different attitudes to leisure and pleasure than their male counterparts. They had to fight for recognition themselves as creators of liberal culture, few women having their musical compositions performed or their paintings exhibited. They were the passive recipients of male-dominated culture. They were also more practical. One of the most brilliant innovators in developing ways of improving the social life of inner-city suburbs was Octavia Hill.[48] She believed, like Barnett, in personal contact between the classes, yet her concern was directed more precisely towards the everyday experiences of the poor. Her method was to buy up dilapidated property and to manage it with volunteer, but professionally trained, lady rent collectors. They had the moral authority to supervise the physical and social environment of the properties. It was Miss Hill who identified the need for small playgrounds for children close to their homes. She planted trees and creepers over her houses to bring some natural influences into a bare brick environment. She recognized the need for regular leisure activities and annual outings. She provided a recreation room for tenants and

reintroduced the traditional festivals of May Day and Harvest Festivals, which the children were taught to celebrate. One of her major contributions was to recognize the need to protect areas of outstanding natural beauty for the recreation of citizens; she worked to save Epping Forest and Wimbledon Common, and went on to be a founder member of a national voluntary organization, the National Trust.[49]

In the huge increase in philanthropic activity which spread from city to city, women became involved in helping the poor, though not always in such a focused way as Miss Hill. There were considerable gender differences in the philanthropic provision of facilities for leisure and pleasure. Women concentrated on housing, on mothers and babies, on gardens and playgrounds. Men recognized the needs of working men and of young boys. The Boys Brigade and subsequently the Boy Scouts Movement were supported in every city.[50] One of the discoveries of the late nineteenth century had been the different needs of different age groups.

Light and air

It is perhaps appropriate to conclude this section on leisure and urban culture before the First World War with the words of J. S. Nettlefold, Chairman of the Housing Committee of Birmingham Municipal Council. Birmingham had been in the vanguard of providing institutions of Liberal Culture and of the attempt to create a great British urban civilization. Since the days of the Civic Gospel preached by Nonconformist ministers to their congregations in the mid-nineteenth century, Birmingham had been the context for experiments in local government administration, drawing especially on the skills of eminent businessmen and their sense of social citizenship. Joseph Chamberlain, as Mayor in the early 1870s, had municipalized the gas industry and was to build an art gallery from the profits.[51] Nettlefold had struggled for decades with the more intractable problem of providing decent houses for those who could only afford the lowest rent. He knew how little all the activities of the previous half century had done to mitigate the worst social consequences of mass urbanization. He wrote, in 1901:

> Millions of English town children have no playground within practical reach except the streets. The young men find it extremely difficult to obtain suitable cricket and football fields . . . Each year makes it harder for men to get allotments on which they can not only get rational enjoyment, but also materially increase the family food supply. The women have no place to go out to where they can enjoy an odd hour, and often find no better choice than the front doorstep, or the nearest public house. We cannot, by legislation, make people healthy and happy, but we can give our town dwellers

fewer temptations to irrational excitement, and more opportunities for beneficial enjoyment than they have at present. We can, if we will, let light and air into our towns; we can, if we will, make the most and not the least of the sunshine.[52]

Letting 'light and air' into British cities became the cultural framework for the modern town-planning movement that Nettlefold helped to establish in Britain.[53] Yet he would have been saddened to know that, almost a century later, there are still areas of physical and social deprivation in British cities and that many young people, far from being concerned with playing football and cricket, are actually without homes.

LEISURE AND TECHNOLOGICAL CHANGE
In the twentieth century, the application of technology to leisure has been claimed to have produced a 'leisure revolution'. Yet, like the impact of urbanization on leisure, the change has been evolutionary rather than revolutionary, although there have been dramatic moments of change. These have mainly stemmed from technological innovations in communication such as the cinema, radio and television. Asa Briggs wrote in 1960 that the cluster of inventions of the last quarter of the nineteenth century

> were as basic to new ways of life in the twentieth century as were the inventions of the last quarter of the eighteenth century in textiles, iron and power, to the new industrial patterns of the nineteenth century. The difference between them is that the eighteenth century inventions transformed the material standard of living and the nineteenth century inventions, the forms of culture.[54]

The subsequent collapse of British manufacturing industry in the last quarter of the twentieth century has given his judgement added strength in that leisure itself has become one of the main industries and sources of employment. Towns and cities throughout Britain have suffered rapid economic decline, and leisure industries (including education and particularly colleges of further and higher education) have emerged as one of the major methods of urban regeneration.[55] This has been happening especially since the 1960s. Yet throughout the twentieth century, punctuated by the experience of two world wars, there has been a transformation in attitudes to leisure which has meant that leisure institutions and activities have had to undergo a constant process of change to meet the demands of each succeeding generation.

There has been a total reversal of the cultural framework fought for by the Evangelicals. Their particular taboos against drink and sex have been gradually broken down, and a sense of liberation and modernity has emerged. It has been the happy task of each generation in the twentieth century to take acceptable forms of social behaviour one step further than their parents' generation, a task which became progressively easier when the strength of beer was weakened by law and women had greater control over their bodies with the development of modern methods of contraception. Perhaps the most outstanding contribution of technology to leisure has been to alter methods of social communication which have both undermined class barriers and, at the same time, exaggerated the differences between people in relation to age, gender and wealth.[56] The most obvious of these changes is the emergence of a youth culture which cuts right across class and indeed, wealth.[57] Its major ingredients – music and sport, against a background of ever greater freedom in social mores – can be enjoyed in some form by all young people.[58] It is not a local, regional or national phenomenon but is truly global. New technology in transport and communications has shrunk the world, and cultural influences, mainly American and European, are felt worldwide. Yet enjoyment of even youth culture is controlled by the point of access and for all young people, often without resources and dependent on their families and the state to provide for their futures, the locality continues to plays a large part in shaping their leisure experiences.

Urban change

The application of technology to leisure in Britain in the twentieth century has thus to be explored in the context of urban change. Nettlefold's ambition to let 'light and air' into British cities has been met by a massive increase in levels of suburbanization. By the turn of the century, the age of great cities was long past, to be replaced by the modern phenomenon of conurbations and suburban sprawl. Before the Second World War, stark contrasts emerged between the Victorian suburbs of great cities and the suburbs of new public and private estates on the periphery. The municipal estates of public housing were built according to the regulations emanating from the Tudor Walters Report of 1919 which was influenced by the Garden City architect planner, Raymond Unwin.[59] The social ideal was to provide low-density housing, no more than 12 houses to the acre. The contrast between the old and the new was extreme. Londoners from the East End, the north and the south of London were decanted into 'cottage estates' built by the London County Council. They felt they were going into the countryside, leaving behind social and cultural networks that had sustained them.[60] It was an experience shared by the new inhabitants of municipal estates built by other local authorities, such as Wythenshawe in Manchester and Kingstanding in Birmingham.[61] Gradually, they became served by cinemas and public houses but a question mark had been left over the issue of how these people should enjoy a place in the mainstream of modern society.

Conditions for those left behind in the inner-city areas continued to deteriorate. The most overwhelming cultural experience of Britain in the interwar period was mass unemployment. The Great Depression of 1929–32 emphasized the social consequences of the collapse of major British industries and the creation of the 'depressed areas'. Whole cities and regions – South Wales, the ship-building areas of Glasgow and Tyneside, the steel and mining towns – all suffered dramatic decline. Where local councils had managed to raise resources for public housing schemes, the result was to make those that were left behind ever more isolated from the countryside. The relationship between town and country is a fundamental one in the leisure revolution. It was the loss of access to open space that had generated the public parks movement. Land, however, was still an economic resource to the urban working classes. The history of the allotment movement provides evidence of this. It was a pre-industrial rural movement that was transferred to the cities and in 1908 an Act was passed which made local authorities responsible for providing land. During the two world wars it was government policy to encourage allotment production, and around one and a half million people became involved. Yet allotments were much more than a means of providing food. Around them developed a culture, mostly male gendered, which touched the lives of many people of the urban working classes.[62] Town and country had a symbiotic relationship in terms of providing leisure resources.[63]

Space as a leisure resource

Controlling space and the countryside as a leisure resource required the framework of state action. In the interwar period the state began tentatively to build on voluntary action in the provision of facilities for sport and recreation. The National Playing Fields Association of 1925 and the passing of the Physical Training and Recreation Act of 1937 were major steps in this direction. Yet progress was very modest. Britain, unlike her European counterparts, especially Germany, did not use the provision of leisure resources as a political means for welding together a mass society.[64] It was not, though, just a political choice. Leisure patterns were already well-established. For example, the inhabitants of industrial cities, especially in the north and Scotland, had for generations used the local moors and hills for recreation and walking. Technology applied to transport was to make these activities possible on a continued basis throughout the century. The working people in Glasgow took the tram to the Trossachs; those of Nottingham, Sheffield and Manchester were able to take the train into the Derbyshire Peak District. The Labour government after the Second World War was to pass the National Parks and Access to the Countryside Act in 1949 to preserve natural regions of outstanding beauty which modern generations now reach by using the motor car. That Labour government also introduced a comprehensive system of town and country planning and subsequently the state has become ever more involved in developing access to the countryside as a leisure resource. In Britain, however, state action has tended to follow voluntary associations and this has been a marked feature of much leisure provision in both town and country. Of key importance has been the reduction in cost in access to leisure.

Technology

Technology has played a part in improving access to leisure, an outstanding example being the invention of the safety bicycle. With ball bearings and rubber tyres, the bicycle became a means of transport within reach of the entire population. In the interwar period, cyclist touring clubs encouraged people to go into the countryside, as did the Youth Hostel Association which set up a network of extremely cheap accommodation.[65] Technology, though, in relation to leisure pursuits, was to play an ambivalent role. As leisure time increased and more people were able to take up a variety of interests, the commercial potential of exploiting enthusiasm was recognized. In every sport, activity and hobby there has been a development of expertise in manufacturing of equipment. New materials, mechanical devices, specially constructed clothing have now become *de rigueur* in many activities. Technology, in this instance, has made the pursuit of hobbies and pastimes ever more expensive, though this has been much more pronounced since the Second World War. In the interwar period the range of leisure pursuits that had been built up over the previous century was still widely evident, from brass bands and male voice choirs to pigeon fancying, greyhound racing and the support of local football teams.[66] Drink and gambling have continued as the longest established and most readily available means of excitement.[67]

The inclusion of women

The working class culture which provided the framework for all these activities was supremely male. One of the most important elements of the leisure revolution in the twentieth century was to be the inclusion of women. For women, a breakthrough came with the cinema.[68] The single most popular new leisure pursuit in the first half of the century was the development of the cinema. By the First World War, there were about 4000 cinemas, many small and locally owned. After the war, giant companies such as the Gaumont British Picture Corporation, Denman Picture Houses, Provincial Cinematograph and the General Theatre Corporation bought many of them up and built new ones in fast-developing suburbs. The Odeon and Rank chains followed. By the end of the 1930s, there were about 100 million admissions each year, which meant that many people were visiting the cinema at least twice a week and many of them were women. This was a leisure activity which cut across gender barriers as did that other enthusiasm of the time, ballroom dancing.[69] Young, single women were able to celebrate their contempt for Evangelical repression by pursuing a passion for dancing. All towns and cities gained dance halls, usually built in a modern style. The music was provided by local bands or sometimes by the new recorded music. Yet, for all these hopeful signs, it was to be a long and complicated process before women were able to take part more or less equally with men in the pursuit of leisure. Two elements kept women from partaking naturally in the pursuit of pleasure: poverty and domesticity. For working-class women the struggle to keep their families fed and clothed was constant and time consuming. Leisure was not a word with any meaning for the female working class.[70] For those women, however, whose husbands were in regular work, there were substantial changes. They were more likely to be amongst those who were able to live in the new housing of the interwar period and to contribute to a domestically orientated development of leisure. In her studies on the relationship between the sexes in the interwar period, Diana Gittins has shown that there were contradictory influences apparent in women's enjoyment of leisure.[71] In youth, women were able to go out to cinemas and dance halls and enjoyed an unprecedented freedom. In marriage, women were more subject than formerly to their husbands. Fewer married women worked and, especially in the environment of the new estates, there was increasing emphasis on making a comfortable home for the husband and children. Fed by the propaganda from magazines, such as *Good housekeeping* and *Woman*, there was a new cult of material comfort which could only be achieved through the constant labour of women.[72]

Technology and commerce, however, were playing an ever more important part in daily life. The housewife had the technology of gas and electricity and the appliances dependent on these sources of energy to help her. She could also listen to the radio while she worked. The radio achieved the most astonishing breakthrough in terms of communication.[73] The ability to communicate directly with individuals in their own homes provided a whole new cultural context for leisure, though it was not until the 1950s, when radios became transistorized and cheap, that all age groups were free to choose their own programmes.

Social groups and leisure

The successful commercial exploitation of leisure has increasingly been aimed at specific social groups defined by age or gender. The transformation of holiday facilities provides another illustration of this. For example, Butlin's Holiday Camps of the interwar period were precursors of a cultural revolution.[74] Seaside holidays for the masses had been established in the wake of the development of the railways. Seaside resorts have been amongst the fastest growing urban areas since the 1860s. Some modelled themselves on the spa towns and offered genteel pleasure gardens, assembly rooms and tea shops, but the most successful catered for the popular market.[75] They offered, with their piers and amusement parks, a context for sustaining many elements of popular culture, such as Punch and Judy shows and street entertainers. What Billy Butlin did was to offer an environment in which holiday makers did not have to choose carefully the entertainment that they could afford but instead were entertained for every minute of the day at a prestated price level. Success was built on the premise that people on holiday wanted entertainment and women, above all, wanted freedom from child care and preparing meals. Stephen Jones has written perceptively on the implications of mass enjoyment of leisure as an indication of working-class solidarity.[76] Since the inception of the Labour Party in 1900, Labour politicians have enthusiastically pursued the aim of securing shorter hours and holidays with pay for the mass of the people. The curious outcome, however, was that the result of their efforts was to build a leisure industry which made fortunes for the capitalists. With continuing affluence, Butlins opened a holiday camp in Torremolinos, Spain, keeping in step with the massive growth of package holidays based on cheap air travel which were to take the British working people abroad on an unprecedented scale from the 1960s.

Post-war developments
The post-war Labour governments of 1945–51 were dedicated to creating a better Britain. Housing and welfare were top of the agenda. There was a great revulsion against the past and the decayed Victorian cities and high unemployment of the pre-war years. The 'better Britain' was modern and ahistorical. Blitzed cities such as Coventry were built on an entirely new pattern and new towns were established to house London's overspill. The standards set by the Labour government proved too expensive if the entire nation was to be rehoused. Harold Macmillan, as the Conservative Minister of Housing in the 1950s, initiated the phase of mass expansion of municipal housing, which was to include high-rise flats. Such a transformation of the urban environment was compounded by the iconoclastic activities of the road builders. Under the impetus of creating urban motorways and improving Britain's road structure, towns and cities were ripped apart and more of the physical environment was destroyed in the 1960s than in the entire Second World War. Once again, Britain's towns and cities were being battered, this time by redevelopment, not war. There was an outcry from the clergy of the inner city parishes and the leaders of organized youth movements, boys clubs, Boy Scouts and many oth-

ers. What was being disrupted was an intricate web of organized voluntary leisure activities, built up over the previous century. In some areas it was lost altogether, in others it was replanted in suburbs further out. Yet the destruction of halls, meeting places and open space was not made good. Inner-city suburbs that somehow escaped the bulldozer were left denuded, and their inhabitants, often now belonging to ethnic minorities, were left with few communal resources.[77]

The only social resource provided in every single locality by the government was the primary school. Provision was made for schools to be, if possible, within walking distance of all homes. There was a revolution in attitudes to education which took root in the primary school system. Education was seen not just as a matter of transmitting information but as a child-centred activity designed to encourage individuals to reach their full potential. Primary school children were to become the most active in exploring their local areas and the social, cultural and leisure facilities available to them. Children explored local libraries, museums and art galleries; their schools were visited by actors and musicians. It was revolution backed up by the latest developments in technology. Most important of these was, of course, radio and television. From its breakthrough in gaining a mass audience in the 1950s, television became the single most important resource of all age groups, young and old. In a dramatically changing and disruptive world it provided the one constant in the lives of many individuals. Radio and television were tools of enormous power for shaping social attitudes, and for those who controlled them the results were sometimes unexpected. For example, in the 1940s the government wanted to reach the more isolated farming communities and encourage them to adopt modern methods of production. One of the means chosen was to mix information with entertainment by instituting a family saga of rural life, 'The Archers'. It was totally unexpected that 'The Archers' would become a constant factor in the lives of millions of people totally unconnected with agriculture. Soap operas have been used on television to capture regular mass audiences with such programmes as 'Coronation Street' and 'East Enders', both built on the myth of an urban working-class social life in an old-established inner-city area. Children's broadcasting has also developed from early radio programmes for primary schools to a non-stop diet of television entertainment to keep children quiet in their own homes. Televised sport has a mass following and has led to the commercialization of the activity itself. Much broadcast entertainment is built on the commercial exploitation of leisure and the encouragement of a consumer revolution.[78]

From the Second World War, the consumer revolution has become ever more pronounced. Retailing is now a sophisticated art and a major stimulus for industry. Breakthroughs in the material standard of living for the working classes from the late 1950s created ever larger markets for the now huge-scale organizations devoted to retailing. Local city department stores, the product of the retailing revolution of the nineteenth century, were replaced by national and international chain stores.[79] With the advent of mass ownership of cars, these organizations have grown out of the need for an urban context and for the past decade have been moving to out-of-town locations, with the creation of shopping malls dedicated to new levels of leisure and pleasure in relation to the act of consuming modern commodities. Mass methods of retailing and mass methods of communication, such as television and now the Internet, have aided the transition of Britain's economic base from being a manufacturing nation to being one where growth areas of employment are in the provision of goods and services. The creation of out-of-town shopping malls, owned by international companies, has put a further question mark over the future economic survival of British cities. Yet over the past quarter of a century the provision of leisure facilities has provided one of the most effective answers. Liverpool, a city destroyed by the collapse of the port and the social consequences of high unemployment, mounted a Garden Festival in 1981. Millions were attracted to an event which was staged on formerly derelict land amongst the old docks. In the wake of this success other cities, such as London, Birmingham, Glasgow and Manchester, have reinvested in their city centres with the kind of optimism shown by their Victorian forebears. New art galleries, museums, libraries, opera houses, theatres, conference centres and the restoration of areas of outstanding historical importance have all contributed to revitalizing local economies and to boosting one of the fastest growing leisure industries – modern tourism.

CONCLUSION

Sustaining these developments and building on the revolutions in education and leisure still depend on the local context. They all need people to use them, to work in them, to administer them, to want them. Most of the leisure activities of the past two hundred years have managed to find a place for themselves despite the changes in urbanization and technology. In the theatre, for example, there has been a revival of local theatres and an encouragement of talent. Yet the most popular performances every year remain the pantomime, full of cultural resonances of a past much earlier than even the nineteenth century. Indeed, in some respects there has been a greater demand for every form of activity, from the popular to the more sophisticated. For most people, the point of access remains what is available within easy reach. Since redevelopment has slowed down, the local institutions that have survived have been able to catch their breath and respond to the changes that have taken place. The local library is no longer just a repository of books. It is a multimedia resource centre sensitive to the needs of a multicultural society.[80] National identity, civic identity and individual identity have all been changing dramatically. At the end of the twentieth century, it is possible to understand more fully the ways in which cultural change has transformed social life. In the wake of the realization of the importance of the leisure industry to our economic survival, there is a new concentration on the form and provision of leisure activities. There is recognition that it has become ever more specialized by age and taste and much of it is still voluntary as well as commercial. Yet many have been excluded, mostly by economic factors. Even further developments of information technology and the Internet will not remedy this. The Internet was invented by the American military to help withstand nuclear attack by making it possible for people to communicate even if the central military headquarters was wiped out. It will have many other uses but it cannot sustain the social and cultural life of the nation, it cannot provide the context for the development of a multicultural society, and ensure the realization of human potential. That is such a complicated task that it needs social and political consent and the revitalization of British urban life. To succeed will require, as a starting point, a sensitivity to the richness of the legacy of the past and the social ideals that have shaped our contemporary institutions.

REFERENCES

1   Clarke, J. and Crowther, C., *The devil makes work: leisure in capitalist Britain*, London, Macmillan, 1985, 1–47.
2   Green, E., Hebron, S. and Woodward, D., *Women's leisure, what leisure?*, Basingstoke, Macmillan Education, 1990.
3   Melling, J. and Barry, J. In: Melling, J. and Barry, J. (eds.), *Culture in history production, consumption and values in historical perspective*, Exeter, University of Exeter Press, 1992, 3–28.
4   Holt, R., *Sport and the British: a modern history*, Oxford, Clarendon Press, 1989.
5   Plumb, J. H., *The commercialization of leisure in the 18th century*, Reading, University of Reading Press, 1973.
6   Bailey, P., 'Leisure, culture and the historian: reviewing the first generation of leisure historiography in Britain', *Leisure studies*, 8 (2), 1989, 121.
7   Cunningham, H., 'Leisure and culture', In: Thompson, F. M. L. (ed.), *The Cambridge social history of Britain 1750–1950*, vol. 2: *People and their environment*, Cambridge, Cambridge University Press, 1990, 279–341; Lowerson, J. and Myerscough, J., *Time to spare in Victorian England*, Brighton, Harvester Press, 1977, 1–22.
8   Seed, J. and Wolff, J., 'Class and culture in nineteenth century Manchester', In: *Theory, culture and society*, 2 (2), 1984, 38–53; Money, J., *Experience and identity: Birmingham and the West Midlands, 1760–1800*, Manchester, Manchester University Press, 1977; Fraser, D. (ed.), *A history of modern Leeds*, Manchester, Manchester University Press, 1980.

9   Borsay, P., *The English urban renaissance: culture and society in the provincial town, 1660–1770*, Oxford, Clarendon Press, 1989.

10 Robbins, K., *History, religion and identity in modern Britain*, London, Hambledon Press, 1993.

11 Storch, R. D., 'Introduction: persistance and change in nineteenth century popular culture', In: Storch, R. D. (ed.), *Popular culture and customs in nineteenth century England*, London, Croom Helm, 1982.

12 Bailey, P., *Leisure and class in Victorian England: national recreation and the contest for control, 1830–1885*, London, Routledge and Kegan Paul, 1978, 35–56.

13 More, H., *Coelebs in search of a wife: comprehending observations on domestic habits and manners, religion and morals*, London, T. Cadell and W. Davies, 1808.

14 Elias, N. & Dunning, E., *Quest for excitement: sport and leisure in the civilising process*, London, Basil Blackwell, 1956.

15 Reid, A. J., *Social class and social relations in Britain 1850–1914*, London, Macmillan (Pamphlet for the Economic History Society), 1992.

16 Cunningham, H., *Leisure and the industrial revolution*, London, Croom Helm, 1979; Bailey, P., *Leisure and class in Victorian England: national recreation and the contest for control, 1830–1885*, London, Routledge and Kegan Paul, 1978; Clarke, J., Critcher, C. and Johnson, R. (eds), *Working class culture: studies in history and theory*, London, Hutchinson in association with the Centre of Contemporary Cultural Studies, University of Birmingham, 1979.

17 Holt, R., *Sport and the British: a modern history*, Oxford, Clarendon Press, 1989, 28–43.

18 Thompson, F. M. L., 'Social control in Victorian Britain', *Economic history review*, **34**, 1981 189–208.

19 Harrison, B., *Drink and the Victorians*, London, Faber, 1971.

20 The pub has continued to meet social demand by changing radically over the past two centuries. For the modern period, see Hopkins, E., *The rise and decline of the English working class, 1918–1990: a social history*, London, Weidenfeld and Nicolson, 1991 especially Ch. 5.

21 Hall, C. and Davidoff, L., *Family fortunes: men and women of the English middle class, 1780–1850*, London, Hutchinson, 1987.

22 Davidoff, L., *The best circles: society, etiquette and the season*, London, Croom Helm, 1973, especially Chs. 3 and 6.

23 Wilson, E., *Adorned in dreams: fashion and modernity*, London, Virago, 1985.

24 McCrone, K., *Sport and the physical emancipation of English women 1870–1914*, London, Routledge, 1988.

25 Prochaska, F., *Women and philanthropy in 19th century England*, Oxford, Clarendon, 1980; Riley, D., *Am I that name?: feminism and the category of women in history*, London, Macmillan, 1988, 44–66.

26 Beckett, J. V., *The book of Nottingham*, Buckingham, Barracuda, 1990; Meller, H. E., *Leisure and the changing city*, London, Routledge and Kegan Paul, 1976; Daunton, M., *Coal metropolis: Cardiff 1870–1914*, Leicester, Leicester University Press, 1977; Reid, C. O., *Middle class values and working class culture in nineteenth century*

Sheffield, unpublished PhD Thesis, University of Sheffield, 1976.

27 Kennedy, M., *The Hallé 1858–1983: a history of the orchestra*, Manchester, Manchester University Press, 1982, 1–7.

28 Lees, A., *Cities perceived: urban society in European and American thought 1820–1940*, Manchester, Manchester University Press, 1985, 59–90.

29 Briggs, A., *Victorian cities*, Harmondsworth, Penguin, 1968.

30 Greenhalgh, P., *Ephemeral vistas: expositions universelles, great exhibitions and world fairs 1851–1939*, Manchester, Manchester University Press, 1988, 52–82.

31 Davies, A. and Fielding, S. (eds.), *Workers' worlds, cultures & communities in Manchester and Salford 1880–1939*, Manchester, Manchester University Press, 1992.

32 Lowerson, J., *Sport and the English middle classes 1870–1914*, Manchester, Manchester University Press, 1993.

33 Meller, H. E., *Leisure and the changing city*, London, Routledge and Kegan Paul, 1976, 96–116.

34 Conway, H., *People's parks: the design and development of Victorian parks in Britain*, Cambridge, Cambridge University Press, 1991, especially Chs. 3 and 4.

35 Nelmes, W., 'A brief history of the Cardiff parks', In: *The Cardiff Naturalists' Society: reports and transactions*, **87**, 1957–8, 5–12.

36 Taigel, A. and Williamson, T., *Parks and gardens*, London, Batsford, 1993, Chs. 7 and 8.

37 Meller, H. E., 'Urban renewal and citizenship: the quality of life in British cities 1890–1990', *Urban history*, **22** (1), 1995, 63–84.

38 For example, see: *City of Birmingham handbook*, 1938, 267–9.

39 *Western Daily Press*, Bristol, 11 March 1895.

40 Information from local archives, Hanley Public Library.

41 Bremner, R. H., *American philanthropy*, Chicago, Chicago University Press, 1960, 115–17.

42 Swetnam, G., *Andrew Carnegie*, Boston, Twayne, 1980, 86.

43 Arnold, M., *Culture and anarchy*, (1859), (ed. Wilson, J. D.), Cambridge, Cambridge University Press, 1966, Ch. 1.

44 Sherborne, J. W., *University College, Bristol 1876–1909*, Bristol, pamphlet of the Bristol Branch of the Historical Association, 1977; Jones, D. *The origins of civic universities: Manchester, Leeds and Liverpool*, London, Routledge, 1988.

45 Barnett, Canon and Mrs S. A., *Towards social reform*, London, Williams and Norgate, 1909, 31.

46 Meller, H. E., *Leisure and the changing city*, London, Routledge and Kegan Paul, 1976, 122–205.

47 Lewis, J., *Women and social action in Victorian and Edwardian England*, Aldershot, Edward Elgar, 1991, 274.

48 *Ibid.*, 24–82; see also Darley, G., *Octavia Hill: a life*, London, Constable, 1990.

49 Jenkins, J. and James, P., *From acorn to oak tree: the growth of the National Trust 1895–1994*, London, Macmillan, 1994.

50 Rosenthal, M., *The character factory: Baden-Powell and the origins of the Boy Scout Movement*, London, Collins, 1986; Eager, W. M., *Making men: the history of boys*

clubs and related movements in Great Britain, London, University of London Press, 1953.

51   Balfour, M., *Birmingham and Joseph Chamberlain*, London, Allen and Unwin, 1985; Davies, S., *By the gains of industry: Birmingham museums and art gallery 1885–1985*, Birmingham Museums and Art Gallery, 1985.

52   Nettlefold, J. S., *Practical housing*, Letchworth, Garden City Press, 1908, 46.

53   Miller, M. *Raymond Unwin: garden cities and town planning*, Leicester, Leicester University Press, 1992, 104–38.

54   Briggs, A., 'Mass entertainment: the origins of a modern industry', *29th Joseph Fisher lecture in commerce*, University of Adelaide, 1960, 11.

55   Bianchini, F. and Parkinson, M. (eds.), *Cultural policy and urban regeneration: the West European experience*, Manchester, Manchester University Press, 1993, 1–20 and 155–76.

56   Hopkins, E., *The rise and decline of the English working class, 1918–1990: a social history*, London, Wiedenfeld and Nicolson, Ch. 5.

57   Roberts, K., *Youth and leisure*, London, Allen & Unwin, 1983.

58   Fowler, D., 'Teenage consumers: young wage earners and leisure in Manchester 1919–1939', *In*: Davies, A. and Fielding, S. (eds.), *Workers' worlds: cultures and communities in Manchester and Salford 1880–1939*, Manchester, Manchester University Press, 1992; Street, J., 'Youth Culture and the emergence of popular music', *In*: Gourvish, T. and O'Day, A., *Britain since 1945*, London, Macmillan, 1991, 305–24.

59   Cherry, G. E., *Cities and plans: the shaping of urban Britain in the nineteenth and twentieth centuries*, London, Edward Arnold, 1988, 83.

60   Rubinstein, A. *et al.* (eds.), *Just like the country: memories of London families who settled the new cottage estates 1919–1939*, London, Age Exchange, 1991.

61   Greatorex, J. and Clarke, S., *Looking back at Wythenshawe*, Timperley, Willow Publishing, 1984; Chinn, C., *Homes for people: a hundred years of council housing in Birmingham*, Exeter, Birmingham Books, 1991.

62   Crouch, D. and Ward, C., *The allotment: its landscape and culture*, London, Faber and Faber, 1988, Ch. 11.

63   Sheail, J., *Rural conservation in inter-war Britain*, Oxford, Clarendon Press, 1981.

64   Mason, T.W., 'Labour in the Third Reich, 1933–9', *Past and present*, **33**, 1966.

65   Prynn, D., 'The Clarion Clubs, rambling and the holiday associations in Britain since the 1890s', *Journal of contemporary history*, **11** (2 and 3), 1976, 65–77.

66   Fishwick, N., *English football and society 1910–50*, Manchester, Manchester University Press, 1989; Mangan, J. (ed.), *Pleasure, profit, proselytism: British culture and sport at home and abroad 1700–1914*, London, Cass, 1988; Bailey, P. (ed.), *Music hall: the business of pleasure*, Milton Keynes, Open University Press, 1986, viii–xxiii and 33–53.

67   Mass Observation, *The pub and the people*, London, The Cresset Library, 1987; Clapson, M., *A bit of a flutter: popular gambling in England 1820–1961*, Manchester, Manchester University Press, 1992.

68   Richards, J., *The age of the dream palace: cinema and society in Britain 1930–1939*, London, Routledge and Kegan Paul, 1984, Ch. 1; Stead, P., *Film and the working*

class: the feature film in British and American Society, London, Routledge, 1989, Ch. 3.

69 Cunningham, H., 'Leisure and culture', *In:* Thompson, F. M. L. (ed.), *The Cambridge social history of Britain 1750–1950*, vol. 2: *People and their environment*, Cambridge, Cambridge University Press, 1990, 311–12; Jones, S.G., *Sport, politics and the working class: organized labour and sport in interwar Britain*, 1992, 52–3; Roberts, K., *Youth and leisure*, Allen & Unwin, 1983, 16.

70 Chinn, C., *They worked all their lives: women of the urban poor in England 1880–1939*, Manchester, Manchester University Press, 1989, 115–21.

71 Gittins, D., *The fair sex: family size and structure 1900–39*, London, Hutchinson, 1982, 33–69.

72 Oakley, A., *The sociology of housework*, Oxford, Basil Blackwell, (1973 reprinted 1988), 135–66.

73 Pegg, M., *Broadcasting and society 1918–1939*, London, Croom Helm, 1983, 7.

74 Ward, C. and Hardy, D., *Goodnight campers! The history of the British holiday camp*, London, Mansell, 1986.

75 Walton, J. K., 'The demand for working class seaside holidays in 'Victorian England', *Economic history review*, XXXIV, 1981; Cross, G. (ed.), *Worktowners at Blackpool: mass observation and popular leisure in the 1930s*, London, Routledge, 1990.

76 Jones, S. G., *Sport, politics and the working class: organized labour and sport in interwar Britain*, 1992. See also McKibbon, R., *The ideologies of class social relations in Britain 1880–1950*, Oxford, Oxford University Press, 1994, 101–67.

77 Bourke, J., *Working class cultures in Britain 1890–1960: gender, class, ethnicity*, London, Routledge, 1994, 138–51.

78 Benson, J., *The rise of consumer society in Britain 1880–1980*, London, Longman, 1994, especially part II.

79 Davis, D., *A history of shopping*, London, Routledge and Kegan Paul, 1966, Ch. 12.

80 Kinnell, M. (ed.), *Informing communities: the role of libraries and information services*, Newcastle, Community Services Group of the Library Association, 1992.

2 Conceptualizing the public library 1850–1919

❖ *Paul Sturges*

INTRODUCTION

Despite the difficulties it has been experiencing in the last decades of the twentieth century, the British public library system is still one of the very best in the world. It has a professional leadership which, although it might not recognize itself in the description, is extremely sophisticated and self-confident. British public library practice is genuinely an example to most of the world, and the professional organizations, professional literature, speakers and consultants, all disseminate this message clearly and effectively. Despite a constant awareness of threats, the profession shows resilience and resourcefulness under what often seem like overwhelming difficulties. Because times are not easy now, professionals naturally remember the fairly recent past, when the prospect of expanding and improving services was a reliable expectation, and they may risk assuming that those days were normal and the present an aberration. This is quite definitely not the case, for very much more of the nearly 150-year history of British public libraries has been devoted to struggle against the odds, than to the enjoyment of plateaux of achievement and opportunity. Many of the problems experienced were quite simply financial: local authorities could not, or would not, vote enough money for adequate library provision. However, underlying this were problems directly attributable to ill-formed concepts of the role which public libraries should perform in society.

We should not allow hindsight to convince us that it has always been clear what a public library was, or what it was supposed to do. The legislators, civil servants, local politicians and administrators who were responsible for the setting up of public libraries very definitely had limited visions of what a public library should be. What is more, the librarians themselves, whose task it was to manage the provision of services, were almost equally unsure of just what they should aim to achieve. There was no relevant professional tradition, and a lack of guidance from cultural theory, political ideology, national policy or legislation. This tended to mean that most problems or opportunities which occurred had to be addressed by those responsible for a particular library service on the basis of their own almost unaided analysis of the situation. Some excellent, inspired responses resulted from this challenge, as did, however, some dismal failures and thoroughly eccentric local forms of practice. A considerable body of published information, ranging from the magnum opus of the late Thomas Kelly[1] to the numerous commemorative pamphlets and articles to be found listed in *British library history: bibliography*,[2] provides the researcher with details of cases in all the profusion that could be wished.

Only with a developing professional consciousness, rooted in the hard lessons of experience and given shape by the forum and structures for the dissemination of ideas provided by the Library Association (founded 1877) and other such organizations, did there emerge a clearer perception of what the public library should do. This hard-won clarity of vision found partial expression in the unappetizingly titled *Third interim report* (1919) of the Adult Education Committee of the Ministry of Reconstruction.[3] The 1919 Public Libraries Act embodied this vision, and effectively formed the basis for modern British public library service. Later, the official report which is referred to as the Kenyon Report[4] gave a full expression to official and professional perception of public library roles and functions. The McColvin report,[5] commissioned by the Library Association in 1942, contained an even clearer vision of the public library system and its future development. Even though this report did not have official status, the quality of its analysis and prescriptions made it an exceptionally influential document.

The route to the 1919 Act, and the Kenyon and McColvin Reports afterwards, was, as has already been stressed here, not at all an easy one. Yet it is arguable that the almost constant need to combat problems and insecurities was part of the reason why the system eventually reached a very realistic and practical set of solutions to the group of questions relating to the best role for a public library service in a particular society. Furthermore, it can be argued that the modern situation, in which the services of the British public library system are so highly developed and well adapted to the needs of its users, owes very much to those early years of struggle. The premise for this book is that there is much to be learned by looking back to the origins of our current system, and this chapter will not shirk identifying the role of inadequate ideas and mistaken directions in the process.

This chapter examines in broad outline the way in which nineteenth century British public librarians explored four main areas of service provision, namely services to scholarship, to learners, both adult and child, services for recreation, and the provision of information for business and professional purposes. First, however, the peculiar circumstances of the legislative enactment of 1850, from which the subsequent events mainly arose, need to be outlined.

THE PUBLIC LIBRARIES ACT 1850

The first thing to understand about the Act of 1850 was that it was not conceived as an element of government policy. Like much important nineteenth
century British legislation, its origin was in the minds of a small group of
reformers who sought to bring about change by promoting particular policies
to the public and influencing Parliament in their favour. In this case, the main
people concerned were William Ewart MP and Edward Edwards, an
employee of the British Museum Library. Ewart had a considerable record of
achievement in promoting social and cultural legislation and Edwards, as a
self-taught former bricklayer, was passionately convinced of the value and significance of libraries. He had set out some of his views in the 1836 pamphlet *A
letter to Benjamin Hawes.*[6] Ewart was equally a believer in the educational potential of freely available library facilities and had brought motions before
Parliament on this subject in 1840 and 1844.

The Select Committee

Ewart contacted Edwards by letter in 1848, when Edwards had just published
his *Remarks on the paucity of libraries freely open to the public*[7] and an article in the
Journal of the Statistical Society of London,[8] in both of which he marshalled a considerable body of evidence in favour of the public library idea. Ewart suggested they should seek legislation for a system of public libraries and to this
end they should encourage the setting up of a Select Committee of Parliament
to investigate the question. He argued that

> Before such a Committee evidence might be given of the number of
> libraries abroad, the number in this country, the facilities abroad, the diffi-
> culties here, the best mode of instituting, maintaining, and effecting the for-
> mation of Libraries – and the Report of the Committee (if favourable) might
> lead, in a subsequent Session, to the action of the Government.[9]

Edwards happily accepted Ewart's proposal and the two began to exchange
ideas and information with considerable enthusiasm.

With Ewart operating from within Parliament and Edwards from without,
the two were well qualified to make the best use of the Select Committee which
was eventually appointed, and which first met to hear evidence on 30 March
1849. The Committee was chaired by Ewart himself and consisted of 15 members, prominent amongst whom were several other radicals. Witnesses were
called to provide information about existing libraries and about the needs of
authors and others who used libraries. The resulting evidence was published
as the *Report from the Select Committee on Public Libraries,*[10] 1849 and 1850. This
document then provided a basis for the framing and debating of legislation on
public libraries.

Edwards was the most prominent witness and, very naturally, his message was that public libraries were conducive to the development of a better educated and better informed populace. This was, however, more or less taken as axiomatic and the chief part of his evidence concerned the contention that, in library provision, Britain was lagging behind those nations, mainly on the continent of Europe, which might be seen as its rivals. As Edwards had put it on an earlier occasion,

> Not that I deem the argument from comparison at all necessary to show that additional public libraries ought to be established in this country – a proposition which might safely rest on its own merits – but because, the utility of public libraries being unquestioned, such a comparison may serve to place their existing deficiencies in a more salient and practical point of view.[11]

Edwards, in his evidence, defined public libraries as

> embracing, first of all, libraries deriving their support from public funds, either wholly or in part; and I would further extend it to such libraries as are made accessible to the public to a greater or lesser degree.[12]

This is a singularly weak definition, which fails to make it clear that it is, in fact, the accessibility of general collections of literature to the whole populace, for the broadest educational and cultural purposes, that distinguishes a public library, rather than its source of funding. Ten years later he defined what he and Ewart had been seeking in 1849 much more effectively, when he wrote that

> They [public libraries] must contain, in fair proportions, the books that are attractive to the uneducated and the half-educated, as well as those which subserve the studies and assist the pursuits of the clergyman, the merchant, the politician, and the professional scholar. They must be unrestrictedly open to every visitor. They must offer to all men, not only the practical science, the temporary excitements, and the prevalent opinions of the day, but the wisdom of preceding generations; the treasures of remote antiquity; and the hopes and the evidences of the world to come.[13]

This might represent a maturer version of Edwards' ideas, but there is the strong possibility that the definition used in 1849 was deliberately framed for a very precise purpose. Using a definition based on public funding, and a subsidiary definition on the basis of free public access, Edwards was able to present evidence showing that London had virtually no public libraries, other than that of the British Museum, and that the provinces were even worse placed. By the same definition, European libraries could be shown to be very numerous and the numbers of books available to the public much more plentiful than anywhere in Britain. Whilst this was true, the books in these libraries were largely of scholarly use and the librarians who cared for them made little attempt to provide a service for the whole public.[14] By ignoring this and making little mention of the wealth of libraries in Britain serving a wide public for payment (the circulating and subscription libraries), Edwards and Ewart were broadly successful in creating the impression that Britain lacked something important which its rivals possessed.

On the strength of this impression, which was reflected in the *Report from the Select Committee*, Ewart was able to pilot a Bill through a rather unenthusiastic Parliament and on 14 August 1950 it received the Royal Assent as the Public Libraries Act. To this extent the exercise begun by the two men in 1848 was a success. But it is important to ask whether it mattered that Edwards and Ewart avoided tackling the case for public libraries directly and relied on creating a positive mood towards legislation by somewhat dubious use of comparative evidence. There is some reason to believe that it did matter.

Early models of provision
In the first place, features of the public libraries which were made possible by the 1850 Act bore a certain unfortunate, but hardly surprising, resemblance to the models which had been cited in evidence to the Committee. The Act permitted, but did not compel, towns of more than 10,000 population to provide a public library if local ratepayers consented. The town council was then empowered to levy a small rate of one halfpenny in the pound to pay for the salaries of staff and the premises and upkeep of a library. Significantly this tax income could not be devoted to the purchase of books, which, it was expected, would be donated by the citizenry. This profoundly static and financially limited concept of a public library was too much like the free, but scholarly and remote 'public' libraries of the European continent for coincidence. A thoroughly limited piece of legislation and a narrow and unhelpful series of models for the public library were the consequences of the way in which the Public Libraries Act was obtained.

Naturally, the newly appointed librarians of public libraries sought to please their employers by providing services which would be acknowledged as meeting their requirements. But the requirements were seldom sufficiently precise as to make this easy, and the librarians themselves were not a group with a coherent understanding of what public libraries might do. The larger cities were able to appoint experienced librarians and scholars to take charge of their new services. Manchester chose the library campaigner Edward Edwards himself as its first City Librarian, and Birmingham Public Library employed J. D. Mullins, the experienced librarian of the Birmingham [subscription] Library in

1865. Such people were not numerous, however, and smaller communities made quite inappropriate appointments. For instance, Martin Finnegan, a former policeman, was appointed at Bolton, and Chesterfield chose Dennis Gorman, whose qualifications or experience were not felt worth recording. Other communities achieved acceptable compromises, Oxford appointing Benjamin Blackwell, former bookseller and father of the founder of Blackwells, in 1854, whilst Cambridge had, in 1853, appointed the 22-year-old John Pink, a bookseller's assistant. Significantly though, Pink's strongest competitor was Thomas Cross, a retired stagecoachman.

Only after the passage of some decades did the apprenticeship schemes in some of the better-run library systems begin to produce significant numbers of librarians grounded in the basics of the work, some of whom could then take their knowledge and experience on into the service of other employers. Some of the more notable figures of British public librarianship emerged from this background. Ernest Savage, though he left school at the age of 12 and had worked in a printing shop before joining Croydon Public Libraries, was able to build a successful career at Birkenhead, Coventry and Edinburgh on the basis of his training there. Other entrants had a better educational grounding: Stanley Jast, for instance, when he joined Halifax Public Library as an assistant in 1887, had studied, unsuccessfully, for the Civil Service examinations. John Potter Briscoe, later City Librarian of Nottingham, had at least continued his schooling until the age of 18 when he joined a Bolton Public Library system which was beginning to gain a reputation for high standards. Other systems, such as those of Leeds and Newcastle upon Tyne, gained the reputation of producing the type of librarian whom other communities might see as a very desirable potential employee. Thus librarians with neither educational background or experience were steadily replaced by successors whose training in the routines of library work was sound.

SERVICES TO SCHOLARSHIP

In the early years after 1850, however, public librarianship was in the hands of a largely inexperienced and untrained workforce. For the most part they did not have the educational background to construct a self-confident consensus on the direction public libraries should take. Such experienced librarians as there were in their ranks came, as noted above, from existing libraries of a scholarly type. It was natural that this experienced minority would feel happiest providing services to scholars, and that their example would influence their less experienced colleagues. However, there was already a well-established pattern of scholarly libraries in both London and the provincial cities. London learned societies and private clubs covered almost every discipline and specialization imaginable and their libraries, many founded as early as the seventeenth century, still serve scholarly research at the end of the twentieth century. In the provinces, specialized societies, such as the Society of Antiquaries of Newcastle upon Tyne, or the Manchester Literary and Philosophical Society, provided similar library facilities. Private subscription libraries, still existing today in Leeds, Manchester, Nottingham and a few other cities, flourished in the nineteenth century, providing general collections with a high scholarly content. This left limited opportunities for public libraries to develop new provision of the kind their librarians tended to feel most drawn towards, either because of their experience, or because of the examples available to them. In consequence, a definite tendency can be identified for public librarians of the day to see themselves as frustrated scholar librarians. This arguably had an adverse effect on the services they were called upon to provide.

Local history collections

Fortunately, there was one scholarly area which all public libraries could, and did, enter effectively. This was local history. In the second half of the nineteenth century, the study of the history of counties, boroughs, parishes, their buildings, families, religious beliefs, pastimes, economic activities and other occupations was losing the purely antiquarian character it had kept since its sixteenth century origins. This kind of study was being taken up by a slightly wider spectrum of the population than the gentry and clergy who had been its main practitioners for centuries. Numbers of the middle class beneficiaries of the more easily available educational opportunities to be found in much of nineteenth century Britain definitely wanted to share in exploring the past of their local communities. For them to take more than a casual interest in the subject, it was necessary for them to have access to the rare books and manuscripts that could at that time be found chiefly in the muniment rooms of country houses, or the vestries of parish churches. In acquiring and making such material available to a wider readership there was a valid scholarly role for the public library.

It was one which the *Report from the Select Committee* had suggested: 'In all our chief provincial towns it is requisite that there should be Topographical Libraries where history may find a faithful portraiture of local events, local literature, and local manners.'[15] It was also something for which the more prescient local historians of the old school, such as George Poulett Scrope, President of the Wiltshire Archaeological and Natural History Society, recognized a need:

> Monuments decay; deeds and MSS are continually destroyed or lost; [private] libraries and collections of drawings etc are broken up and dispersed. Is there no spirit of antiquarian and local research left in the country that

will struggle to save from oblivion what yet remains decipherable of the relics of our past history?[16]

Public libraries responded to this need by setting up local collections, among the first of which were those at Manchester, Liverpool, Rochdale, Bristol, Leicester, Birmingham, Plymouth, Warrington, Cambridge and Derby.

They were frequently able to get such services off to a good start by acquiring accumulations, of the kind referred to by Scrope, from local owners by bequest and purchase. Thus in its very first year, the Liverpool Public Library, founded in 1852, acquired the Binns collection of maps, drawings and engravings, which formed the nucleus of its future local collection. From many other examples which could be cited, one more – that of Derby – will be sufficient to show that Liverpool was not unique. In 1878, the Duke of Devonshire donated to the borough library a collection of Derbyshire books which had been in his personal library at Chatsworth House. To this the library added, in 1914, the personal library of local material of Sir Henry Howe Bemrose, purchased from the proceeds of a public subscription.

Such was the speed with which local history collecting spread amongst public libraries, that it was possible for a remarkably complete rationale for this type of work to be set out as early as 1878, at the Second Annual Meeting of the newly formed Library Association, held in Oxford. This was done in a paper by William Wright (1844–1915), who had been appointed Librarian of Plymouth only two years previously, having before that served as librarian to the Plymouth Working Men's Association.[17] Wright has been described as the 'father' of public library local history collections,[18] but the significant thing is that this 'father' was such a young man and that he had such short experience of public library work. His paper obviously drew on an expanding body of experience and precedent from throughout the public library service, to discuss acquisitions, cataloguing, development of the librarian's specialist knowledge, and the stimulation of local research and publishing.

However, the success of British public libraries in local studies work, which Wright's paper effectively announced and which has continued to the present day, must not be allowed to obscure the fact that there was, for the most part, no major role in scholarly librarianship for the early public libraries. Such experience as there was in their ranks of public librarians might have been derived from scholarly work, and they might have shared a sentiment that work with learned books and periodicals was the respectable thing for a librarian to do, but if libraries were to succeed in providing services that their community would accept and appreciate then they would have to look for other types of function. With the British population increasingly literate and faced with opportunities for moving into employment which required a sound general education, provision for those involved in formal education, both at adult and school level, was a role which offered itself very naturally to public libraries.

SERVICES TO LEARNERS

Public libraries very quickly involved themselves in services to learners, and it was service to adults which they took up first, and with the most marked enthusiasm. There was a model here, the Mechanics Institutes, and there was indirect government encouragement. A new Department of Science and Art was created in 1853, under the aegis of the Board of Trade. The Department was based at South Kensington, in the museums complex which originated from the ideas and finance created by the Great Exhibition. The Department in 1857 became part of the new Education Department. It worked by providing grants to pay some of the expenses of the organizers of classes in science and art. The classes themselves sprang from a great variety of private efforts by organizations such as scientific societies, schools and Mechanics Institutes. Amongst this confusion of different attempts to provide technical education, some of the new public libraries began to get involved to the extent of not merely providing books for adult learners, but organizing adult classes themselves.

Warrington, a northern industrial town, was one of the most progressive communities in the matter of libraries and adult education.[19] It was also one of the very first communities to organize adult classes in its library, after the 1850 Public Libraries Act. By 1855 a sufficient number of library services were organizing classes to induce Parliament to include in the new Public Libraries Act of that year a clause to the effect that science and art classes could be provided by Public Libraries. This recognition of something that certain libraries were already doing was in financial terms not a great step forward for either libraries or adult education. Both services had to be provided from the same rate of one penny in the pound. The Act was, however, to be the only legislation for over 30 years which did anything to aid the provision of adult education by local authorities.

What this meant for a particular community was that it had to balance two legitimate and related activities within fixed funding limits. For instance, in Cardiff the Public Libraries Act was adopted in 1862 and science and art classes were added by 1865.[20] John Ballinger, the librarian of Cardiff at this time, later revealed the consequences of this arrangement. A penny rate in Cardiff produced £1510 annually, from which £422 went to pay loan charges on the building provided. The library, museum and science classes all had to be maintained from the remaining £1088. However, since the Council regularly voted less than the product of a penny rate, the sum was notably smaller. In fact most of the money went towards administration and a totally inadequate sum was available for book purchase (now at least permitted under the 1855 Act). This was not an untypical consequence of the linking of library and classes, and the effects could be much more severe in a smaller, less wealthy town.

Yet the Public Libraries Act of 1884, which had clarified the right of libraries to organize Schools of Science and Art and to claim Department of Science and Arts grants, encouraged more authorities to do this. Only with the Technical Instruction Act of 1889 was the raising of a separate rate of one penny for the support of classes allowed. This relieved the impossible burden that classes placed on the library rate of many communities. Although this new legislation did not solve all the problems created by library provision of technical classes, the Act placed the arrangement on something more like a rational footing. It was not, however, the Act which made the most significant difference to the funding of technical education by another almost wholly contingent legislative intervention. The 1890 Local Taxation Act raised a duty of 6d. per gallon on spirits which the Government had at first no fixed view on how to spend. This so-called whisky money was in fact allocated as grants for local expenditure on technical education.

The effect of these measures could be substantial. In Hanley, for instance, the product of a penny rate was £250, so that after 1889 two sums of that amount were available for libraries and technical education respectively.[21] Hanley's whisky money was £840 over and above this. The scale of financial improvement was obviously enormous and Cotgreave's collection of pictures of library buildings of 1901 shows imposing joint Library and Technical School buildings in Darwen, Ashton under Lyne, Chesterfield, Leigh, Lancaster, St. Helens, Doncaster, Longton, Poole, Bromley and Newport.[22] By this time, of 330 Technical Schools in England, about 100 were connected with libraries and this arrangement was used in communities as varied as Launceston (population 4345 in 1900) and Liverpool (population 518,000 in 1900).

That the legislation now made it possible for such an arrangement to work better than before should not obscure the memory of the totally unsatisfactory way it worked before the Technical Instruction Act. Nor should it be assumed that the arrangement always worked well in the 1890s. The natural expansion of library collections placed demands on space in libraries such as those of Newcastle and South Shields and created pressure for the removal of classes from the building. There were undoubtedly still many librarians and teachers cursing the arrangement almost as heartily as they had before 1889. This type of link was effectively terminated by the Education Act of 1902. This measure obliged Library Committees to transfer control of Technical Schools to the new Education Committees created to administer the whole of each local authority's educational provision. Any final ties were cut by the 1919 Public Libraries Act.

Children's services

At the same time as public libraries were deeply involved with adult education, through arrangements arguably detrimental to the service as a whole, they showed comparative reluctance to serve school-age learners. The first fully fledged service provided for children seems to have been that which was set up in Manchester in 1862.[23] Manchester's initiative seems not to have been followed by any great rush of other library authorities anxious to serve young readers. Birkenhead began similar service in 1865, and by 1869 Birmingham had children's material at its central library and two branches. The subsequent spread of this type of service did gradually speed up after the passing of a new Education Act in 1870, but by 1891 an informed estimate, by Butler Wood, of the number of children's collections put it at only about 40.[24] This contrasts quite sharply with the 100 or so Technical Schools connected to libraries at this time. What is more, the children's services varied in size, form and quality.

The children's collections identified in 1891 ranged in size from Leeds' 24,000 volumes with 207,000 issues, down to Brentford's 56 volumes, which achieved 531 issues. Most collections were actually in a range from about 500 to 3000 volumes, but the average number of times each book was used per year varied from two to 35. Approaches to this type of service varied from authority to authority. Nottingham and Reading rented buildings specifically as children's libraries, but Leeds, Norwich and Plymouth placed their services in the schools, with teachers acting as 'librarians'. Where specifically designated children's service was provided in the main library, a separate children's counter might be provided, as at Cardiff, but more usually children were served along with the rest of the users. In these cases a separate catalogue was printed, listing material bought specially for children and material in the general collection which might appeal to them. By 1885, librarians could read a strong statement of the case for children's libraries, and an outline of recommended ways to provide service, by Potter Briscoe.[25] Briscoe's library at Nottingham was generally regarded as an example of what children's libraries should be like.

Yet only a minority of libraries followed the example of Nottingham and the other more advanced authorities. Wood did point out that

> We find a large number of young borrowers in all our libraries, and if the books suitable for them are not separated from the rest of the stock, they are there all the same and are freely used by the young readers. It would therefore be an injustice to those libraries where no such arrangements exist to suppose that the claims of the children are neglected.[26]

This was too kind or somewhat disingenuous. The age at which children were allowed to join the library was prescribed, and often set amazingly high by present opinion at 14 years (it was still nine years when the writer of this chapter wanted to join his home town library in the 1950s). The collections were closed access and selection could only be made from the catalogue. A child wishing to read would have to rely on a parent or older companion to borrow a book on their behalf. The book would then have to be selected just on the basis of author and title, from collections which contained nothing bought with children specifically in mind. It is not unfair to suggest that, despite the exceptions discussed above, librarians generally turned their back on service to children. The lesson that this type of service is a cornerstone of public library activity was only slowly learnt.

RECREATION

Even though, to modern eyes, the involvement of public libraries with services to learners was unduly skewed towards adults, it is clear that librarians, councillors and other opinion-formers believed that an essential aim of the public library was to serve formal education. At the same time, the issue of informal education, and more particularly, the role of recreational reading in personal development, was one which gave particular problems. This issue will be dealt with in more detail in Chapter Four, but another useful approach to the question of provision of recreational reading material in nineteenth century public libraries is the evidence of issue statistics for fiction.

This reveals that the percentage of fiction issues from public libraries was huge. An article of 1890,[27] using a cross-section of 25 libraries in England and Scotland, identified an average fiction issue (with certain qualifications) of 74% of total issues. Such a figure is broadly confirmed by statistics from a small sample of 13 lending libraries (both small and large) for the years 1876–7 examined by Thomas Kelly.[28] He found only two in which fiction issues amounted to less than 50% of total loans; for the remainder, the range was between 57% and 83%. Throughout the period, fiction remained the overwhelming first choice in lending libraries, and indeed percentages have stayed towards the upper end of this range to present times. What the 1890 article, quoted above, also revealed was that whilst it represented 74% of loans, fiction only represented 37.5% of the stock of the libraries examined. Even bearing in mind that the non-fiction lending stock may very probably have been read quite often on the library premises, these figures illustrate a serious mismatch between demand and provision. The significant point is that this represented deliberate policy.

Professional responses

The reaction of librarians to the evidence of statistics and, indeed, of their own experience, can be discovered from a steady sequence of articles on the topic which appeared in the newly emerging professional press. Peter Cowell, who was librarian at Liverpool, a large and progressive authority, addressed the issue at the first conference of librarians in Britain in 1877. His paper 'The admission of fiction in free public libraries'[29] drew attention to Liverpool's lending statistics which showed fiction at about 75% of the issue. His reaction to this was to regard it as basically a problem, since much of the fiction chosen was not of the most edifying kind on offer. He confessed himself very sceptical towards the argument, often presented when such facts were revealed, that readers progressed from inferior to superior fiction in a gradual improvement of their taste and understanding. His attitude was that 'Free libraries were primarily intended to carry on the education of our schools and enable the poorer classes to develop any latent talent or ability they might possess of a literary, a scientific, or an artistic kind.'[30] Only a few of the 'better' novels would fit this scheme and the drastically reduced issues that would result from restricting fiction collections should be accepted in the interests of 'good quality'.

Two years later, J. T. Kay, of Owens College, Manchester, in a paper to the 1879 Library Association Conference, went even further, declaring that 'Much has been said of the value of reading; but reading per se is not valuable, and in the case of many of these novels it is dissipating and valueless.'[31] In his experience 'Schoolboys or students who took to novel-reading to any extent never made much progress in after life. They neglected real practical life for the sensually imaginative and suffered accordingly from the enervating influence.'[32] Perhaps this distaste for fiction as a whole and the more popular types of fiction in particular was best summed up by W. E. Doubleday, of Hampstead Public Library, whose title 'The fiction nuisance and its abatement'[33] is enough indication of the tone and content of his contribution. What Cowell, Kay, Doubleday and others effectively proposed was the active pursuit of reduced proportions of fiction lending.

Many librarians actually aimed at fiction issues close to 50% of the total issue in their libraries, largely on the basis that percentages of this kind had been 'achieved' in some public libraries. For example, when in Stockport during the period 1877–8 fiction issues reached 80% of the total, determined efforts were made to reduce the level.[34] Opinion seemed to be that people would read what was available, and that if levels of fiction were reduced library users would read other more 'beneficial' material. Not surprisingly, Stockport's experiment in providing more 'substantial' material did succeed as fiction issues began to decline. The cost of this reduction of the percentage of fiction loans in terms of what it meant to total issues and to the breadth of general interest in the library's services was clearly not regarded as the significant part of the equation.

It is true, of course, that a more open-minded view of fiction reading in general, and the reading of popular fiction in particular, was also held by librarians. There was also some defence of the utility of reading as the exercise of a useful skill. As L. S. Jast put it 'The basic proposition that it is better to read than not to read may be taken as a sound generalization. There is – alas! – no law against bad taste.'[35] An even more wholehearted version of this line, which came from Frederic Perkins of Boston, Massachusetts, Public Library, had been quoted by Cowell, with the intention of refuting it. This suggested that

> It is desirable that the habit of reading should be formed. A habit of reading is more necessary than any particular line of reading, and to form that habit, easy reading – that is, reading such as people want, such as they enjoy – must be furnished first, and afterwards that which requires more effort.[36]

Ernest Savage, when librarian of Edinburgh Public Libraries, claimed that his own personal experience showed a process of improving taste in action and said that 'A single book, even a rubbishy book, will start a line of reading, or study, extending over years, if the subject arouses interest in the reader.'[37] Probably the least apologetic case for fiction, in all its manifestations, seems to have been put by the economist Sydney Webb, who took a great interest in library matters. He suggested that 'There is absolutely no argument, on grounds of economic or political science, why public libraries should not purvey recreative or amusing books, if the ratepayers so desire.'[38] Practising librarians seldom offered such a hearty justification for positive treatment of popular fiction. This is despite the observation that public libraries did quite often lend fiction of a more popular variety than some commercial circulating libraries, particularly the most dominant of these, Mudie's.[39] Whatever it was that they did in practice, the generality of public librarians clearly found it hard to reconcile the pressures of public demand with their idea of what librarians ought to be doing.

Not until 1908, at the Library Association Conference, was a compromise position reached, balancing the message of reader demand against librarians' sentiments about their true role. A. O. Jennings, the Chairman of the Brighton Library Sub-Committee, proposed three resolutions which were adopted without dissent.[40] They stated that:

> 1. The function of a public lending library is to provide good literature for circulation amongst its readers, and that the same test must be applied to its works of fiction as to the books in its other departments: they must have literary or educational value.
> 2. Every public library should be amply supplied with fiction that has attained the position of classical literature.
> 3. The provision of mere ephemeral fiction of no literary, moral or educational value, even if without offence, is not within the proper province of a public lending library.

The resolutions seem to have provided a formula which librarians could accept and after this debate the topic declined noticeably. In subsequent years, public libraries came to accept that they could legitimately add 'mere ephemeral fiction' to their collections, and that the consequences would be positive rather than harmful.

INFORMATION SERVICE

The final category of service that will be discussed is 'information service', but that is a term which is to be used with caution. Much of the service provided in the early public libraries was 'reference service', in the sense that many books were to be consulted in the library rather than to be borrowed for home use. Indeed, a few libraries began with a reference collection, but no lending collection at all.[41] Ipswich, for instance, began a library service in 1853 and did not provide lending facilities until 1887 or 1888, whilst at Maidstone the library opened in 1858, acquired as many as 20,000 books for reference use, but did not lend any until 1890. In cases where material was kept for consultation in the library only, it tended to be a mixture of more costly books with varied subject matter and genuine works of reference, such as encyclopedias. The works of reference were almost invariably kept in closed access with the rest of the collection, so that it was necessary to request items specifically to be able to refer to them. The main honourable exception to this was Cambridge Public Library. A collection of reference books was made available to readers on open access as early as 1870. The collections of reference material in the libraries of large cities became extremely large and valuable at this time, but were still kept on closed access. Thus Liverpool in 1886 had a reference collection of 89,000 volumes and that of Manchester was nearly as large. The utility of a closed access reference collection is, of course, somewhat questionable.

It is not unfair to suggest that reference departments were a neglected aspect of library service in these early years. Why this should be is hard to explain, since, like provision for local history, it had a satisfyingly scholarly aspect. The neglect took various forms. Collections were not carefully selected, they were poorly catalogued, and specially trained staff were not usually available to help users to trace the information they required. Regarding the latter problem, James Duff Brown declared in 1903 that there were 'Plenty of municipal reference libraries at the present time, whose service is in the hands and at the mercy of the frivolous small boy or helpless girl.'[42]

All of these, coupled with closed access in the great majority of cases, amounted to an inadequate service in national terms. The Kenyon Report of 1927 found that, in general, the situation was still unsatisfactory and made a number of specific recommendations for the upgrading of reference services.[43] There had, however, already been some change in attitude amongst a minority of libraries. In particular, the value of specialized commercial and technical services had been recognized in a number of cases.

This had not been the case as late as 1883, when John Southward declared, at the Library Association's Conference, that an investigation of public library collections by studying their catalogues showed that 'technical books, in which ninety per cent of the readers are most distinctly concerned, do not exceed ten per cent of the whole'.[44] Whilst one might question his grounds for assuming that so many of the public were interested, his figure for the technical part of the collections may even have been a little optimistic. However, it was definitely the case that in the bigger cities the reference collections included large quantities of material that was of value to business and industry. In 1911 this was explicitly recognized by Glasgow, which, when its main reference library was moved from the business district of the city, kept the directories and other business reference materials in the original building. This was designated as a Commercial Library in 1916.[45] In following this approach Glasgow was doing something which was already advocated in the library press.

Ernest Savage and Stanley Jast both discussed this type of service in print, whilst, in 1912, W. E. Doubleday – previously cited as an opponent of fiction – suggested that a broadly defined information function was the prime responsibility of the public library.[46] British advocates of this approach were able to cite American instances of reference libraries successfully taking on an active role as disseminators of information. Indeed arguing from American precedent was a frequent and very effective way of encouraging moves towards improved library practice in Britain. However, it was the First World War (1914–1918) which made the difference in this particular area. Public libraries, whether the librarians liked it or not, were used for the distribution of official materials, such as those produced by the Parliamentary Recruiting Committee and the Director of Food Economy, and other literature contributing towards the war effort. The role of near-propaganda institution may not have appealed to librarians nurtured in a more open tradition, but it did initiate them in the techniques of a more active information role. This possibly contributed to a greater receptivity to the idea of commercial and technical information services during the war years.

The necessity for an improved and more innovative industrial economy in a country at war was certainly recognized by many library services. Commercial and technical information services were set up in a number of major cities, notably Liverpool in 1917, Bradford in 1918, and Leeds in the same year. Ernest Savage, who became chief librarian at Coventry in 1915, almost immediately set up a commercial section of the reference library, and also had a technical section in operation in 1916. These services compiled bibliographies, subscribed to journals relevant to local business and industry, and collected newspaper cuttings.[47] Savage's success in Coventry led him to suggest action on this topic by the Library Association. A Special Committee on Technical and Commercial Libraries was set up in 1916, which conducted an enquiry into the way in which libraries were dealing with this type of material. This Committee's report, submitted to the Department of Scientific and Industrial Research, did not produce a dramatic change in Government policy. It was, nevertheless, an important contribution to the continuing process of defining and redefining the role of public libraries. When at the end of the war, The Library Association campaigned for new and improved legislation for public libraries, the work on commercial and technical services was effectively cited as the type of progress which made such legislation necessary. The Public Libraries Act of 1919, to which these services indirectly contributed, was arguably the first really strong piece of legislation for public libraries which Britain had seen. It came at the end of 70 years of struggle and was itself a product of that struggle.

CONCLUSION

The original Public Libraries Act of 1850 was little more than a shell within which a library service could grow or wither. The public, through the librarians who served them, slowly obtained services which were extremely appropriate, useful and, eventually, well-loved, within the scope of this legislation and the later Acts which amended it. This came about, however, despite the tendency of librarians to provide for an idealized reader, preferably a scholar or adult learner, rather than the actual schoolchild, fiction-reader or information seeker who entered their doors. This account of some of the vicissitudes of that process is given because the difficulties experienced by British public libraries in attaining a mature and effective role have something to tell us about the essential elusiveness of a fully developed concept of the role of the public library in any society.

It may seem, in retrospect, obvious that public libraries could really only play a limited part, mainly through work with local history, in serving scholarship. The validity of the public library's function as a support for formal education, particularly adult education, is also indisputable. What was a problem in the early years was the balance of that role against others, and the extent to which taking on the role demanded an institutionalized link with education. The provision of recreational reading, particularly fiction, was much more contentious and a rationale which would satisfy librarians and their employers emerged only with extreme difficulty. Yet here, more than in any other area of public library service, the message of demand was unequivocal. However, it was not easy to reconcile what public demand made plain with orthodox views of the value, or rather lack of value, of fiction and other recreational material. An informational role for the public library was developed last of all, ultimately under the malign stimulus of war. In this type of service the library accepted a necessity to anticipate demand – indeed to stimulate demand – in the interests of national development. In taking up this challenge, the British public library can perhaps be seen for the first time as a fully mature institution, understanding its relationship to other forms of library and information service, acknowledging and responding to the public's calls upon it, yet also identifying new missions which it could undertake for the general good.

The process by which this occurred can be observed taking place in a number of ways. The proceedings volumes of The Library Association's conferences, the texts of papers presented to the monthly meetings of The Library Association, as published in journals such as *The library*, and books and pamphlets by librarians and supporters of libraries, all show debates in process and dominant views emerging. A number of substantial works on public libraries, perhaps most significantly those of Thomas Greenwood 1851–1908,⁴⁸ sum up and codify the developing concept. The emergence of leaders, such as Ernest Savage and Stanley Jast, gave authority to particular approaches, and the mobility of library staff spread ideas and practices from one library authority to another. A professional concept of public librarianship gradually came to dominate debate in a wider forum, to the extent that the Public Libraries Act of 1919 can definitely be seen as a professional's Act first and a politician's second.

The purpose of this chapter is not to advocate the utility of 70 years of ill-directed exploration and struggle as a means to obtain a public library system which offers a close match to public need. These were often wasteful and unsatisfactory years, but their value lay in the opportunity that the search for a role gave librarians to experiment with types of service and ways of delivering service. Successes could be compared with false directions and mistaken initiatives so as to allow others to learn lessons which would enrich the totality of service provided throughout the system of public libraries. A process of evolution – the survival of the most appropriate – produced many libraries well adapted to the peculiar circumstances of their own localities. The surveys conducted by Kenyon and McColvin could identify these successes – the favourable trends and the worthwhile initiatives – so as to point national planning in similar directions. British public library achievements, post-1919, were a triumph based on the results of British empiricism. It is an approach which has its costs, but which, by harnessing professional initiative and the public will, in the end promises services of the highest standards, matched to need in the closest possible way.

REFERENCES

1   Kelly, T., *History of public libraries in Great Britain 1845–1975*, 2nd edn, London,

Library Association, 1977.

2   *British library history: bibliography* 6 vols., in progress, 1972–present.

3   Adult Education Committee of the Ministry of Reconstruction, *Third interim report*, Cd. 9237, 1919.

4   Board of Education, Public Libraries Committee, *Report on public libraries in England and Wales*, Cmd. 2868, 1927.

5   McColvin, L. R., *The public library system of Great Britain*, London, Library Association, 1942.

6   Edwards, E., *A letter to Benjamin Hawes: being strictures on the Minutes of Evidence taken before the Select Committee on the British Museum*, London, 1836.

7   Edwards, E., *Remarks on the paucity of libraries freely open to the public in the British Empire*, London, 1849.

8   Edwards, E., 'A statistical view of the principal public libraries in Europe and the United States', *Journal of the Statistical Society of London*, **11**, 1848, 250–81.

9   Munford, W. A., *Edward Edwards, 1812–1886: portrait of a librarian*, London, Library Association, 1963, 57.

10   House of Commons, Select Committee on Public Libraries, *Report*, London, HMSO, 1849 and 1850.

11   Edwards, E., *Remarks on the paucity of libraries freely open to the public in the British Empire*, London, 1849, 4.

12   House of Commons, Select Committee on Public Libraries, *Report*, Minute 10.

13   Edwards, E., *Memoirs of libraries*, London, Trubner, 1859, Vol. 1, 776.

14   Sturges, P., 'The use of comparative data in librarianship: an Anglo–French case study, 1848–1850'. *Libri*, **39** (4), 1989, 275–83.

15   House of Commons, Select Committee on Public Libraries, *Report*, x–xi.

16   Scrope, G. P., *History of the ancient manor and barony of Castle Combe*, London, J.B. Nichols, 1852, vii.

17   Wright, W. H. K., 'Special collections of local books in provincial libraries', *In: Transactions and proceedings of the First Annual Meeting of the Library Association of the United Kingdom, 1878*, London, Chiswick Press, 1879, 44–50.

18   Ansell, R., 'The historical development and present structure of public library local studies provision in the United Kingdom', *In:* Dewe, M. (ed.), *A manual of local studies librarianship*, Aldershot, Gower, 1987, Ch. 3, 27–51.

19   Stephens, W. B., *Adult education and society in an industrial town: Warrington 1800–1900*, Exeter, Exeter University, 1980.

20   Ballinger, J., *The Cardiff free libraries*, Cardiff, City Council, 1895.

21   Hunter, E. J., *The role of the public library in the development of technical education in Great Britain and Ireland during the nineteenth century*, Sheffield University dissertation, 1973, 127.

22   Cotgreave, A., *Views and memoranda of public libraries*, London, Truslove Hanson, 1901.

23   Ellis, A., 'Public libraries for children during the nineteenth century', *Library Association record*, **69** (7), 1967, 230–5.

24   Wood, B., 'Three special features of free library work: open shelves, women read-

ers, and juvenile departments', *The library*, **4**, 1892, 105–14.

25 Briscoe, J. P., 'Libraries for the young', *Library chronicle*, **3**, 45–69.

26 Wood, B., 'Three special features of free library work: open shelves, women readers, and juvenile departments', *The library*, **4**, 1892, 112.

27 Mason, T., 'Fiction in free libraries', *The library*, **2**, 1890, 178–81.

28 Kelly, T., *History of public libraries in Great Britain 1845–1975*, 2nd edn, London, Library Association, 1977, 84.

29 Cowell, P., 'On the admission of fiction in free public libraries', in: *Transactions and proceedings of the conference of librarians held in London, October 1877*, London, Chiswick Press, 1878, 60–7.

30 *Ibid.*, 66.

31 Kay, J. T., 'The provision of novels in rate-supported libraries', in *Transactions and proceedings of the second annual conference of the Library Association of the United Kingdom, Manchester, 1879*. London, Chiswick Press, 1880, 42–6.

32 *Ibid.*, 43.

33 Doubleday, W. E., 'The fiction nuisance and its abatement', *Library world*, **3**, 1903, 206–8.

34 Smith, R. E. G., *The first fifty years of public libraries in Stockport*, Library Association thesis, 1950, 79.

35 Jast, L. S., *Libraries and living*, London, Grafton, 1932, 124.

36 Perkins, F. B., of Boston Public Library, USA, quoted in Cowell, ref. 29, 61.

37 Savage, E. A., *A librarian's memories*, London, Grafton, 1952, 34.

38 Webb, S. J., quoted in 'The municipal librarian's aims in bookbuying', *The library*, NS **7**, 1906, 70.

39 Keating, P., *The haunted study: a social history of the English novel 1875–1914*, London, Secker and Warburg, 1989, 280–2.

40 Jennings, A. O., 'Fiction in the public library', *Library Association Record*, **10**, 1908, 534–41.

41 Kelly, T., *History of public libraries in Great Britain 1845–1975*, 2nd edn, London, Library Association, 1977, 33.

42 Brown, J. D., *Manual of library economy*, London, Scott, Greenwood, 1903, 424.

43 Board of Education, Public Libraries Committee, *Report on public libraries in England and Wales*, Cmd.2868, 1927, 60–2 and 194–6.

44 Southward, J., 'Technical literature in free public libraries', *In: Transactions and proceedings of the Library Association of the United Kingdom; Sixth Annual Meeting 1883*, London, Trubner, 1886, 82–7.

45 *Descriptive account of the Corporation Public Libraries of the City of Glasgow*, Glasgow, Glasgow Public Libraries, 1924, 35.

46 Doubleday, W. E., 'Public libraries and the public', *Library Association record*, **14**, 1912, 537, 541.

47 Olle, J. G., *Ernest A Savage, librarian extraordinary*, London, Library Association, 1978, 83.

48 Greenwood, T., *Free public libraries: their organization, uses, and management*, London, Simpkin Marshall, 1886. Subsequent editions under the title *Public libraries*.

3 Local politics and national provision

❖ *Alistair Black*

A 'LOCAL' NATIONAL SERVICE

The municipal public library has always held an ambivalent position in the context of national–local tensions and relations. It is a common and familiar feature of city, town and village life, and its services, of both the 'buildings-based' and 'outreach' type, constitute a shared – universal even – experience for citizens from across the socio-economic spectrum. Yet today's public library is conceptualized and managed mostly as a local rather than as a national institution. As such, the public library can more convincingly be regarded as a civic rather than as a state phenomenon. At the same time, the public library has a legitimate claim to being part of the complex structure of the welfare state which generates a national political discourse and has as its foundation a centralizing ideological project.

THE POST-FORDIST PUBLIC LIBRARY

In recent years, the welfare state's 'national', centralizing, ideological project has come under sustained attack from both libertarians and reactionaries. Politicians, planners, theorists and, indeed, large sections of public opinion, have become increasingly pessimistic about the efficacy of the social policy constructed as part of the post-war settlement. Arguments particularly persuasive in this regard are those concerning 'dependent' citizens, wasteful public spending damaging to the forging of an enterprise culture, and the unresponsive, distant nature of service provision and bureaucracy. As a result, the welfare state has undergone over the past generation, a shift towards a post-Fordist configuration in social policy.[1] The model of the Fordist welfare state mirrors Fordist production, the chief characteristics of which are mass consumption, mass markets, central planning, bureaucratic rigour, standardized components and inflexible production.[2] The post-war Fordist welfare state, paralleling chronologically the era of classic Fordist production between 1945 and about 1970, was similarly organized, with emphasis being placed on Keynesian demand management, liberal welfare provision, high social spending and free collective bargaining, each aimed at priming the pump of welfare and prosperity. It also emphasized the need for rationally planned and centrally directed social provision, where social products/consumption took on a homogeneous form and where choice was marginalized. In its place, mirroring revolutionary changes in economic production, and in particular the growth of 'flexible accumulation', the post-Fordist welfare state is said to offer socio-economic flexibility.[3] Here, emphasis is placed on responsiveness, pragmatism, organizational decentralization, strategic (as opposed to bureaucratic, directing) central control and choice in service delivery. These departures are complemented by ideas about the transformation in our culture from modern to post-modern modes of thinking and living: the emergence, in essence, of diversity, difference and repetitive discontinuity in our lifestyles and social practices.

Post-Fordist restructuring has been clearly visible in high profile welfare state institutions like the health and education services. A process of fragmentation has also been experienced in the less contentious area of public library provision. The credentials of the modern public library, emergent in the period from its inception to about the mid-1970s, are easily identifiable. By that time public libraries had been subjected to the universalism of the 1964 Act; organization into large authorities offering economies of scale by local government legislation implemented in 1965 (in London) and 1974 (elsewhere); infusion with the ideology of social democracy as evident in the McColvin Report of 1942;[4] and given the support of a unified, graduate profession whose identity was solidified by controlled entry through The Library Association. Thereafter, a process of differentiation and dispersal has set in. Thus, key characteristics of the post-modern public library model are: the recognition of segmented social groups requiring special 'needs auditing' and provision through innovative models of service like community librarianship; the arrival of compulsory, competitive tendering; the increased stocking of non-print materials; a relaxation in attitudes to popular culture, cultural relativism and the 'direction' of readers; the organization of professionals into flexible teams, and into 'core' and 'periphery' workers; and the threat to professional identity posed by both emerging markets in information work and the surrender of idealist purpose to the hidden pragmatic workings and ethics of the market.

Post-modern prescriptions for the operation of the public library are based on perception of the shifting demands of an increasingly sophisticated and pluralistic user body. This user body has grown impatient with the promises of experts and of authority to deliver the services they require. Distrust of the expert–professional librarian – a marked contrast to the relatively high status achieved by many Victorian and Edwardian town librarians – is seen in the persistent comic image, in reality of recent origin, of the detached, socially-irrelevant librarian–bibliophile. Moreover, it is a distrust possibly compounded by the continued proximity – in terms of corporate image – of public libraries and their staff to the world of municipal government. The latter's political representatives, like their counterparts at the national level, have suffered from a post-modern scepticism as to their ability also to 'deliver the goods.'[5] People have begun to withdraw their confidence in politicians and invest it in grass-roots action mobilized around specific, not party issues. Faith in municipal government has been eroded by the post-modern suspicion of monolithic systems and structures. Clearly, this has placed the public library in a difficult position, and may explain why in the late twentieth century, despite often adopting an 'up-market' pose, it retains such a powerful anachronistic image. For historically the institution has been, if nothing else, a civic entity. Whereas post-modern culture and post-Fordist organization stand for the decentralization of services to the extreme periphery, modern culture and Fordist organization entertain an opposition to centralization only as far as the 'civic'. In the formative era of modernity in the nineteenth century, therefore, the idea of the civic and the existence of civic consciousness found intense support, especially in the context of the historic distrust of central authority. Nowhere was this celebration of 'civicness' more clearly visible than in the establishment of free municipal libraries at the heart of urban culture.

MUNICIPAL GOVERNMENT, THE CIVIC IDEAL AND LOCAL POLITICS

The history of the public library can be viewed through a number of lenses. One obvious lens, that of local government, affords an analysis which focuses on important issues contiguous to public library development, such as local politics, civic pride, ideological perspectives on state action, relations between local and central authority, and even religious belief. It is not the purpose of this discussion to either chronicle the statutory framework or describe the local government structures in which public libraries evolved; that has been done elsewhere.[6] Rather, attention is paid to the ways in which the library question intersected with attitudes to the collective provision of culture and knowledge, thereby encouraging an informed assessment of today's perceptions of the public library.

Britain has a long tradition of local government, to the extent that it has been 'part of the constitutional structure of government and of politics, for rather longer perhaps than there has been a recognizable central government.'[7] Against a background of suspicion of central power arising from the constitutional struggles of the seventeenth century, national government has always had to negotiate with those making claims for local sovereignty. As a manual on local government in 1922 declared in respect of this 'bargaining' relationship: 'There is no strict line of demarcation between central and local government; the limitations of each being effected by compromise'.[8]

Relations between central and local government, in the period since public libraries first appeared on the political agenda in the 1820s, are complex and difficult to trace in detail. Only a brief, general assessment can be afforded here. In the early nineteenth century traditional local bodies were not without significant power; between 1800 and 1845, for example, nearly 400 Local Improvement Acts were passed by parliament. However, it was not until the Municipal Corporations Act (1835) that the power of localities was placed on a formal and solid administrative footing, with the inauguration of the institution of the elected local council we recognize today. Aimed at defeating the forces of the 'old', 'closed', corrupt society – not least its Tory representatives – this Act enabled a reformed local government, in the course of the nineteenth century and for much of the twentieth century, to exercise a vastly increased control over the lives of citizens. At the same time, central government became not just more powerful and interventionist in its own right, from the earliest utilitarian reforms of the 1830s and particularly after the First World War, but was also increasingly involved in the operations of local government in an advisory, regulatory and inspectorial capacity. Moreover, central government has become a crucial source of finance for local government, to the advantage of the latter, but also for its own benefit in attempting to manage the overall pattern of demand in the economy.[9] In this positive process of interaction between central and local government there have obviously been numerous shifts to and fro in the balance of power between the two. In recent years, however, there has occurred a violent movement away from local sovereignty. Local government has attracted a bad press since the late 1970s. It is said to be in abrupt decline.[10] Whilst the record shows that real expenditure on social services (mostly dispensed through local government) did not fall in the 1980s, any increase has been given in a grudging fashion, local services being perceived as a drag on economic prosperity not a complement to it – a view not entirely in keeping with nineteenth and early twentieth century attitudes which generally praised civic achievements as resulting from and contributing to heroic, pioneering economic initiatives.[11]

Public libraries have suffered as a result of the recent swing away from a once resilient support for, and belief in, the workings of local government. For better or worse, the public library has always evinced local credentials. Whilst the Municipal Corporations Act did not include public libraries in the list of services that local authorities could legitimately provide, this oversight was soon remedied by the Public Libraries Act (1850). Public libraries emerged from this legislative beginning as a local institution. However, it should not be concluded from this that they operated with unrestricted local autonomy. The restriction of expenditure for library purposes to one penny in the pound until

1919 (a half-penny between 1850 and 1855) is indicative of the operation of central government power in the area of social provision; much the same is being said about today's rate-capping and expenditure restriction mechanisms. The direct grants that pioneers like Ewart and Edwards envisaged in the 1840s but which, unlike the case in education, were not forthcoming, would have perhaps made the public library more susceptible to central control, and would certainly have pushed the process of inspection beyond the returns of data to parliament that public libraries were asked to make periodically. In the absence of direct assistance, therefore, early public libraries were allowed to develop according to local desires, though only as far as the relatively restrictive framework established by central government allowed. The result was patchy, parochial provision, not a national service.

The permissive nature of library provision, which lasted until 1964, was created by the perception of centralization as 'un-English'. Suspicion of taxes extended to the local level. Hence, early library provision was tied closely to the democratic desires of citizen ratepayers. Obtaining ratepayer consent was a persistent and major obstacle to the building of anything approaching a national service. Explaining why in some areas the proposal for a public library found stiff opposition, yet in others was embraced wholeheartedly, requires extensive research into local conditions. Key variables for analysis are: local social structure, especially the presence of the petit-bourgeoisie; the state and structure of the local economy; the level of rateable value; the influence of local individuals; and, to be discussed below, patterns of local politics and of religious belief. It is sufficient to say here that controversy over the public library was generally a pre-adoption issue. Once a library had been established, the issue tended to fade from the local political agenda. This phenomenon was noted by Darlington library activists in a report on library provision nationally: 'The rate is nowhere a matter of complaint. When first imposed it may be grumbled at by a few, but when the library has been established a little while, such a thing as a complaint respecting the rate for its support is never heard of'.[12] Similarly, a representative of the Walsall Library Committee cited by the Darlington report explained: 'The fact is . . . it is not surprising if some grumble at first. It is a tax.' He went on to describe the 'ungrudgingness' with which the rate was paid in his town.[13]

As the century progressed, adoption legislation strengthened the hand of local government and of those seeking to establish a public library. Public Library Acts (for England) of 1855, 1866 and 1893 permitted adoption by, respectively, a public meeting (serving to intimidate opponents of the library cause), a simple majority instead of a two-thirds endorsement, and the council itself. By the twentieth century, therefore, the direct sanction of the citizen ratepayer had been replaced by the indirect functionalism of the local franchise. In particular, the library question was subsumed by the civic ideal. Civic pride became an important flywheel driving the early public library movement. This is illustrated by the slow pace of library development in London.[14] As early as 1856, William Ewart could assert that 'in London they do not know what a Free Library means.'[15] By the last decade of the century there existed a confusing collection of parishes and districts, as well as other bodies like the Metropolitan Board of Works, the London School Board, and the London County Council.[16] This mishmash, as well as providing obstacles to setting up a library service, obviated against the formation of the civic pride that elsewhere enriched the public library ideal.

Nineteenth century local government was based on a nostalgia for the Greek 'polis' and for the 'Gemeinschaft' notion of society – both essentially pre-modern, pre-industrial models of organic social relations.[17] As the Fabian educator and political scientist Graham Wallas proclaimed in celebrating the first hundred years of municipal government: 'For the average citizen . . . the possibility of health, of happiness, of progress towards the old Greek ideal of 'beautiful goodness' depends on his local government more than on any other factor in his environment'.[18] Under the civic banner, intervention by the local state developed rapidly in 'survival' services associated with sanitation, the maintenance of public order and education which, once dealt with, opened the way for the provision of 'additional' amenities like swimming baths and libraries. This development of local services by urban elites was, in the political sense, largely unconscious, and not usually motivated by ideology.[19] It is only in recent years that, generally speaking, partisan political wrangles have come to taint local government to the degree seen in national politics. Before 1914, conflict between organized political groups was by no means absent. Leeds, for example, was a fierce battleground for party politics and for control of the council from 1835 onwards. Whilst in Birmingham, Chamberlain's Liberal Association (founded in 1865) inaugurated the political 'caucus' devoted to the implementation of a publicized programme – a strategy inherited by the new Labour politics in the 1890s. However, despite the increasing tendency to draw battle-lines according to party allegiance, it was not until after the First World War that the mass local politics we recognize today began to emerge. Rather, local political conflict very often cut across party lines, with cliques, factions and pressure groups vying for influence on specific issues.[20]

The public library was one such specific issue, either debated in defiance of party position or, more likely, deemed to be outside the boundaries of party friction. To a degree, today's public library would seem to have inherited that political neutrality. Recent work by Usherwood has revealed that local politicians are by no means inclined to toe the party line on public library issues, such as compulsory competitive tendering, for example. Nonetheless, says

Usherwood, 'It is no longer possible to study the workings of a public body such as a "library committee" without taking politics, often party politics, into account'.[21] The impacting of formal party politics upon the public library issue is not an entirely new development. In the nineteenth century Liberals were noticeably supportive of the public library movement. The library promoter and publisher Thomas Greenwood was active in Liberal politics;[22] as was the library benefactor John Passmore Edwards, who served as a Gladstonian Member of Parliament between 1880 and 1885.[23] The Liberal John Lubbock (from 1900 Lord Avebury) took over from William Ewart as the public library movements chief parliamentary advocate.

There is evidence too of the Liberal leanings of librarians. As Thomas Aldred wrote to Walter Powell in 1906, warning him not to seek a librarianship in London, 'Work in London is not near so pleasant as in provincial towns, especially in liberal boroughs. Administrations here (in London) take their duties very seriously and liberals, in particular, worry officials. You are better off in Birmingham if you attach any value to peace of mind'.[24] There were those, indeed, who viewed the public library as an envoy of Liberalism. As an Oxford citizen, naming himself 'Fair Play', wrote in the 1860s: 'Here is a Public and Free Library, to which all ratepayers, Whigs, Tories, Radicals and Constitutionalists, are obliged to subscribe, whether they like it or not'. Yet, he continued 'The management is no doubt in the hands of the "Liberals" ... This is a truly "Liberal proceeding".'[25]

Nevertheless, despite some evidence of partnership in respect of proposals for public libraries and, once established, their management, the most common signal emanating from the library debate was that of consensus. Thomas Greenwood believed that 'The Free Library movement is perfectly free from suspicion of belonging to party, class or sect'.[26] He, like many others, thus echoed Charles Dickens' much cited consensual view that the public library was an institution 'knowing no sect, no party, no distinction – knowing but the public want and the public good'.[27] Some aspects of provision were particularly reflective of the desire to lower political tension. Strenuous efforts were often made to produce balanced library committees, as well as to depoliticize them. It was said that 'A mixed committee, composed partly of members of the Town Council, and partly of gentlemen who were not members of the Council, seems to be the most popular and likely to be most efficient in working a Free Library'.[28] This imperative was echoed in Doncaster, where it was thought a good idea that:

> The committee should be so formed as to consist of two sections, one the Corporation and the other the non-Corporation section. This did away with any appearance of exclusive management, and afforded all a fair opportu-

nity of being fully represented. There is nothing at all in these two sections of an hostile or antagonistic character, save so far as might create whole-some opposition, and would act as a check of one party upon the other.[29]

Coopted members, often professionals and individuals of cultural achieve-ment, were no doubt important to keeping the peace in potential flash-points like book selection subcommittees, the reasoned arguments flowing from cul-ture and knowledge being marshalled against censorial partisanship. Wholesome opposition was also encouraged through the provision of news-papers. Public library newsrooms were an instrument of political consensus. As the Dean of York was reported to have explained to a pro-library public meeting in 1881:

> on politics and religion, he thought a man who read only one paper each day or week, who took his views of men's words and actions and the pol-icy of this or that nation from one paper only was a very feeble creature indeed... He thought that it was a very good thing for him, as a Tory, to read Radical newspapers, and a very good thing for him as a Churchman to read Nonconformist papers. The more they examined each others' views the more reason they had to find for their differences, and the less they had to suspect one another on account of those differences.[30]

Whilst there might be a danger of exaggerating the degree of consensus engendered by the public library – conflicts over adoption are, after all, one of the more colourful aspects of public library history – the overriding impression is one of subdued political controversy. A good deal of apathy surrounded the library issue. As Thomas Greenwood stated: 'Frequently not one in ten of the ratepayers has voted where the method has been by voting papers, and in some cases where it has been settled by statutory meeting there has been an even worse evidence of the want of interest in the movement'.[31] In those cases where apathy was not so visible, political friction – occurring invariably before adoption – rarely reflected formal party political allegiances. As a library cam-paigner in Oxford in 1852 stated, albeit at a time when even national party lines were faintly drawn:

> The adoption of this act is not a party question, but one of knowledge against ignorance; of means of enlightenment against utter destitution, of means of self-improvement felt by the masses of society. Literature, Art and Science ought to belong to all classes, and to all sects and parties... let no improper feeling characterize us in attempting to carry out so useful a mea-sure.[32]

The political antagonism – the 'improper feeling' – against which this campaigner warned was not a dominant feature of local government, especially as the century progressed and as civic power and culture became more and more revered. Gradually, public libraries became a way of life, serving to disseminate national culture (more of this later) in towns and cities throughout the country. By 1883, Stanley Jevons was able to declare, in respect of public libraries, that: 'Perhaps it might be said that they are ceasing to be a matter of opinion at all, and are classed with town halls, police courts, prisons and poor houses as necessary adjuncts of our stage of civilization'.[33]

Significant sections of middle-ranking opinion would not, of course, have agreed with Jevons' message of political anonymity and civic neutrality. Anti-expenditure, anti-collectivist attitudes to local public affairs should not be underestimated. However, a clear distinction should be made between, on the one hand, economizers (mostly typically of the shopkeeping class, as well as artisan ratepayers) and, on the other, the expenditure-orientated bourgeoisie (comprising middle-class reformers, professionals and substantial entrepreneurs). Those in favour of local public expenditure did not derive their support from any dogmatic belief in collectivism. Rather, they supported intervention pragmatically:

> specific proposals, like public libraries, received attention if they were believed to coincide with their value systems and moral agendas. This was most clearly the case with regard to religious enthusiasm for the public library ideal. It is true that in the formative era of public library development many Anglicans opposed libraries associated with secular institutions, like mechanics' institutes and municipal government.[34]

However, as the control attractions of educational institutions like public libraries became more obvious, even the established church joined Nonconformists in praising the manifest efficacy of free literature. The Vicar of Doncaster, in support of the town's new library thus asserted that 'Knowledge, like all God's gifts, is free for all – free as the air we breathe, free as the sunlight which streams upon us.'[35] Unitarians were extremely active in promoting free libraries in Manchester and Birmingham; whilst in the economist, Stanley Jevons, the creed found a formidable intellectual ally.[36] For most religious activists, the moral message of individual effort and responsibility was extremely important, thereby always casting doubt on the value of state help. However, as Greenleaf has argued in his exhaustive history of collectivism, 'the Christian spirit which was first moved in the sphere of voluntary action came to realize the need to substantial public help. Personal philanthropy could never itself be enough and had to be supplemented or supplanted by an extensive system of charity by state proxy'.[37]

Support for public libraries came from across the religious spectrum. Unlike education, the library issue rarely provoked political antagonism between religious groups. As such, religious opinion was illustrative of an apolitical approach to the establishment and management of local municipal libraries, notwithstanding some informal political opposition from economizers, and occasional formal political posturing and positioning, as one would expect in the embryonic phase of party politics before 1914.

LEEDS, BIRMINGHAM, YORK: CIVIL WAR, CIVIC RESPONSE, CONSENSUS POLITICS

Although it can be dangerous to draw general conclusions from particular evidence, specific examples of how local politics interacted with the public library issue help the historian to reach a fuller understanding of shared, even national, attitudes to what was, for most, a parochial institution. Contrasting evidence is presented here from the political-library history of three manufacturing towns: Leeds, Birmingham and York. It was in progressive local economies such as these that the philosophical underpinning of, and opposition to, the municipal public library were often most sharply articulated.

The shifting allegiances of local politicians on the library question is seen in the fight to secure a public library for Leeds. Liberals in Leeds were split on the issue. In 1868 the Town Council decided to adopt the Public Library Acts, the idea having first been raised in 1861 but thrown out partly on the grounds that the working classes had opportunity enough for acquiring the knowledge they needed and 'should be taught to rely a little more upon themselves'.[38] However, the proposal encountered heated opposition at an ensuing public meeting. The anti-library lobby was led by a Liberal town councillor, a pawnbroker. Such was the presence of the anti-library faction that it needed a second count at the meeting for the pro-library resolution to be passed by a narrow majority. Later that year at the local elections, the Municipal Reform Association, a newly formed body 'with a view of lessening expenditure and securing greater municipal purity', took its revenge by making gains at the expense of 'ruling' Liberals. It was said to be a contest conducted 'not for party purposes, but for the principle of economy'; and it was further explained that the 'upper section' of the Liberals 'had paid rather too little consideration to the lower section.' In Leeds, therefore, Liberal was found pitted against Liberal over the library question, formal party allegiances – to the extent that they existed in the mid-Victorian era – counting for little.[39] Of less importance on this occasion was the historic rivalry in Leeds between Tory and Liberal. To be sure, the middle classes of early industrial towns were divided by religion and party. This was emphatically the case in Leeds, where sectarian divisions were highly visible. In the first half of the nineteenth century the Whig-Liberal alliance in the town fought a running battle with the Tory–Anglican elite.[40] Amongst other matters, this was reflected in the struggle for control over the

Leeds Private Library – the second oldest proprietary library in England, established in 1768 – a struggle exemplified by the controversies surrounding the censoring of liberal–entrepreneurial texts promoting the new market society.[41] However, despite the long tradition in Leeds of Liberal–Tory animosity, the issue of the establishment of a public library in the town did not generate heated debate along formal party lines, but rather civil war within one political grouping.

For nearly 60 years after the Municipal Corporations Act, Leeds was 'essentially a Liberal town'. Between 1835 and 1894 (when they finally lost control of the Council), Liberals won approximately two-thirds of both the parliamentary and municipal seats available.[42] Although the town experienced relatively little public disorder during this time, despite the activities of the Chartists, it did encounter its fair share of formal political conflict. However, the extent to which elected representatives were strictly dragooned into party camps in support of a coherent set of policies should not be exaggerated. In the second half of the nineteenth century, party politics, as we know it today, was in its infancy. Yet as the century progressed, party loyalty in local government did strengthen.

The embryonic model for programmatic party government at the local level was the agenda set by Liberals in Birmingham under the leadership of Joseph Chamberlain. The civic innovations set in motion in Birmingham in the 1860s and 1870s had by the 1880s become extremely influential elsewhere in the country. Of significance in this respect is the support given by Birmingham's political and social elite to public libraries. Chamberlain described the public library as 'a kind of Communism which the least revolutionary among us may be proud to advocate'.[43] This ideological position was most forcefully broadcast by the Baptist minister George Dawson, who believed the public library to be the embodiment of God's will. At the opening of the Birmingham Reference Library in 1866, Dawson took the opportunity to preach what he believed to be the near-metaphysical nature of civic administration.[44] For Dawson, a public library was 'all things to all men'. Like the civic corporation of which it was a part, it was 'at the service of the whole people'; it was a 'Holy Communion, a wise Socialism'. He proclaimed that 'a town exists here by Grace of God, that a great town is a solemn organism through which should flow, and in which should be shaped, all the Highest, Loftiest and truest ends of man's intelligent and moral natures'. Dawson stressed the social healing that the 'spirit of corporate ownership' could bring, explaining that a civic community was not 'a fortuitous concourse of human atoms, or a miserable knot of vipers struggling in a pot [each] aiming to get its head above the other in the fierce struggle of competition'. A library, he said, was itself a healing mechanism. In his own library he placed divergent opinion side by side; he put Radical beside Tory, laying them together 'as the wolf and the lamb'.

In this environment of civic optimism, public library provision in Birmingham progressed more rapidly than in most places, including towns with a much longer history. In York, for example, despite its ancient tradition, civic feeling evolved only slowly. This was reflected in the late arrival of the library question in York, and in the decade of debate that preceded the eventual adoption of the Public Library Acts in 1891. The background to the debate in York was the unbroken period of Liberal control of the municipality between 1850 and 1894.[45] This lengthy period of political hegemony led, in the 1880s, to accusations of 'interested' party management of the corporation: Liberals were said to be placing party before municipality. Hence, throughout the 1880s more and more politicians of a conservative persuasion replaced their Tory label with that of Independent, their aim being to break up the Gladstonian majority and substitute in its place a body pledged to serve the ratepayers independently of party considerations.[46] In 1891, one independently minded member 'decided not to identify himself with either party, believing that in municipal affairs ... there should be neither liberals nor conservatives'.[47]

Whereas before the 1880s municipal elections in York reflected national issues and national patterns of political control, thereafter local issues found their way onto the local political agenda. This was to the liking of Independents seeking to depoliticize municipal affairs, and it was a development which the ruling liberal bloc was forced to accommodate, the more so as Independents cut deeper into their long-standing majority. One depoliticized battle-ground upon which Liberals found themselves forced to fight was the proposal for establishing a public library in York, first raised in 1881.[48] Despite wearing the cloak of independence, Tories were identified as the focus of opposition to the public library idea, most forcefully supported by the Liberal body. The debate centred on the issue of economy. One Liberal supporter wrote that the leader of the corporation's Tory group:

> and his party have always been the advocates of economy, whereas it is notorious that he and his party introduced one of the most extravagant schemes that has been brought before the Council in the present generation. I refer to the Castlegate improvement, and had it not been for the action of the Liberal party in frustrating this costly scheme the public debt of the city would have been largely increased . . . The Tory cry of economy is a sham and a delusion, and is intended as a trap to catch the votes of the working classes [in the library adoption poll] . . . but probably they will be found to have more intelligence than the Tories give them credit for. It is part of a deep laid plot to recover Tory ascendancy and arrest the political progress of the city, which will receive the ignominy which it deserves.[49]

In general, however, Liberals appeared to adopt a conciliatory tone, one which attempted to convey consensus and non-partisanship. Thus, it was reported that Joseph Rowntree 'confessed himself a Radical and Nonconformist, and said it had been his duty to commend a policy of economy not only in municipal matters, but also in relation to the Imperial Parliament. He claimed to be as true an economist as anyone present, and thought that every penny expended in rating ought to be vigilantly watched.'[50] At the same library campaign meeting in 1881, another Liberal declared that 'he was not going to speak that night as a city councillor, but simply as a ratepayer', adding that citizens should determine the matter 'not as Conservatives, not as Liberals, not as Churchmen or Dissenters, but as citizens of no mean city'.[51]

A poll of ratepayers the following year rejected the proposal for a public library. This result was repeated in 1887, but in 1891 a majority of nearly 3000 in favour of adoption was recorded, and a library was finally opened in 1893. The reasons for this change of heart on the part of York ratepayers is not clear. Certainly, the fact that for a cheap price the public library was to occupy the premises of the York Institute, with the latter's subscription library stock being transferred free of charge, must have appeared as a good deal for York ratepayers. There is also the key factor of improving economic conditions – clearly conducive to a 'yes' vote – to be considered. However, the depoliticization of the library issue would seem to offer the most plausible explanation. As the voice of independence in York took hold, party controversy declined, issues like the establishment of a public library being treated more on their merits than on party lines. In the 1890s political partisanship declined. In 1894 the Liberals lost their majority and progressive government of the corporation was halted. That same year all properties in York had their rateable value reduced, thereby instituting a regime of retrenchment that retarded the development of library and other services in the town.

The history of the adoption debate in York began in a way that resembled the political intensity which marked the struggle to establish a public library in Leeds, though in York the ruling Liberal group was not split on the issue. Liberals in York were firmly united, as occurred in Birmingham, in support of progressive local government, including public library provision. However, Liberals only found it possible to obtain a free library for York once the issue had been drained of its party political significance and imbued with the neutral ideology of civic pride, which social elites, like the paternalistic Rowntree family, promoted. Civic purpose, in York and elsewhere, became the guiding force behind public libraries. The aim was to build a broad consensus operating in differentiated local societies. Public libraries, preaching the civic gospel of social unity and class cohesion, fitted this objective tightly. This sense of civic solidarity and consciousness was in stark contrast to the radical alternative in town management seen in some towns in the first half of the nineteenth century, for example in Sheffield and Oldham.[52] In the late 1840s, Sheffield Chartists won control of the town and instigated a method of government wholly opposed to the influence of civic elites and executive functions. In many areas of Sheffield, local parliaments were established, public affairs being run close to the people at the neighbourhood level. Proposed institutions like municipal libraries were viewed as 'a massive and alien imposition'.[53] It was a form of local government that stood little chance of success in competition with the civic gospel, as preached by men like George Dawson and supported by urban elites like Chamberlain and Rowntree. It was civic, not neighbourhood, consciousness that came to dominate local affairs. The imperatives of consensus inherent in the civic approach obviated against conflictual politics in many areas of municipal provision. This was patently the case in respect of public libraries, which embodied the politics of incorporation central to the civic ideal. Civic pride took the politics out of public libraries, certainly once they had been established and had opened their doors.

TOWARDS A NATIONAL SERVICE?

The civic purpose underpinning Victorian and Edwardian public libraries served to emphasize their status as local rather than national institutions. By 1914, the idea of a truly national library service barely existed. Localism reigned supreme. This is not to say, however, that the public library was discussed in isolation from national issues. On the contrary, those promoting local municipal libraries, especially in the late nineteenth century, stressed their importance to national well-being. As Britain's international economic hegemony began to be challenged, from about 1870 onwards, public libraries were advocated as a means of correcting industrial malfunction. Their value, in terms of technical and general education, was offered as a partial panacea to national economic instability. As education itself grew into a national issue, public libraries benefited accordingly, not least in respect of their proposed role as disinterested sources of information for a widening electorate requiring schooling in national and international political knowledge and current affairs. Public libraries were also advocated as generators of a national code of moral respectability, as well as social (including class) consensus: as envoys, in short, of a universal culture of civilized living. They were, as one source proclaimed, 'one of the highest ways of educating, elevating, and promoting our best national life'.[54] Linked to this notion of a 'national', civilized existence is the emergence of a dominant middle-class consciousness. Although much has been written in recent years both supporting and denying the idea of the 'failure' (political, cultural and economic) of Britain's middle class, the latter's emergence in the second half of the nineteenth century as a significant social force is undeniable. The public library was an institution which reflected the rise of middle-class power. Contrary to the received image, public libraries were not merely instruments of middle-class social control of a troublesome middle class. They were also institutions for use by the middle class itself, this being particularly true of the central libraries of large provincial towns. Public libraries were arenas where middle-class divisions on religion and politics could, to a degree, be healed, and where an emergent bourgeoisie could help educate itself into a position of national social prominence.

Before 1914, urban civic culture and its various agencies, municipal libraries among them, became a symbol of a confident, advancing middle class. To the extent that the bourgeois moral agenda of universal respectability was a national one, the early local public library can itself be considered to be a national institution, invested with a national task of continuous moral and material regeneration. However, despite the fact that it possessed national objectives, the early public library could not have claimed to be a wholly national institution until after the First World War. Not until 1919 were counties given powers to provide a service in rural areas, thereby paving the way for coverage nationwide. Further, it was only between the wars that many homogenizing practices and techniques – such as Dewey classification as the complement to the increasingly common feature of open access – were instituted. Finally, it was also only in the inter-war period that librarians came to speak with any great conviction of a national service. Thus, by 1939 Stanley Jast could refer to the public library as a key component of what he called 'the library grid', a term derived no doubt, from the recently inaugurated national programme of electrification and the construction of a national grid for electricity.[55] Earlier, in 1924, Ernest Baker had hoped that the local public library would undergo a 'centralizing and systematizing process' in terms of, firstly, being organized into larger and more economically viable authorities and, secondly, being incorporated into a cooperative network for the purpose of interchange of materials. In addition, Baker called for 'national and systematic inspection', and the organization of librarianship on a civil service basis. Urging public libraries to assume the status of a national project, he was scornful of the 'parochial methods that had retarded its development to date'.[56]

Pleas such as this for increased centralization were not to be realized until the construction of a welfare state, inclusive of public libraries, after 1945. Even then, the public library retained a strong spirit of localism. Recently, that localism has been challenged. Calls for a national coordinating body appear to threaten the much-cherished local sovereignty of public library provision. Even more worrying for champions of localism is the suggestion that a main task of such a national body should be the identification of 'core' services, a strategy that, by definition, marginalizes periphery, 'non-core' provision; for as 'soon as the concept of "core" is used . . . this becomes the accountant's bound-ary to restrict activities'.[57] This spectre of oppressive central power contrasts sharply with the civic consciousness associated with the early public library. Although the cry of economy was rarely silent, the philosophy that under-pinned the early public library was one of an idealist belief in collectivism – instituted philanthropically or via taxation – as the helpmate of individualism and of the self-guided effort of individuals to realize their potential and ambi-tions. This philosophy was extended, through increased state intervention, onto the national stage after 1945. Both civic culture and welfare state models of library provision were characterized by an absence of political controversy. There was a widespread consensus that the public library was a non-nego-tiable 'public good', and should operate, essentially, as an apolitical institution uniting opposing political groupings behind a doctrine of 'individual self-real-ization through collective security'.

For most of its history, the public library has not been a political football, in the context of formal party political activity. Support for the public library has mostly cut across party lines (though the enthusiasm of many pre-1914 library advocates for Liberal politics has been noted in this discussion). The fact that the public library precipitated political struggle of an informal kind – evident in the tensions in the public library arena between middle and working classes, if not between elements of the middle class itself – might lead to the surpris-ing, if not bizarre, proposition that the institution represented, in effect, a post-modern political issue in the age of modernity, one which attracted within 'pro' and 'anti' stances a cluster of varied social philosophies and motivation. In other words, the controversy surrounding the establishment of early public libraries was, as is characteristic of post-modern politics, issue-driven and not instigated by formal, mass political structures, either local or national.

This history contrasts markedly with the current dogmatic, ideological attack on the ethos and practice of the public library. In an era of post-modern culture, where emphasis is placed not on uniformity but on difference, a post-Fordist configuration in public library provision, constituting flexibility and imagination to meet shifting and niche cultural needs, is surely appropri-ate. Instead, the prospect is one of a strengthening adherence to a reactionary neo-conservative interpretation of post-Fordist social provision, where market forces serve as the main determinant of social policy. Not until the resurrection of the Victorian and Edwardian shared political gospel of 'individualism through collectivism', as preached by early public library protagonists, will the local public library once again be viewed as a vibrant and valuable social insti-tution of national significance.

REFERENCES

1   Burrows, R. and Loader, B. (eds.), *Towards a post-Fordist welfare state*, London, Routledge, 1994.

2   Murray, R., 'Life after Henry', *Marxism today*, **32** (10), October 1988, 8–13.

3   Loader, B. and Burrows, R., 'Towards a post-Fordist welfare state? The restructuring of Britain, social policy and the future of welfare'. *In:* Burrows, R. and Loader, B. (eds.), *Towards a post-Fordist welfare state*, London, Routledge, 1994.

4   McColvin, L. R., *The public library system of Great Britain*, London, Library Association, 1942.

5   Declining trust in political representatives and in established political structures is a central theme of Beer, S. H., *Britain against itself: the political contradictions of collectivism*, London, Faber and Faber, 1982.

6   Kelly, T., *A history of public libraries in Great Britain 1845–1975*, London, Library Association, 1977; Morris, R. J. B., *Parliament and the public libraries*, London, Mansell, 1977.

7   Loughlin, M., Gelfand, M. D. and Young, K. (eds.), *Half a century of municipal decline 1935–1985*, London, G. Allen and Unwin, 1985, xii.

8   Clarke, J. J., *Outlines of local government of the United Kingdom*, London, I. Pitman, 1922, 12.

9   Greenleaf, W. H., *The British political tradition*, London, Methuen: Vol. 1 *The rise of collectivism*, 1983, 96; Vol. 3, Part 1 *A much governed nation*, 1987, 73–4.

10 Loughlin, M., Gelfand, M. D. and Young, K. (eds.), *Half a century of municipal decline 1935–1985*, London, G. Allen and Unwin, 1985, xii.

11 Lowe, R., 'The welfare state in Britain since 1945', *Recent findings of research in economic and social history [Refresh]*, **18**, Spring 1994, University of York, Department of Economics.

12 Johnman, W. A. P. and Kendall, H., *Report of a [Darlington] commission appointed to enquire into the conditions and workings of free libraries of various towns in England*, Darlington Central Public Library, Local Studies Department, c.1885, 15.

13 *Ibid.*, 10.

14 For a discussion of the history of public libraries in London see the special issue of *Library review*, **33**, Summer 1984.

15 Letter from William Ewart to the chairman of the Oxford Public Library Committee (3 May 1856), Oxford Central Public Library, Local Studies Department.

16 'Prologue: the wen', *Library review*, **33**, Summer 1984, 77.

17 Mouffe, C., *Dimensions of radical democracy: pluralism, citizenship, community*, London, Verso, 1992, 4–6.

18 Laski, H. J., Jennings, W. I. and Robson, W. A. (eds.), *A century of municipal progress 1835–1935*, London, G. Allen and Unwin, 11.

19 Greenleaf, W. H., *The British political tradition*, Vol. 3, Part 1, *A much governed nation*, London, Methuen, 1987, 35.

20 Gyford, J., *Local politics in Britain*, London, Croom Helm, 1984, especially Chs. 1 and 3.

21 Usherwood, R., 'Politics and the public library service', *Journal of librarianship and*

information science, **23** (2), June 1991, 75; Usherwood, R., *Public library politics*, London, Library Association, 1993.

22 Carlton, G., *Spade-work: the story of Thomas Greenwood*, London, Hutchinson, 1949.

23 Baynes, P., *John Passmore Edwards 1823–1911: an account of his life and works*, unpublished, deposited with the British Library Reference Division, 1994.

24 Letter from T. Aldred to W. Powell (26 February 1906), uncatalogued collection of letters to the librarian Walter Powell, deposited with the British Library Information Science Service.

25 Newscutting, source unidentified (*c*.1860), Oxford Public Library Scrapbook. Oxford Central Public Library, Local Studies Department.

26 Greenwood, T., *Free public libraries*, London, Simpkin, Marshall and Co., 1887, 8.

27 *Ibid.*, 24.

28 Johnman, W. A. P. and Kendall, H., *Report of a [Darlington] commission appointed to enquire into the conditions and workings of free libraries of various towns in England*, Darlington Central Public Library, Local Studies Department, *c*.1885, 16.

29 Doncaster Borough Free Library, words of Charles Jackson in *Catalogue and inaugural ceremony*, Doncaster, *c*.1869, 14.

30 *A public library for York*, handbill, York Central Public Library, Local Studies Department, 1881.

31 Greenwood, T., *Public libraries*, London, 1894, 77–8.

32 Oxford pro-adoption handbill, produced by Joseph Taylor (1 October 1852), Oxford Central Public Library, Local Studies Department.

33 Jevons, W. S., 'The rationale of free public libraries', *Contemporary review*, **39**, 1881, 385.

34 Pinfield, S., *Labour, literacy and libraries: a survey of the provision for working class readers in England 1800–1850*, unpublished MA dissertation, School of Library, Information and Archive Studies, University College London, 1991, 41.

35 Doncaster Borough Free Library, words of Rev. F. Pigou, *Catalogue and inaugural ceremony*, Doncaster, *c*.1869, 8.

36 Holt, R. V., *The Unitarian contribution to social progress in England*, London, G. Allen and Unwin, 1938.

37 Greenleaf, W. H., *The British political tradition*, Vol. 3, Part 1, *A much governed nation*, London, Methuen, 1987, 294.

38 Hand, T. W., *A brief account of the public libraries of the public libraries of the city of Leeds 1870–1920*, Leeds, 1920, 3.

39 Hennock, E. P., *Fit and proper persons: ideal and reality in nineteenth century urban government*, London, Edward Arnold, 1973, 210; Barber, B., 'Municipal government in Leeds 1835–1914', in Fraser, D. (ed.), *Municipal reform and the industrial city*, Leicester University Press, 1982, points out that in mid-Victorian Leeds an atmosphere of economy pervaded the discussion of projected amenities like libraries, baths, parks and street improvements. The group most staunchly opposed to increased expenditure on urban amenities were the shopkeepers who, in order to protect the purchasing power of their customers, became a significant political factor in Leeds.

40   Morris, R. J., *Class, sect and party. The making of the British middle class: Leeds 1820–1850*, Manchester, Manchester University Press, 1990, 277.

41   *Ibid.*, 171 and 284–5.

42   Burt, S. and Grady, K., *The illustrated history of Leeds, Derby*, Breedon Books, 1994, 187–8.

43   Greenwood, T., *Free public libraries*, London, Simpkin, Marshall and Co., 1886, 75.

44   Borough of Birmingham, *Opening of the free reference library . . . inaugural address by George Dawson*, Birmingham, 1866.

45   A succinct account of the city's local politics is given in *A history of Yorkshire: the city of York*, The Victoria History of the Counties of England, Oxford University Press, 1961.

46   *York Herald*, 3 November 1891.

47   *York Herald*, 2 November 1891.

48   For a sketch of the adoption conflict between 1881 and 1891 see Tomlinson, O. S., 'Libraries in York', in: Stacpoole, A. (ed.), *The noble city of York*, York, Cerialis Press, 1972.

49   *York Herald*, 31 October 1881, Letter from 'a liberal elector'.

50   *A public library for York*, handbill, York Central Public Library, Local Studies Department, 1881.

51   *Ibid.*, words of Councillor Coning.

52   Gyford, J., *Local politics in Britain*, London, Croom Helm, 1984, Ch. 3.

53   Smith, D., *Conflict and compromise: class formation in English society 1830–1914*, London, Routledge and Kegan Paul, 1982, 75–9.

54   *A public library for York*, handbill, York Central Public Library, Local Studies Department, 1881.

55   Jast, L. S., *The library and the community*, London, Thomas Nelson, 1939, Ch. 10.

56   Baker, E. A., *The public library*, London, Grafton, 1924, Ch. 5.

57   Gee, R., 'Who should run public libraries', *The library campaigner*, **50–51**, Winter-Spring, 1995, 9.

4   Home reading

❖ *Robert Snape*

THE PUBLIC LIBRARY AS A LEISURE INSTITUTION
The public library is a major public sector leisure institution. Statistics show that most of the books issued by public libraries are borrowed primarily for leisure purposes; adult fiction forms the largest category of books borrowed, but many non-fiction titles on sports, hobbies and foreign travel are also read – directly or indirectly – for leisure purposes. Tapes and compact discs are available in most larger libraries as are informal and hobby magazines, and while there is a significant degree of information and reference use, the fact remains that for most of the people most of the time the public library is a leisure-orientated resource. Leisure, however, is not as highly valued by librarians as other elements of the library service. Throughout the past 15 years the library profession has redefined its self image in close alignment with information, and particularly with information technology, which was reflected in a campaign to change the title of the Library Association to include the word 'information'. In marked contrast to its information function, the public library's leisure function has not featured largely in the professional press, and current research in librarianship – a word rapidly being displaced by the phrase information science – is heavily biased towards information management. Allowing for the fact that some of this trend can be attributed to the existence of academic and special libraries with a more obvious preoccupation with information than public libraries, the low status and esteem of leisure still remain, and it is clear from the contents of professional journals and the nature of in-service training courses that the majority of librarians are more interested in information. Indeed, it is not difficult to gain the impression that extensive loans of fiction are sometimes seen as an embarrassment rather than as an indicator of achievement.

Why, given the predominance of leisure in public library use, should there be a divergence between the ways in which the majority of borrowers use libraries and the image of the library service which is promoted by the profession? This dichotomy is historical and forms one of the strongest elements of continuity in the evolution of the public library service. This chapter explains how the tension between the leisure demands of the public and the ideology of the library profession originated in the nineteenth century and suggests that the issue is still important today as the public library service faces the uncertainties of local government structure and funding, exposure to competitive tendering, and a social environment in which leisure provision and participation are undergoing great changes.

LIBRARIES AS LEISURE INSTITUTIONS

As was pointed out in Chapter Two of this book, the lack of a precise definition of role has been a perennial problem for public libraries. This was particularly so during their early years, for the widely held but mistaken view was, and is, that they were introduced solely for the purpose of providing working class readers, in particular those employed in manufacturing and technical industries, with access to educational books. This was certainly one function they were expected to fulfil, but it was not the only rationale for their introduction. The first public libraries were in fact used for a wide range of purposes, many of which were related to leisure rather than education; indeed, if education was meant to be their principal function, why did they provide so much popular fiction and light miscellaneous reading? To answer this question it is useful to see the first Public Libraries Act in 1850 not as a beginning but as the endpoint of a process, and to focus upon the role of the social 'problem' of popular leisure and its reform in the introduction of libraries.

Leisure reform in the nineteenth century

The transition of Great Britain from an agrarian to an industrial society, which occurred between approximately 1780 and 1850, was a gradual process which brought profound social changes. New modes of production, the movement of population from the countryside to the burgeoning industrial towns, and the evolution of new employer–employee relationships brought with them a number of problems, many of which were related to popular leisure activities. In the new urban conditions, squalid, dirty and cramped, facilities for popular leisure were somewhat restricted, and the public house became a major focus for leisure activity, incorporating not only drinking but gambling, prize fighting, cock and dog fighting and prostitution. Popular leisure was frequently characterized by drunkenness, and was a threat to the economic system when it prevented men and women from working efficiently. Leisure was also notorious through its associations with immorality and petty criminal activity. By the 1830s popular leisure was widely recognized as a social problem and its reform appeared on the political agenda. Percipient observers realized that repressive measures would be effective only to a degree, as the root of the problem was that very few alternative leisure facilities existed. This was noted in a number of Parliamentary Select Committees which were established to research the extent of the leisure problem and to recommend solutions. The *Report from the Select Committee on Public Walks* in 1833 presented a graphic account of working class leisure activity, as did the *Report from the Select Committee on Drunkenness* in the following year, which suggested that the problem of leisure would be alleviated only if facilities were provided, and specified public libraries as one such form. A number of contemporary politicians, amongst them Robert Slaney and Lord John Manners, advocated the building of libraries as a means of solving the leisure problem, though no action resulted immediately.

By the late 1840s, however, the campaign to provide public libraries had gathered sufficient momentum to establish a Parliamentary Select Committee to investigate their feasibility. The potential benefits of libraries in effecting changes in popular leisure patterns form a continuous theme in the Committee's report. Edward Edwards informed the Committee that libraries would not only provide instruction, but would offer a means of 'rational amusement' and would entice people away from the several forms of degrading and immoral leisure which were pursued in most industrial towns. Samuel Smiles also foresaw that libraries would assist leisure reform by facilitating home reading:

> ... give a man an interesting book to take home with him to his family, and it is probable that the man will stay at home and read his book in preference to going out and spending his time in dissipation and idleness; and, therefore, the formation of those libraries would be favourable to the improvement of the moral and intellectual condition of the working population.[1]

The Report contains several similar references to the role of the public library in reforming popular leisure.

When public libraries were established, they were used predominantly for leisure purposes, chiefly fiction borrowing, and anticipations of home reading similar to those expressed above by Smiles were largely fulfilled. Thomas Greenwood, a tireless campaigner for public libraries in the later decades of the nineteenth century, related how, when he was a practising librarian, women and children would ask him to choose a book for them: Please pick me a nice one, sir, for if I take home an interesting book, my husband (or father, as the case may be) will stop in during the evening and read it aloud'.[2]

Novels were the books which were most requested, and even reference departments provided substantial stocks of fiction as well as light magazines. The reference department in Liverpool's public library, for example, issued

almost 200,000 novels and romances in 1868.[3] However, it was lending departments, sometimes disparagingly referred to as 'jug and bottle' departments,
which were the major providers of fiction. As the provision of public libraries
expanded, the greater proportion of the urban-based reading public increasingly had access to an ample supply of novels which could be taken home to
be read. The demand for fiction was enormous, so much so that several public
libraries were hard-pressed to satisfy it. The imprecise classification systems
used by early public libraries present difficulties in quantifying exactly the
amount of fiction issued, but there can be no doubt, from figures which do
exist and from comments and observations by contemporary librarians, that it
was huge. It was unusual for fiction to account for less than half of the total
issue, and in many places it represented as much as 80–85%. The available statistics suggest that, on average, most public libraries had a fiction issue which
constituted between 65% and 75% of their total issue. Public libraries thus had
a great recreational appeal, and some of them enhanced their leisure provision
through experimenting with such leisure attractions as games and smoking
rooms.[4] Although most of these were abandoned before the turn of the century, fiction retained its popularity and has done so to this day.

The function of the public library as an agency for leisure provision and the
validity of fiction provision, were certainly recognized in wider society, if not
in the library profession. In his speech at the opening of the St. Martin in the
Fields public library in 1891, Gladstone spoke of libraries, baths, museums and
gymnasia as institutions waging a war against idleness, brutality and ignorance. Speaking of libraries specifically, they were, he said, in direct competition with the public house; libraries provided the working man with

> the means of employing his leisure, not only without difficulty or disad-
> vantage, but with the greatest satisfaction to himself . . . His leisure may be
> employed in these libraries, and how happy it is to see with what zeal and
> promptitude all over the country the working population have exhibited
> their readiness to take advantage of the opportunities when once afforded
> them.[5]

Public library fiction often featured in national and local newspapers and
here again, although opinions differed, it was not unusual to discover attitudes
more liberal than those found within the profession. The *Manchester Guardian*,[6]
for example, felt that by providing ephemeral novels, libraries offered a valid
form of leisure to city dwellers who, by and large, had limited access to recreational opportunities. Although the popularity of the public library was virtually totally dependent upon its leisure appeal, its attractiveness as a provider
of fiction was not generally welcomed by librarians. Many were acutely
embarrassed by the overwhelming demand for fiction, for they saw their own

claims to professional standing to be undermined by what they perceived as a non-purposeful and non-profitable use of libraries. As Henry Tedder, a founder of the Library Association, noted,[7] only if librarians made the educational value of their work more apparent would their social status rise, but the extent of novel borrowing was instead promoting a perception of libraries as storehouses of fiction. The debate as to whether libraries should provide fiction was prolonged and bitter and very nearly split the profession. The history of the Great Fiction Question, as this debate came to be known, reveals how a divergence emerged between the ways in which librarians conceptualized the nature of the service and the ways in which the public used it.

THE GREAT FICTION QUESTION

The Great Fiction Question became important not simply because librarians were troubled by the demand for popular novels, but because fiction was, in its own right, an important social issue in the four decades preceding the First World War. At a national level, much of the debate of the fiction question was concerned with literary merit and cultural values, but at a local level other factors came into play. The nature of the interaction between libraries and fiction and the ways in which libraries responded to the popular demand for fiction suggest that libraries were not always neutral but could be instrumental in the maintenance of cultural values and social structure, and that fiction provision could be manipulated in ways which promoted the interests of a library committee rather than those of the individual reader.

Popular reading and literary culture

The English novel of the mid-nineteenth century was much more culturally and socially important than its modern counterpart. Novelists of the stature of Scott, Dickens, Thackeray and George Eliot were central figures, and in many ways the spokespersons of their time. The educated reading public was essentially middle class, and there were strong links between literature, morality and social structure. However, since at least the 1840s there had been a growing concern about what working-class people read for pleasure, which was, in the main, not the standard English novel admired and promoted by middle-class readers, but cheap sensation fiction. Works of notoriety such as Reynolds' *The mysteries of London* and weekly penny publications such as *Varney the vampire* caused much hand-wringing amongst the middle classes. In the case of Reynolds, this was partly based upon his candidly expressed anti-establishment and republican views, but even publications with milder political overtones were criticized because they were felt to be morally harmful. Attitudes to popular reading were similar to those towards any form of popular recreation: it ought to be useful, improving and morally instructive. The appearance, at the end of the 1860s, of the sensation novel, which was immediately popular amongst all classes of society, provoked a fresh wave of moral indignation, as did translations of French novels which many critics thought unsuitable to have in a family house.

The expansion of the reading public in the last quarter of the nineteenth century and the accompanying growth in the output of cheap novels accentuated the split between literary fiction and fiction produced for the mass commercial market. Literature and the literary novel retained their cultural status, and the literary reviews, which were publications with an important political significance, were written and read by those in positions of power and influence. Mass-market fiction was seen by many critics and librarians as a threat to social harmony because it did not promote the moral and cultural values of the middle class and the establishment in the way that literary fiction did. John Ruskin laid some of the blame for this upon urbanization, in which alienation from nature, over-crowding and monotony of existence had eroded people's ability to obtain excitement other than from fiction which provided a studied arrangement of 'the daily bulletins of their own wretchedness, in the prison calendar, the police news, and the hospital report'.[8] Another contemporary observer felt that popular novels and magazines which displayed imaginary vice and immorality would undermine public morals and respect for intellectual culture, and stated that 'Free libraries should entirely discard books of bad influence, and educate and elevate the tastes of the reading public by putting before it only those works which are calculated to effect these objectives'.[9]

Such views were shared by many librarians, though it is only fair to point out that a few had a more positive attitude. James Duff Brown, for example, published a splendid defence of public library popular fiction and the validity of its appeal to working-class readers.[10] The feeling that popular fiction was in some way problematical to public libraries persisted, however. In the inter-war years Queenie Leavis observed that although libraries provided the works of most popular novelists, they seldom stocked what was considered by a critical minority to be fiction of literary significance and commented that 'A librarian who has made the experiment of putting "good" fiction into his library will report that no-one would take out South Wind or The Garden Party, whereas if he were to put two hundred copies of Edgar Wallace's detective stories on the shelves, they would all be gone the same day'.[11]

Yet it was often not simply the inherent qualities of a book itself which were at issue, but its readership. Just as the 'problem' of leisure was, in essence, focused upon the working classes, so the concern about reading was related to the social class and educational status of the reader. This was significant to libraries because they were intended for, and used predominantly by, the working classes, and librarians often adopted a patronizing approach on account of this. There was a feeling that public libraries had a missionary duty to improve the reading habits of their working-class borrowers and to protect them from certain forms of fiction. For example, one librarian's solution to the vexed question of whether to provide French novels was to stock original copies but not translations as a reader able to cope with the original was more likely to be sufficiently mature and intelligent to remain uncorrupted.[12] Broadly similar distinctions were made when open access was introduced in 1893 and borrowers were allowed, for the first time, to browse amongst the shelves of lending departments. Although some librarians welcomed it, open access was greeted with suspicion in many sections of the profession because of a fear that it would increase the already present tendency to borrow fiction, as uneducated readers would be drawn to the more garishly bound popular adventures and sensation novels. Far from welcoming the fact that more and more people were reading, many librarians, and indeed some literary critics,[13] were deeply concerned that they were reading purely for pleasure in random and non-systematic ways which did not reflect contemporary concepts of recreation as utilitarian, uplifting and improving.

Fiction in libraries

It is virtually impossible to find a volume of a professional library periodical published before 1939 which does not contain references – direct or oblique – to the fiction question, which shows that it was of central importance to the public library movement. The Great Fiction Question, or the 'fiction nuisance' as it was sometimes called, was really two questions in one: should public libraries provide fiction and, if so, what type of fiction? This issue was never seriously debated in the parliamentary processes through which libraries were introduced, and because for the first five years of their existence libraries could not buy books but had to rely on donations, most acquired novels through gifts and bequests. Many libraries took over the bookstocks of Mechanics Institute libraries, and as these almost invariably contained substantial proportions of recreational literature, the majority of public libraries quickly developed stocks containing fiction and light literature. Once fiction had been provided, demand and public expectation were such that it was difficult to stop doing so.

Library committees and book selection

The intensity of the fiction debate within the library profession sometimes screens the fact that the processes of book selection were largely the preserve of library committees, and that it is only since the Second World War that librarians have had general autonomy in selecting and purchasing the stock. Selection by committee was a source of irritation to many librarians because it often happened that a committee would act in a way which was diametrically opposed to the librarian's philosophy. The main object of many committees was to make the library a popular institution, and they often selected large numbers of popular novels to attract the public, whereas the librarian would have preferred to have kept popular fiction at a minimum and to have developed a more scholarly and culturally elite standard in the stock. Committees were generally composed of people drawn from the employing and middle classes, and included not only elected members but coopted members, often invited as a mark of social favour, and representatives of the clergy. Committees did not always possess literary knowledge or an interest in books, and the professional press of the later nineteenth and early twentieth centuries published several critical letters and articles about them and their tendency to buy books which had little literary merit or educational utility but which were guaranteed to have a popular appeal.

Librarians were frequently side-lined in the selection processes, and their impotency fuelled a resentment of a perceived excessive supply of fiction over which they had little control. Their responses to the fiction question varied, but three main strands can be identified: the abolition of fiction, the admission of all fiction, both of which were minority views, and the majority view that some fiction should be provided, but not the more popular and ephemeral sorts.

The anti-fiction lobby

There was a view that libraries should abandon fiction provision, even though the extent of public demand rendered such a measure impractical. This was forcibly expressed at the Library Association's second annual conference in 1879, when it was proposed that a 'hard and fast line' should be drawn by refusing to stock fiction, as novels were becoming cheaper and more affordable to the individual, and as the extent of their supply was undermining the public's respect for the educational work of libraries. Although the motion was defeated, the anti-fiction lobby continued to express its animosity to the leisure function of libraries, as indeed it does to this day. The professional press carried numerous articles and letters of protest against fiction, and the issue came to the fore once more at the Library Association's 1908 conference when the chairman of the Brighton library committee proposed that libraries should not buy popular or ephemeral fiction; this time the motion was carried almost unanimously, and although, as it was not binding, it had little practical effect, it nevertheless reflects the strength of anti-fiction feeling in the profession. Despite its failure to exercise any real impact on library policy on fiction provision, the anti-fiction lobby persisted, and as late as 1958 an *Assistant librarian* editorial proposed that 'worthwhile fiction' be made a separate category for issue purposes so as to portray a better image of the public library in issue statistics.[14] Although the call to abandon fiction has not been prominent in recent decades, it remains relevant as part of the larger question concerning the role of the library as a leisure provider.

Outside the profession, there was a politically motivated anti-fiction lobby similar in ideological conviction to the right wing of the modern Conservative party. Occasionally this was sufficiently strong to prevent the local adoption of the Public Libraries Acts on the grounds that ratepayers' money would be used to subsidize fiction purchases for the benefit of the working classes. Its principal spokesman, M. D. O'Brien,[15] likened public libraries to a 'socialists' continuation school', arguing that while he had no objection to fiction per se, it was not a 'luxury which should be paid for out of the rates'. Even where the public library service flourished, as it did in Sheffield, the Lord Mayor of the city told The Library Association's annual conference that he did not expect to get his light literature any more than his amusement in the form of sport paid for by the public.[16] There was also a minor degree of criticism of fiction from within the book trade, although not sufficient to be considered a major factor.

Rationales for fiction provision

Most librarians adopted the pragmatic view that it was useless to attempt to get rid of fiction altogether, and either promoted it positively or tolerated it in varying degrees. Much as there was a principled distaste for popular fiction amongst a large proportion of the profession, the fact remained that the provision of educational and reference materials by itself was not sufficient to attract the desired numbers of readers to the library. As Bramwell, the librarian at Preston, pointed out, 'People seem to make a great to do about fiction, and some libraries won't have any at all – and nobody goes to them as a result'.[17]

Attitudes to fiction were rarely absolute, and although popular fiction and sensation novels were widely considered unsuitable as public library materials, there was a considerable degree of respect for the works of Scott, Dickens and Thackeray and other literary novelists. Most librarians believed in the existence of a literary hierarchy, and by implication, a hierarchy of reading in which some forms were superior to others. As Victorian recreation was essentially a utilitarian process, reading for pleasure was expected to yield some result beyond mere enjoyment. There was always a chance that readers who used libraries for obtaining popular novels and romances might progress to a higher level of the hierarchy, and this was always cited when libraries were criticized for providing popular fiction. As early as 1869, Edward Edwards claimed that those who started out with lesser books often acquired 'an appetite for the more substantial and wholesome kinds',[18] although Peter Cowell, the librarian at Liverpool, maintained that this was not borne out by his own experience.[19] Some librarians had a more open-minded approach to fiction and felt that libraries, as public institutions, should give the borrowers what they wanted; as one pointed out:

> ... we are bound to supply books of healthy recreation in the form of light literature ... if we stock one kind of book to interest and entertain one class, we can legitimately be called upon to stock another kind of book for another class. The class of lowly education has quite as good a claim to consideration as have their more highly educated brothers.[20]

Positive approaches to fiction provision such as this appeared more commonly towards the end of the nineteenth century, as social attitudes to leisure became more liberal. Newspapers and magazines sometimes published editorials affirming the right of working people to simple amusement as an antidote to the monotony of mechanical employment.

Fiction and the popularization of libraries

To judge from the statistics of issues, which show that almost everywhere more novels were borrowed than any other sort of book, most library committees must have felt that the provision of popular fiction was a valid public library function. It was virtually guaranteed to draw the general public into the library in a way in which reference books and scholarly tomes would not, and was equally certain to result in high issues. All libraries adopted a policy of stocking novels, and as the demand for fiction grew, some library committees responded positively by buying yet more fiction. An ever-increasing demand for novels made it imperative that more should be purchased if a library were to retain its popularity and, to judge from their readiness to buy more novels, many committees recognized this. Many of the writers in demand are barely remembered today, but they included the most popular novelists of the time, amongst them Mrs Henry Wood, Emma Worboise, James Payn, Mary Braddon, Rhoda Broughton and Mayne Reid, and many public libraries contained several copies of all their works. A comment by one librarian in a report from this period shows how a policy of fiction purchase was adopted to popularize the library when he wrote of how the committee continuously bought new books and new editions of books, with multiple copies of titles in high demand, to maintain the 'usefulness of the Institution'. Although this approach to the public library service was exactly of the type that was so roundly disparaged in the professional press, it was one which made the library directly responsive to what the public wanted.

Fiction purchase policies designed to popularize libraries were usually devised by library committees rather than by librarians. Library committees were composed primarily of local politicians who, in some towns, represented almost exclusively the major employers. Sometimes such hard-headed and practical men had a lack of regard for literary merit which, together with a willingness to provide working-class borrowers with easy access to popular fiction, reflected a local culture of paternalism. This paternalism, which expected and received in return a degree of social and political deference, was largely expressed through providing for various leisure interests. Many large employers provided factory libraries and reading rooms for their employees as well as outings, picnics, games and sports facilities and occasional parties. The provision of popular fiction through the municipal library was a corporate extension of this practice; it demonstrated an awareness of working class readers' desire for fiction and a willingness to react positively to it. In such a case the rationale for fiction provision had little to do with cultural values or the imposition of the literary standards of the committee upon the public, and neither was it based upon professional idealism; the objective was to make the library popular by making it relevant to the recreational interests of the local community.

Restricting the range of fiction
A further approach to the fiction question was to concede both that fiction had a rightful place in libraries and that borrowers were entitled to read novels, but to do so within limits. The simplest way of restricting the availability of ephemeral or controversial fiction was through censorship, and few things have contributed more than this to the negative stereotyped image of the public library and the librarian as prim and fastidious.

Public libraries were more assertive in censorship in the past than they are today. Some felt they had a duty not to provide certain novels, and either refused outright to stock them or kept them in a special cupboard to be issued only upon application to the librarian. Novels by Fielding and Smollett were frequently treated in this way, while those by Wells and Hardy were in some places either transferred to the reference department or not bought in the first place. As a contemporary writer pointed out, a particular difficulty was presented by realist and naturalist authors whose names had not yet become hallowed by time, but as he went on to say, it was impossible

> to keep out of a library all books which deal in any way with the seamy side of life, [as that would] prevent the institution from fulfilling one of its most important functions: the placing of the world's great literary masterpieces within the reach of everybody. To be consistent, too, not only the more frank foreign writers such as Zola and Anatole France, but even Thomas Hardy must be banned'.[21]

There was no coordination on a national scale, other than what was not allowed by law, of what was permissible in a public library, and the fact that decisions on what was to be excluded were made at a local level portrayed the library as a guardian of public morals and censor, then as always an honour of dubious distinction. Practices of this type were extremely widespread and continued well into the twentieth century.[22]

Overt censorship of the sort described above was usually undertaken in the case of novels which had fallen foul of literary critics, committee members or Mrs Grundy. Most librarians were more interested in keeping out or reducing the numbers of inoffensive but non-literary cheap romances and popular novels of ephemeral appeal. As was noted above, many committees preferred to provide popular novels, but some were prepared to use their power to promote their own literary standards and religious beliefs in selecting the library's books.

This occurred in differing ways, but one interesting manifestation is found in the development of the public library service in Darwen, Lancashire, where a committee with a strong sense of social mission used the provision of fiction through the library service as a means of promoting a civic gospel. Like the full council, Darwen's library committee was dominated by a Liberal/Congregationalist group, the members of which occupied socially and economically important positions in the town. The religious element was especially significant, for it was within Congregationalism that the concept of the civic gospel evolved. In the words of Robert Dale, the most prominent Congregationalist preacher of the mid-nineteenth century, members of the denomination had a religious duty to become involved in public affairs as councillors and aldermen, and to encourage the provision of rational and harmless amusements.[23] The Congregationalists who dominated Darwen's library committee were also well known in the town through their activities in the church itself. Most of Darwen's nine Congregationalist churches provided a wide range of recreational activities for their members, including the promotion of reading. One of them commented in its magazine that it was important to persuade young people to read 'good and wholesome literature', and this mission to influence popular recreational reading was adopted by the library committee.

In the 1890s the Congregationalist influence on the library committee became more prominent, and the extensive borrowing of ephemeral and sensation fiction from the library became of concern. In 1901, Ralph Yates, the Congregationalist chairman of the library committee, announced that the library intended to take action against the use of the library as an agency for popular fiction. His initial attack focused upon the lack of discrimination shown by both readers and writers, and was typical of a widely encountered attitude amongst librarians and committee men of the time:

Unfortunately, the average reader is not over critical about the creations of the artist, either with respect to incident, plot, descriptive power, or historical or philosophical allusions which in the best tales point the moral and adorn the tale. The writer may violate almost every canon of his art and produce the most vapid and enervating rubbish if he will only give the reader a 'thrill'.[24]

The committee decided that as popular fiction did not, in its opinion, offer moral instruction and innocent amusement, the library would no longer buy new popular novels until at least one year after publication, in the hope that by this time they would have been forgotten. The fact that the embargo was placed upon popular fiction and not upon fiction in total is significant, for the decision as to what was 'popular' and what was 'literary' would be made by the library committee alone; as Yates pointed out, the average reader was not 'over critical' about fiction, and would read almost anything as long as it provided a thrill. It was also a decision which had the greatest impact upon working-class readers, who constituted the bulk of the library's membership. The ban provoked a considerable reaction, and the local newspapers published numerous letters from users protesting against the imposition of the cultural values of the library committee upon the leisure activities of novel-readers. One correspondent said that as the purpose of a library was to provide pleasant recreation for working people, the library's refusal to buy novels by authors such as Annie Swan, Guy Boothby and their like could not be justified, while another posed the blunt question '. . . who has constituted the few members of the Library Committee as the judges of what is or what is not readable?'.[25] Even local newspapers that normally supported Liberal politicians and the council felt that the library committee had taken a step too far. Nevertheless, the ban was implemented and adhered to for some time before it was relaxed and abandoned.

The treatment of fiction in Darwen Library reveals a number of interesting aspects of fiction provision in the period. First, the social function of English literature and the concern about what people read could be important at a local level as well as at the national level as reflected in literary reviews and quarterlies. This meant that in providing fiction, all public libraries were involved in a form of popular recreation to which a range of values were attached. To some committees this was not of primary importance, but to others it was a major factor in rationalizing fiction provision. There was also a tension between the perception of leisure as freedom of individual choice and the view that leisure – or recreation, as this was the more widely used term – should be purposeful in promoting cultural and moral values. It would be an overstatement to suggest that this amounted to a class struggle over the control of leisure through the library, but the censorship of popular fiction was certainly something that working-class readers perceived as being against their interests and wishes, and it did not pass without notice or comment.

Subscription departments and class privilege

The provision of home reading did, however, become a class issue in Warrington Public Library through the exclusion of working-class readers from the subscription scheme in operation there. A number of nineteenth-century public libraries operated subscription departments alongside their 'free' lending departments, usually as a means of raising income to support the library. Newly published novels were lent only to subscribers paying an annual fee; after a period, usually 12 months, these novels were then transferred to the lending department where they were available to the general public under normal public library conditions.

When it opened in 1848, Warrington Public Library inherited the bookstock of a local subscription library, and ran a lending service on a subscription basis. Readers wishing to borrow a book could do so only by paying a subscription fee of half a guinea per annum; in 1887 this was modified to a charge of one penny per book. Subscribers clearly preferred fiction, for in 1876, a typical year, they borrowed 21,965 novels, largely by popular authors such as Mary Braddon, Ouida, Mrs Henry Wood and Emma Worboise, and these accounted for 78% of the total subscription issue. Readers unable or unwilling to pay the fee were not allowed to borrow books but could read them in the library, and this resulted in the subscription department being patronized by the higher social classes. A letter in the *Warrington Examiner* noted that the scheme created a barrier which was 'just high enough to keep out the vulgar herd' though easily met by the wealthy minority.[26] Despite the fact that this practice clearly ran counter to the spirit of the Libraries Acts, the Conservative-dominated library committee abided by a system which placed working-class readers at an obvious disadvantage. The public were less happy with this state of affairs and gradually a campaign evolved to have the library made truly public. This met with strong resistance, however, from the library committee, who insisted that the loss of income which would result from the dissolution of the subscription scheme would render the whole library a non-viable concern. There was also some expression of disquiet from subscribers who wished to retain their privileges; as one of them pointed out, 'If books are lent for home use to those who cannot or will not pay the trifle required, they must get into the hands of the careless and improvident classes, and the damage and cost of renewals will be greatly increased.[27]

Eventually, after a deal of pressure and argument, the library was made free in the conventional sense of the word in 1891, a full 40 years after it opened.

There seems little doubt that the subscription scheme placed working-class readers at a disadvantage at the same time as it provided a useful fiction-lending service – the staffing and housing of which were funded through the rates – for middle-class readers able to pay the required fee. The evidence of subscription departments in other towns[28] also shows that they resulted in class privilege in terms of access to leisure reading, and this provides some useful insight to the potential effects of their reintroduction, a possibility which has been widely voiced in political circles in recent years.

CONTINUITY AND CHANGE

What significance does the above have to the public library of today? Since the period discussed in this chapter, reading has continued to be one of the most popular and widely enjoyed leisure activities, and public libraries have continued to be major providers of fiction. Forecasts that radio and television would displace reading have proved to be erroneous, for, if anything, they have helped to promote fiction. At first glance it may seem that the pre-First World War arguments about popular reading and fiction provision can be of little relevance: most libraries provide novels in ample quantities and, as literature has lost much of its cultural importance, there is little social concern about the range of novels supplied by libraries. Within the profession, fiction is, at worst, tolerated as a necessary evil, and there is no realistic expectation that libraries could now relinquish its provision altogether. In a more positive light, there have been some innovative marketing and publicity campaigns to promote fiction in cooperation with arts bodies and cultural organizations, though libraries do not figure prominently in Arts Council strategies to promote literature.

The relevance of the Great Fiction Question becomes much clearer if it is considered not in the narrow context of fiction provision but in the wider context of the leisure role of the modern public library. In terms of library practice, the fiction question was concerned primarily with a public demand for recreational reading and with the selection and provision of novels. However, at a more theoretical level, it was a debate about the role and social function of the public library and the status of the library profession, and it is these issues which provide the strand of continuity with today's public libraries.

During the period reviewed in this chapter, the public library was struggling to define its role and to gain social agreement on priorities in its functions, and there is still considerable debate in this area today. The 1964 Public Libraries Act referred to education, information and recreation, but did not commit libraries to providing anything more specific than a comprehensive and efficient service. This absence of specificity did not seem to be too disadvantageous while funding levels were relatively healthy, but the intensity of the cuts in public spending and the advances in information technology have forced public libraries to consider, once again, their purposes and functions. Whether this will result in a more positive approach to their leisure role remains to be seen, but it is worth noting that in times of financial stringency, many libraries identify the fiction budget as the first to be reduced.

In terms of the ways in which public libraries are used, remarkably little seems to have changed in the last century. The books borrowed from public libraries are still taken predominantly for leisure purposes, and for many the library is essentially a source of entertaining fiction and other recreational reading; in branch libraries the service is often nearly totally leisure-orientated. Before the First World War librarians disliked this fact and certainly no more than a small minority regarded it as a positive and constructive type of use. The more common occurrence was to seize upon even the most minor decrease in the fiction issue as a sure sign that public libraries were at last becoming purely educational, and it was always quickly pointed out that novels borrowed were not necessarily always read, whereas a non-fiction title might be borrowed with a more definite purpose in mind. The animosity towards fiction, which was characteristic of that period is not present to the same extent today, but fiction provision and leisure aspects of the service still sometimes appear to be viewed as a harmless by-product rather than as a core element: it is still possible to hear senior librarians refer to fiction dismissively as 'non-purposive' and, by implication, as something not to be considered seriously by library managers.

The evidence available in the professional press shows that in the decades preceding the First World War there was a widespread desire that public libraries should be placed under the control of education departments, in the belief that this would enable them to become clearly and formally associated with a function of recognized social importance and would enhance the standing of the profession. Some alignment of libraries with education did in fact occur when county libraries were introduced in 1919. However, although they were able to develop strong links with schools, county libraries too were heavily used for leisure purposes and were rarely seriously integrated in education. Although there seems to be little desire that the public library service should now be operated through education departments, there have been major moves to redefine the service in the context of information provision, in which the public library is promoted as a core agency in community information provision and as a gateway to electronically stored information on a global scale. Whether this will become a reality remains to be seen; libraries will continue to have an information role, but if the viability of the service is to be judged according to volume of use it may be that the increasing availability of CD-ROM packages for use on home computers, and other developments in information technology such as the ability of the Internet to offer home-based access to information which would previously have necessitated a visit to the library, will have an impact on this type of library use. In such a scenario the leisure aspects of the service would need to be maintained, and indeed enhanced, to retain relevance to the wider community.

The history of the public library shows that its leisure function is vital to its popularity. Critics may argue that the provision of fiction has not been a sufficiently strong inducement to persuade the majority of the population to be active members of public libraries, but if it were not for fiction it seems safe to assume that far fewer people would use them than currently do so. The library profession seems never to have been fully comfortable with this fact and, in the context of the past, this is perhaps understandable given the different attitudes to leisure and to popular fiction which then prevailed. However, changes in patterns of employment and production, combined with demographic shifts and altered social attitudes to leisure, have produced a markedly different leisure environment in which public libraries will have to readdress the older questions concerning their leisure role and function.

REFERENCES

1 Great Britain, *Report from the Select Committee on Public Libraries*, evidence presented by Samuel Smiles, London, 1849.
2 Greenwood, T., *Public libraries*, 4th edn, London, Cassell, 1894.
3 Edwards, E., *Free town libraries*, London, Trubner, 1869.
4 Snape, R., 'Betting, billiards and smoking: leisure in public libraries', *Leisure studies*, **11**, 1992, 187–92.
5 Greenwood,T., *Public libraries*, 4th edn, London, Cassell.
6 *Manchester Guardian*, 4 April 1903.
7 Tedder, H., 'Librarianship as a profession (1884)', *In:* J. L Thornton (ed.), *Selected readings in the history of librarianship*, London, Library Association, 1966, 212–24.
8 Ruskin, J., 'Fiction fair and foul, part one', *Nineteenth century*, 7, June 1880, 941–62.
9 Hopkins, T. M., 'A protest against low works of fiction', *Westminster review*, **149**, January 1898, 99–102.
10 Brown, J. D., 'In defence of Emma Jane', *Library world*, **11** (29), 1908, 161–6.
11 Leavis, Q., *Fiction and the reading public*, London, Chatto & Windus, 1932.
12 Baker, E. A., French fiction in public libraries', *Library world*, **2**, 1899, 68–70.
13 Collins, J. C, 'Free libraries: their functions and opportunities', *Nineteenth century*, **53**, June 1903, 968–81.
14 *Assistant librarian*, **51**, 1958, 171–2.
15 O'Brien, M. D., 'Free libraries'. *In:* T. Mackay (ed.), *A plea for liberty: an argument against socialism and socialistic legislation*, London, Murray, 1891, 329–49.
16 *Sheffield Daily Telegraph*, 22 September 1909.
17 Bramwell, W. S., *Reminiscences of a public librarian: a retrospective view*, Preston, 1916.

18   Edwards, E., *Free town libraries*, London, Trubner, 1869.
19   Cowell, P., 'Experientia docet; or, the thoughts and experiences of a public librarian', *Library chronicle*, **5**, 1888, 157–66.
20   *Manchester Guardian*, 24 September 1909.
21   Kirby, S., 'The question of censorship', *Library world*, **14**, 1912, 257–9.
22   Thompson, A. H., *Censorship in public libraries in the United Kingdom during the twentieth century*, London, Bowker, 1975.
23   Hennock, E. P., *Fit and proper persons. Ideals and reality in nineteenth century urban government*, London, Arnold, 1973, 154–69.
24   *Darwen Gazette*, 16 February 1901.
25   *Darwen Gazette*, 2 August 1902.
26   *Warrington Examiner*, 13 March, 1886.
27   *Warrington Examiner*, 19 May, 1886.
28   Snape, R., *Leisure and the rise of the public library*, London, Library Association Publishing, 1995.

5   Built to last

❖   *Michael Dewe*

INTRODUCTION

More than anything else, perhaps, the construction of a library building demonstrates a firm commitment to providing a public library service, although there is a danger of seeing a commitment to such a service as resting largely on the provision of a building. For example, although quickly resolved by the legislation of 1855, the first Public Libraries Act of 1850 did not permit the purchase of books. It was expected that these would flow in as donations. The initial cost of making that building commitment, however, can be seen as one of the stumbling blocks to the spread and development of a nation's library system, especially where its complete cost must be borne locally. It is for this reason that the work of the public library buildings benefactor was so important for the UK in Victorian and Edwardian times, and later in the shape of the Carnegie United Kingdom Trust (CUKT).

An initial financial commitment, however funded, must, of course, be sustained over time. And so for any public library system and its buildings, money should be regularly available for new and replacement libraries and the modernization, possible extension, and maintenance of existing buildings. Building activity on such a wide front may be financially difficult at certain times but the planned approach over a period of years currently adopted by some public library systems can achieve a great deal.

Nowadays, not all library service is provided from static service points and due regard must be given to the provision, renewal and maintenance of the road vehicles used to serve both urban and rural communities and particular individuals and groups, such as the elderly and housebound, the under-fives and school children. This aspect of library service will only occasionally be referred to in this chapter.[1]

It is tempting to see the history of public library building activity, particularly in the twentieth century, as a series of extreme peaks and troughs. The author's impression, gained during the preparation of this chapter, is that, perhaps with the exception of the first 25 or so years after 1850, there has been a fairly constant stream of public library building activity over the decades (with understandably less during the 1920s and '40s). This activity may favour smaller, converted, modernized or prefabricated buildings in times of financial difficulty, but there have been at least two periods of more intense endeavour (1890–1910 and 1960–80) when financial and other conditions were right for more and bigger building projects, particularly new construction.[2]

Change and development

The use of converted buildings – those not originally built for library service – has been a feature of public library development in the UK since its mid-nineteenth century beginnings. In many instances, a library's first accommodation was in a converted house or other building and in some cases this was occupied for a number of years before being replaced by purpose-built accommodation.

Today, however, the majority of public libraries have come to occupy purpose-built buildings often standing independently on their own site. Indeed, influential American and British public librarians have stated that public libraries should not share a building with other agencies. Nevertheless, alongside this 'purist' approach to the location of the public library building in the UK, runs a strand of development that has placed the public library in a complex (civic, arts or shopping), sited it in association with another building, such as a community centre, or housed it with other facilities such as a museum or theatre. Another variation is the dual-purpose or joint-use library, a mix of public library branch and school library. The reasons for such varied siting may have as much to do with government prompting, practical necessity and finance, as with ideas of an enhanced public library role, encouraging a wider range of users, or the benefits of a close association with non-library facilities.

Not only does a library building show a commitment to public library service, but it also provides a physical expression of what the role of that service is seen to be at a particular point in time. New public library buildings thus provide the opportunity to perpetuate existing and accepted ideas or to reconsider the role of a public library and to implement change and engage in experimentation. Such change and experimentation may well be picked up on and followed by others in existing buildings or new ones being planned elsewhere. Some changes may be of long-term significance, others may be seen as relatively short-lived trends, while others may take time to develop and mature. The size, location and nature of some existing library buildings may make it difficult to accommodate change and cope with increasing demands, and these pressures create the demand for new, replacement accommodation.

Thus, over the decades, the changing role of public libraries, including their access policies and operational methods, the increasing variety of formats of library material, and changing constructional techniques and materials have led to considerable changes in the appearance of their buildings, their spatial make-up (the types of spaces provided), and their layout and arrangement.

A constant feature of change is architectural style which is always moving forward or looking back – or doing both. Public library buildings cannot escape, therefore, the dress of the time when they are built. The look of library buildings of the 1980s and the early '90s is very different, especially externally, to those of the 1960s and '70s. Earlier buildings may now be thought to present an inappropriate library image, perhaps by looking too institutional or too utilitarian .

As public buildings, it has to be recognized, however, that local authorities want libraries they can be proud of architecturally and which are not designed merely to serve their utilitarian purpose. These requirements – function and appearance – can be a source of conflict between politicians and librarians in approving a design. A proposed library design may attract adverse comments from local residents, even when politicians and librarians agree. The public controversy over the design of a proposed new library at Brighton is a case in point.

Library buildings are inevitably products of their time, both architecturally and in the way the public library service responds to the concerns, problems and changes in society. In recent years, these matters have included disadvantaged groups, reductions in public spending, energy saving, conservation (of buildings and library materials), information technology, and customer satisfaction. Other factors, as will be seen, shaped the public library service and its buildings of earlier years. Encouragement to respond to change is stimulated by legislation and professional and government reports, such as those produced by the Library Association and the former Department of Education and Science, whose *Library information series* has been of particular significance.

While the following chronological account will demonstrate the effects of change on the public library building, it will show that a new building may also represent both continuity, where old traditions are maintained, and innovation, where new ones are established. The chronological approach has its drawbacks as some ideas may be somewhat older than the decade in which they become more generally adopted. Indeed, it might be argued that a certain amount of time has to pass before change is more universally adopted.

This chapter concentrates on discussing the major public facilities provided in public library buildings since their establishment. The development of special services in respect of different groups, such as children, or of different collections, such as music and local studies, or of different formats, audiovisual materials, for example, is only treated very generally as regards their impact on buildings.

1845–1886: A PLACE TO READ

Following the Museum Act 1845, the Public Libraries and Museums Acts of 1850 and later, and some local acts, 31 rate-supported public library services came into operation in England, Wales and Scotland in the years 1850–70, utilizing 55 buildings. Of these, 38 were converted premises and 17 were purpose-built libraries.[3] Of the converted buildings, the most popular for library use were houses, former Mechanics Institutes and allied institutions, single rooms in town halls, chapels, and proprietary and subscription libraries.[4]

Reflecting the Victorian battle of the styles, and the demand by local authorities for grand public buildings, two-thirds of the 17 purpose-built libraries were in a classical or Italianate style, while the remainder were Gothic.[5]

An analysis of these early 55 libraries and their departments shows: three cases of libraries dominated by museums, with museums provided in ten other buildings; art galleries in two buildings and schools of art or science in three others; the reference library dominating 11 central libraries, the lending library nine and in five the newsroom. Other facilities provided included: 'two ladies' newsrooms, one students' newsroom, two subscription lending libraries, one youths' library, one children's library, the patent room at Nottingham and the Shakespeare Memorial Library at Birmingham. No doubt many other special collections existed in libraries but these probably formed part of the reference library.'[6]

Manchester was the first public library established under the 1850 Act; a lending and reference library opened in September 1852 in a building originally opened as the Hall of Science in 1840 and considered by its first librarian as not well suited for a library.[7] Of particular interest, however, is the large Liverpool Central Library and Museum (1860), paid for by William Brown, and containing newsrooms, reference library, museum and other accommodation.

In the decade that followed, the number of public libraries increased to 80[8] and there was some expansion and development amongst existing services. Liverpool added the Walker Art Gallery (1877) and the Picton Reading Room (1879), a room for students and for literary research and enquiry, thus creating an impressive group of buildings for education and art.

The 1880s saw the opening of the new Birmingham Central Library, declared 'the finest building of its kind in the United Kingdom,'[9] and other buildings, for example, in Newcastle upon Tyne (1884), and Oldham (1885), the latter a central library, museum and art gallery.

In his *Free public libraries* (1886), Thomas Greenwood, the public library propagandist, records that libraries at Darlington, Leek, Northwich and Preston, among others, owed their existence to what he called 'private munificence'.[10] Of these, probably the most impressive was the Greek temple of a building at

Preston, the Harris Free Library and Museum, whose foundation stone was laid in 1882, the library opening in 1892. Greenwood also records Carnegie's first gift in 1883 of the Free Library, Dunfermline, perhaps sounding as much like a club as a library. There were separate reading rooms for ladies and gentlemen, and recreation and smoking rooms in addition to lending and reference departments.

By 1886, Greenwood was suggesting that the public library should consist of at least three separate departments – lending and reference libraries, and newsroom – and, where possible, a separate room for ladies. If all of these could be placed on the ground floor, it was argued, with the lending library and staff at the centre, and partitions appropriately arranged, then the librarian could supervise all departments. In addition to the provision of lavatories, committees were strongly urged to follow Manchester's example (begun with Ancoats Branch in 1878) and provide boys' reading rooms: 'how many lads would be kept from running about the streets, and falling into all sorts of mischiefs and pernicious influences, if they had a reading-room to which they could resort?'[11] Boys were seen as the ratepaying townsmen of the future.

Statistics for the period show that in the mid-1880s a number of places provided branch libraries. Birmingham and Bristol had five each, Bradford had seven, and Manchester had six branches, while Leeds had 22. Some towns provided separate reading rooms in addition to or instead of branches; Nottingham, for example, had three branches and nine reading rooms.[12]

The first 35 years of the public library building already provides exemplification of the variety of possible roles that the public library could play. It could be:

- a mix of library, museum and possibly art gallery (where not too large it could be housed in 'one good room', according to Mullins[13]);
- a library with club facilities, as at Dunfermline or Hindley, Lancashire (where it was proposed that the basement of the library and museum be utilized as a working-man's club[14]), or
- a library consisting of a number of reading rooms, lending and reference libraries.

The latter model was the one most generally adopted, and (because it was cheap to do so) catered principally for the reading of newspapers, magazines and books on the premises. The overriding purpose was an educational one, including some libraries' educational activity, e.g. science and art classes, sponsored by the library and aimed at the population at large. Nevertheless, the library was considered as a counter-attraction to 'this and that improper place for recreation,'[15] and this role should not be overlooked.

1887–1918: THE OPEN ACCESS REVOLUTION

For a variety of reasons, these years were to be an era of great growth for the municipal library service. Because of their number (348, including extensions and conversions built or begun before October 1913[16]), the term 'Carnegie library' came to be used to dismiss aesthetically and functionally many of the library buildings of those years, whether Carnegie funded or not, although this attitude has changed, to some extent, more recently. It has been demonstrated that the best of these buildings, can, if approached with imagination, still serve as satisfactory library buildings a century or many decades later. Dunfermline has recently been extended and Hammersmith (opened 1905) has been refurbished.

Whilst Andrew Carnegie was pre-eminent amongst benefactors, the generosity of men like Tate and Newnes in London, Passmore Edwards in London and the south-west of England, and local donors of sites and/or buildings elsewhere in the country, continuing a tradition noted earlier, should not be overlooked. Indeed, it is tempting to conclude that the public library movement in Britain would not have expanded and established itself so successfully without these many and often substantial gifts that created an inheritance of library bricks and mortar for future generations to add to.

An investment in a building, however, whether donated or local-authority funded, could result in inadequate returns if restrictive legislation (the penny rate limitation did not disappear until 1919), or a local authority's lack of, or unwillingness to spend, money, meant that it could not receive sufficient resources of books and staff. Carnegie went some way to ensuring the basic financial resources for the work of the library service in the buildings he funded by the conditions he laid down for the acceptance of his offers, e.g. a debt-free site, the adoption of the Public Libraries Acts and the levy of at least the penny rate.

By the mid-1890s, the constituent parts of the public library building started to undergo some major developments. For example, Greenwood was now less in favour of separate reading rooms for boys and ladies, for, amongst other reasons, it would decrease the number of rooms that staff had to keep an eye on. He was also wary about including lavatory accommodation. He advocated, however, that the plans for new buildings should, if possible, include a lecture hall.[17] Comment was made on 'the ever-extending number of [public libraries] . . ., which are including as part of their operations lectures and science and art classes.'[18] Greenwood had noted the provision of 'free library lectures' eight years earlier and urged their commencement but had not advocated special accommodation for them.[19] He also asked that: 'Wherever possible, juvenile libraries should be started. These are extending everywhere, with specially selected books and catalogues, and are doing good service.'[20] In his recommendations and comments, Greenwood is clearly reflecting changing practice and provision, but it would be a few years, even where new buildings were constructed, for these ideas to be followed.

Burgoyne's *Library construction*, published in 1897, summarizes the accommodation possibilities for the town library as at least reference and lending departments, a reading room (or separate reading rooms for newspapers and magazines), and the necessary working rooms for the librarian and his staff. Other accommodation could include separate reading rooms for boys, girls, women and students; a lecture hall; a museum and art gallery; residences for the librarian and caretakers; a strongroom for manuscripts, incunabula or local collections; and rooms for the binding and repairing of books.[21] Surprisingly, unlike Greenwood, Burgoyne does not mention a library for juveniles, although separate reading rooms for boys and girls are offered as a possibility; the author knows of no library ever making separate provision for girls before or after this period.

Open-access provision

While giving almost a whole chapter to the varieties of indicator available to record the availability and loan of titles in closed-access libraries, Burgoyne surprisingly offers no discussion of open-access libraries and the implications of this new operational method for library service and design. Clerkenwell, erected in 1890, was, in 1893, the first British public library to open up its lending department to borrowers and allow them to select their own books. This method of operation was slow to be adopted more widely, and the question of whether lending libraries and, to a lesser degree, reference libraries should be open- or closed-access libraries, became one of the major professional issues of this period.

Open-access libraries allowed readers free access to the bookstock, while closed access (the traditional approach) meant there was no such direct access but, by means of a catalogue (showing what was available), indicator boards in lending libraries (showing what was not on loan), and library staff, readers were handed their requested book across a counter. The use of one method or the other for operating the library had implications for the role of its staff, space allocation and layout. For example, open-access lending libraries required lower shelving, ample circulation space, a system of arrangement by author or subject, and a layout that allowed for supervision from the staff enclosure, with wicket gates controlling the entrance and exit of readers. The radial arrangement of bookcases made supervision more complete but wasted space, except in a semi-circular room.

While there is no doubt that the introduction of open access was a major influence on public library interior design (and a step towards a change of emphasis from reading on the premises to the lending of books), the controversy aroused by the debate over its rightness or otherwise has perhaps overshadowed other developments in public library provision which were under discussion at this time, e.g. the lecture hall and juvenile library. These ideas were to be physically exemplified in the library buildings of the early twentieth century, such as those of Islington (1907) and Fulham (1909) central libraries.

Interestingly, in addition to Clerkenwell, Burgoyne records only two open-access libraries in 1897: at Worcester (with museum, art gallery and technical and art school, 1895), and at Croydon (with municipal buildings, 1896).[22] Worcester provided seats for 80 readers and stands for 28 newspapers in its reading room; the reference library also seated 42 persons. Clearly, provision for reading on the premises continued to be a major objective.

In 1913 it was noted that branch libraries should always have a lending department and a news and periodical room, and possibly a children's department and a small collection of quick-reference books.[23] The same writer also advocated delivery stations for districts with a scattered population on the outskirts of towns which did not currently warrant a branch library. A carefully selected stock of books could be housed in a busy shop, post office or school.[24] Almost 20 years earlier, Greenwood had argued for board schools to be used as branch libraries where the expense of building, stocking and maintaining a branch could not be afforded.[25]

In spite of open access, and a greater variety of space provision in some libraries, e.g. for children and lectures, the newsroom was still the best patronized facility, although there was the beginning of a decline in the space given over to reading-room provision. Open access, with its underlying concept of self-service by users and the importance of lending books over that of reading on the premises, did not begin to assert itself, however, until the following decades, by which time many existing lending libraries had converted to open access. This change of method also heralds, perhaps, the emergence of the staff as assistants to the public rather than attendants policing the library.

1919–1939: EXPANSION, CONSOLIDATION, AND SPECIALIZATION
The passing of the Public Libraries Act 1919 empowered county councils in England and Wales to adopt the acts and many did so during the 1920s, some assisted by the CUKT. The act also abolished the one penny rate limitation, although this did not mean that substantially more would be spent immediately on public libraries. The concept of service that was developed by the new county services was that of a headquarters building, invariably in some sort of adapted building, with village centres to which boxes of books were sent and regularly exchanged. To improve upon this very basic service static purpose-

built service points were needed to serve the more populous areas but it would be some years before this would be possible: 'it was not until the middle and late 1930s that a short period of extensive building programmes coincided with easier economic conditions and that purpose-built branch libraries were erected in market towns and urban areas'.[26] This development was also assisted by the CUKT, whose grant of £25,000 to mainly 11 counties, assisted the development of libraries on new housing estates.[27] Other towns within the county were often independent municipal library authorities. Students and others, whose requirements were beyond the branches and centres, were encouraged to visit the headquarters building or were sent books by post.

Of the buildings of the 1920s, it was remarked that when Hendon Central Library was opened in 1929 it 'was very generally quoted by librarians as being an example which very nearly approached the ideal of what a conveniently planned library should be. I had heard great accounts of the building . . . and was not disappointed when I had the opportunity to visit it.'[28] It was, without a doubt, conveniently planned, but in terms of service provision or the organization of the interior space, it showed no real development, mirroring, as it did, the progressive central library buildings of the century's first decade. Even the neo-Georgian facade was a throwback to the exteriors of earlier libraries like Kingston and Fulham.

1930s developments

Following the post-war inactivity of the 1920s, the 1930s saw a spurt of major central library construction that ended with the outbreak of the Second World War: Burnley (1930), Birkenhead, Manchester, Sheffield (all 1934), and Huddersfield (1939). All confirmed, in terms of space and location, the primacy of the lending library and the need to provide a service to children. Special departments for local studies, music, and commercial and technical information were also to be variously found in these buildings.

Anthony Thompson wrote in 1963 that 'the 1920s in the USA saw the development of subject departmentalization and of buildings specially designed for it', and also that 'In this period the so-called "open plan" also spread in America', the two approaches 'developing into a general principle for the arrangement of large multistorey libraries'.[29]

The arrangement of the 1934 Manchester building is that of subject departments round a central bookstack,[30] but it was an idea that did not blossom generally in the UK until after the Second World War. An important and earlier milestone, therefore, was the introduction under Ernest Savage in 1932 of subject departments in Edinburgh's replanned central library.

A number of larger branch libraries from the 1930s provide examples of the lack of major changes in this area of provision. Firth Park (Sheffield), Yardley

Wood (Birmingham) and Norris Green (Liverpool) were all branches with similar butterfly plans, all with centrally placed counters and compartmental-ized interiors that included a children's department and considerable reading-room provision. The 1930s saw the planning of the UK's first modular library (Manor Branch, Sheffield) which was begun in 1939 but not opened until 1953. An adult library was divided off from the children's library (with separate entrance) and the small reference library by floor-to-ceiling glass screens.[31]

It has been suggested that 'The design of the smaller branch libraries tended to be more experimental than central libraries, and several, for instance, the Purley branches . . . showed a mix of neo-Georgian and moderne styles'.[32]

A survey of libraries, made by the Library Association during 1936–7, pro-vides a useful snapshot of the state of public libraries in the latter part of the decade, including the position as regards buildings.[33] It mentions favourably a number of specific buildings, but the general points made fairly frequently by contributors could be summarized as: old buildings were hindering change; many building were dull and dingy and in need of redecoration, and the accommodation for staff was poor but better in modern buildings.

This between-the-wars period saw the expansion of the public library ser-vice to the county areas, providing essentially books for loan. Purpose-built county branches began to be established, particularly in the latter half of the 1930s. Municipal libraries benefited from a small number of major buildings and the erection of a significant number of branches that consolidated the changes in provision begun in previous years, although reading-room provi-sion continued to be a major feature of many libraries. While the need to pro-vide special collections, such as those of local history, local industry, music, and books for the blind was clearly recognized earlier in the century,[34] it was not until the major public libraries built in the 1930s that this was reflected in their accommodation. In spite of this expansion, consolidation and specializa-tion, this transitional period for public libraries between the wars had much that required improvement, including the buildings, and this was a theme that was to be taken up in the following decade.

1940–1959: LIBRARIES IN WAR TIME AND AFTER

Lionel McColvin's *The public library system of Great Britain*[35] was published in 1942 and provides a one-man picture of their then condition with proposals for their future, post-war development. Philip Whiteman has brought together McColvin's views on the library buildings he saw at the time of his report: 'The majority were "unsuitable, inappropriate, inadequate, expensive or ill-sited", many being "ugly, uncomfortable, cold, badly lit, dreary, undecoratable mon-uments", though the best of modern libraries were well designed and fur-nished. Some libraries were seriously short of space, both for storage and to make possible proper working conditions for staff.'[36]

While putting his finger on much that would be in need of change – such as the abolition of the newsroom – or improvement, e.g. service to 'special classes of readers' when times were more propitious, McColvin's rather limited concept of the role of the library (he was not keen on the library as a cultural or educational centre) was one that would be challenged by some of the buildings of the post-war years.

However, in the light of McColvin's comments it is interesting to look at the St. Marylebone Central Library, planned in the late 1930s and opened in May 1940. Designed in a classical style as an extension to the existing town hall, the building contained a lending library on the ground floor, with reference library, quick reference hall, local collection room and reading room on the first floor. The lower ground floor housed the children's library, with a separate side entrance, and it was said that 'much thought has been expended on the amenities of this particular department. There is a projection room for lantern talks. All fittings are movable and on casters so that the room may be cleared in a very short space of time and seating provided by means of stackable metal chairs . . . No washing facilities are offered . . .'[37]

Storage was also provided on this lower floor and in a basement level. The care given to the children's library and the scale of lending-library provision are clearly symbols of change, as perhaps is the absence of a newsroom and lecture hall.

In the immediate post-war period, housing, schools and hospitals took priority over libraries. However, the 1950s saw the provision of at least 203 new service points[38] as well as the repairing of war-time damage. The 1910 central library in Plymouth was destroyed by enemy action in 1941 and rebuilt in 1954–6. In the rebuilt library no separate provision was made for reading newspapers and periodicals, confirming the post-war trend to do away with such rooms, and the whole of the ground floor was given over to lending provision for adults and children (served by a common desk), plus some office and staff accommodation. The first floor continued to accommodate the reference library (with study room), and local collection, with a lecture room (for extension activities), music and drama library, plus some office and staff facilities. The basement housed the city muniments and local history archives.[39]

The immediate post-war period saw the last vestiges of closed access disappear: in England at Holborn in 1947 and in Scotland at Dumbarton in 1951.

1960–1979: CULTURE, COMMUNITY AND COMPUTERS

The 1960s opened with a pamphlet from The Library Association entitled *Public library buildings: the way ahead*. The pamphlet stated that 'The use of public libraries has increased by 75 per cent since 1939; book stocks by 110 per cent;

staff by 80 per cent; but the provision of new library buildings and the extension and improvement of existing premises has been virtually at a standstill.'[40]
While noting that only three purpose-built central libraries had been built since
the war, it later states that only 236 branch libraries were built between 1945
and 1958 – hardly a standstill – but that some of these were of a temporary
nature. It reckoned that a further 750 branches were required to meet the needs
of post-war housing estates alone.

Later sections of the pamphlet briefly comment about siting, architectural
style, etc., and suggest what should be provided; the newsroom got the
'thumbs down' as 'a relic of the past and a waste of space today'. The pamphlet
offers standards for calculating library size – an important new development –
seemingly based on those of the International Federation of Library
Associations.

Major initiatives

British public library buildings, published in 1966, noted that since 1960 no fewer
than 350 new public library service points had been provided in Britain and
that there could well be more.[41] This figure represents a major step forward,
given The Library Association's suggested requirements published six years
earlier. Later, the authors of *British public library buildings* comment that 'the
British public library is at that state of its development historically when most
of the major main library buildings are due for replacement, but the problem
has not yet been tackled bravely enough'.[42] The book records, therefore,
because of post-war financial conditions, the emphasis that was placed on
municipal and county branch library construction and laments the lack of purpose-built county library headquarters and new municipal central libraries,
although the latter were represented in the book by Holborn and Kensington
(1960), Guildford, Luton, Norwich and Nuneaton (1962), Eastbourne and
Hampstead (1964), and Hornsey (1965).

In the first half of the decade, county library headquarters (HQ) were completed at Staffordshire (1961) Montgomeryshire and Durham (1963), Kent and
the West Riding (1964). Such HQs could also have public service facilities as
well as those for administration, distribution, storage and garaging. West
Riding's was the largest, but Kent's HQ, with its ten-storied book stack above
a two-storied administrative block and decagonal and galleried students'
library, was a unique public library architectural solution.

Both municipal and county branch libraries ranged in size from small one-
room libraries of just under 100 m², to those, sometimes on more than one floor,
of 500–700 m². The counties also designated some larger branch libraries as
regional or area libraries, for example Mansfield Woodhouse
(Nottinghamshire, 1961) and Kirby (Lancashire, 1964). Branch libraries were

often erected to serve housing estates and would, in many instances, be close to or on a housing development, sometimes with flats above the library. Branch libraries were also built in association with accommodation for the elderly, but more commonly with a health, child welfare or other clinic, or possibly adjoining a community hall or community centre. Another favoured location was near or in the local shopping area. The usual strange bedfellows occurred: a library above slipper baths and launderette; a library and police station; a library housed with changing rooms for a sports ground. Provision of, or proximity to, car parking facilities began to be of importance.

In the 1950s the majority of building projects were conversions, in the 1960s this represented about one-quarter of such projects.[43] However, extensive use was made of prefabricated structures and, in some authorities, the use of standard or model designs to provide many buildings quickly and economically, for example Liverpool, Nottingham, and West Riding.

The impact of service changes

Many libraries continued to use the Browne issue system but many others were using photocharging, which required much smaller issue desks. This, along with other equipment such as telex, telephone exchanges and photocopiers, heralded the arrival of a different way of running libraries that was to change even more markedly in the 1960s with the use of the computer.

From their inception there had always been a cultural dimension to the work of the public library through lectures and classes, and associated museums and art galleries. The post-war period saw this develop further, particularly in buildings in towns of some size. For example, of the buildings constructed in the years 1960–6, 'twenty of the thirty one main libraries, both municipal and county, provided special rooms for extension activities, but that only twenty four out of 224 branch libraries provided such rooms or even mentioned adaptations to allow part time use of the library rooms for cultural purposes'.[44] By 1967–8, the limited evidence seemed to indicate better provision, with at least a meeting room.

There were some interesting examples of this cultural dimension: for example, Wythenshawe Forum (Manchester), where library and theatre formed part of a social and sports complex; St Pancras Library which incorporated the Shaw Theatre; and Thurrock (1969 and 1972) with theatre, local history museum, exhibition area and refreshment facilities. Branch libraries too, it was recognized, had also a role to play.

This cultural role was formally acknowledged and its continuance encouraged by the 1975 publication *Public libraries and cultural activities*.[45] In espousing the library as a cultural centre (rather than an arts centre), the publication recognized the need for it to work in association with others and to reflect local needs and other available provision. Through their libraries, it was felt that local authorities could provide finance, facilities and expertise.

Major buildings of the 1970s included the following. Birmingham, which at the time of completion in 1973 was the largest public library building in Europe, consisted of a seven-storey reference library, arranged by subject department (and including an archives department), and a three-storey lending library, with movement through the large building provided by escalator.[46] Sutton (1975), embraced the concept of the market place and serving the needs of the whole community, and included a gallery, sales area, coffee bar and five subject departments each one using individual colour coding for everything from shelf guides to upholstery. Dundee (1978) was built as part of a major shopping centre on two large floors, with cinema/lecture hall and lending, arts and music, and children's libraries on the lower floor, and reference, commerce and technology, and local history on an upper floor. Portsmouth (1978) was said to be liner-like in appearance, and was a well sited library on five levels with a popular library and exhibition area on the ground floor, a children's library on a lower ground floor, and integrated lending and reference stock, as well as more specialized collections and services (e.g. Patents Collection, Naval Collection and online services) on the floors above, the third floor housing a cafeteria, meeting rooms and a lecture hall.[47]

The libraries choice, published in 1978, drew attention to the work then going on in creating another public library access revolution, this time for the disadvantaged. The disadvantaged were seen as hospital patients, the housebound and handicapped, residents in homes for the elderly, prisoners, ethnic minorities, adult illiterates, and those in deprived areas. The publication suggested 'that while significant numbers of authorities might be providing for some disadvantaged readers in their areas few were providing services in any comprehensive way'.[48] In deprived areas, library authorities were encouraged to give priority to the redecoration of library buildings, to seek better sites, be welcoming to library-based community activities and be hospitable to other information-providing agencies, such as Citizens' Advice Bureaux. Reaching out to the community during this period included the provision of 'bookbuses' for children and parents, for example.

Much of the library work just described became known as 'community librarianship' and has come to be regarded as a particular phenomenon of the 1970s and the '80s. While recognizing that this term is capable of a variety of interpretations, it has been characterized as 'freedom of access and of delivery, responsiveness to the needs of local communities and availability to all, regardless of location, ethnic or cultural origin, or level of income or education'.[49]

The 1960s and 1970s saw a considerable increase in public library building, a delayed post-war recovery and expansion helped by the optimism engendered by the Public Libraries and Museums Act 1965 and the more prosperous but gradually worsening financial climate of the times.

1980–1995: LIBRARIES AS SHOPS

In spite of the financial problems of the 1980s, capital projects were not halted. The decade saw the construction of a number of large, outer London libraries (Bexley, Ilford and Uxbridge, for example), the completion of the extension to the Mitchell Library, Glasgow (1981), the biggest reference library in Europe, and the opening in 1988 of the largest public library in Wales at Cardiff.[50] Other buildings of note were, in the early 1980s: Calderdale (minimum use of glazing on upper floors); Runcorn (a four-floor library adjacent to a shopping centre and built following a major market research study of user needs, probably the first of its kind in the UK); the Barbican (part of the City of London Barbican Centre that included, as well as a library, a concert hall, theatres, cinemas, art gallery, restaurants, conference facilities, trade exhibition halls and rooms for private functions), and Rotherham Library and Arts Centre (lending, reference and local studies facilities together with a multipurpose hall, a variety of meeting and activity rooms, galleries, cafe and bar). Buildings of interest from the later 1980s were: Hounslow, Rhyl Library, Museum and Art Centre, Reading, Chesterfield, Telford, and Willesden Green Library Centre.[51]

Libraries in association with shops or in shopping centres have been a siting feature since the 1930s. The library as a constituent of an enclosed shopping mall is largely, however, a product of the 1980s and '90s, reflecting a major change in the way retail and some community facilities are presented to people. There can be significant advantages for such siting in terms of use, car-parking facilities, and finance (through planning gain), but disadvantages in that accommodation is not purpose-designed, space may be limited and the library (other than a dedicated entrance) may be entirely at first-floor level or above. Examples of shopping centre libraries were to be found at Hounslow, Enfield and Havant.

Whether linked with shopping facilities or not, additions to traditional library materials – compact discs, computer software and videos – and the furniture to display them, together with new designs for library book shelving, have encouraged the creation of libraries with the informal, browsing atmosphere of the bookshop. These changes, as well as those to the library layout, reflect a more reader-orientated arrangement and display of books and other material. Some libraries have also been concerned with providing space for revenue-producing activities, such as a library shop, a sales point, or for advertising, adding to the feeling of a changed library environment. Facilities for open learning are also becoming increasingly common.

Computer loan and catalogue systems became firmly established, and librarians, obliged to recognize the unacceptable stock losses from open access, have often combined a security system with the issue counter. This marks a return to the earlier idea of open access with appropriate safeguards. In children's libraries, play and display furniture – displaying library materials and often providing somewhere for children to sit – became very much in vogue, with animal and transport vehicles as popular themes. There have been increasing amounts of equipment in public libraries, e.g. public telephones, coin-operated photocopiers, television sets, computers and fax machines. This technology is a major resource for developing the information role of the public library and a significant feature of Croydon Central Library, opened in late 1993.

Gone in the 1980s were exposed concrete, and large areas of glass and undecorated surfaces to be replaced by brick, pitched roofs, less fenestration and some external decoration, as seen at Rhyl, for example. Some library buildings were designed in a low key – almost domestic vernacular in approach – in order to fit in with the local environment.

Writing half-way through the 1990s it is difficult to forecast how it will be seen in terms of library buildings in the first decade of the new millennium. Many of the changes noted above will continue and will be consolidated. One trend that appears to be emerging is the greater use of refurbished and converted buildings over new buildings.

CONCLUSION

In 1993–4 the number of service points in the UK, both full- and part-time, was 1682.[52] While many of these will be post-1950 or more recent, a number still date from the pre-Second World War period and back to the late Victorian and Edwardian eras. The stock of public library buildings, both central and branch, is thus very varied as regards age. While the current building may be the only building a community has had, many of the former municipalities have buildings which have replaced their earlier Carnegie library. In those authorities with a long history of public library service, the latter may well have replaced a converted building where the service first began.

Those Victorian and Edwardian buildings that continue to provide a satisfactory library service can be said to have been built to last. What determines their continuing use? They survive because they have always been fundamentally good buildings of which some of the key characteristics are a suitable and spacious site, and generous and well-distributed interior spaces that permit change every 25 to 30 years. Additionally, they have become well-loved landmarks in their community and some may also be protected because of their architectural or other attributes. There is a kind of natural selection that operates amongst public library buildings – survival of the fittest is bound up with the capability to adapt.

Not all library buildings have been built to last, some, usually branch libraries, have been seen as temporary structures, erected until something better can be provided by way of building and library services. However, at least one library authority places a planning life on its branch library buildings that relates to its expected usefulness. Perhaps we are still concerned to build to last so that the opportunities to do otherwise are missed. There may be a place for planned obsolescence in the public library building and it has been suggested that there is a trend towards the demise of the separate library building. One thing is certain; it will be fashionable to be very critical of the buildings of a particular period, as was the view of Victorian and Edwardian libraries in the 1950s and earlier. Views can change, however.

Gone are the words 'free' and 'public' from a library exterior, except where they remain carved indelibly on some earlier building still in use. The word 'library' emblazoned on a building has come to signify the local public library, whether branch or grander edifice, and free in most respects they continue to be. This chapter has also demonstrated that behind the 'library' designation are a whole range of different and changing interpretations that are reflected in the varied range of buildings, both large and small, that have been and continue to be provided. This was true at the beginning of the public library movement and continues to be so today.

REFERENCES

1   The development of this aspect of library service is given in Eastwood, C. R., *Mobile libraries and other public transport*, London, Association of Assistant Librarians, 1967; and Orton, G. I. J., *An illustrated history of mobile library services in the United Kingdom*, Sudbury, Suffolk, Branch and Mobile Libraries Group of The Library Association, 1980.

2   Figures compiled in 1970/71 show the number, age and type of library buildings in use at that time; the ratio of new to converted was 60% to 40%. For full details see Taylor, J.N. and Johnson, I A., *Public libraries and their use*, London, HMSO, 1973, 57–8.

3   Keeling, D. F., 'British public library buildings 1850–1870', *Library history*, **1** (4) 1968, 109.

4   *Ibid.*, 120.

5   *Ibid.*, 122, 124.

6   *Ibid.*, 121.

7   *Ibid.*, 116, 118.

8   Mullins, J. D., *Free libraries and newsrooms: their formation and management*, 3rd edn, London, Southeran, 1879, 4.

9   Greenwood, T., *Free public libraries: their organisation, uses, and management*,

London, Simpkin, Marshall, 1886, 63.

10   *Ibid.*, 187–232,

11   *Ibid.*, 164–5.

12   *Ibid.*, Ch. XXII.

13   Mullins, J. D., *Free libraries and newsrooms: their formation and management*, 3rd edn, London, Southeran, 1879, 12.

14   *Ibid.*, 105.

15   Mullins, J. D., *Free libraries and newsrooms: their formation and management*, 3rd edn, London, Southeran, 1879, 1.

16   Smith, A. J., *Carnegie library buildings in Great Britain: an account, evaluation and survey*, thesis submitted for Fellowship of the Library Association, 1974, vol.1, 28.

17   Greenwood, T., *Public libraries: a history of the movement and a manual for the organization and management of rate-supported libraries*, London, Cassell, 1894, 386–7.

18   *Ibid.*, 470.

19   Greenwood, T., *Free public libraries: their organisation, uses, and management*, London, Simpkin, Marshall, 1886, 358–67.

20   Greenwood, T., *Public libraries: a history of the movement and a manual for the organization and management of rate-supported libraries*, London, Cassell, 1894, 372.

21   Burgoyne, F. J., *Library construction, architecture, fittings and furniture*, London, Allen, 1897, 8.

22   *Ibid.*, 187–9, 205–11.

23   Rae, W. S. C., *Public library administration*, London, Routledge, 1913, 42.

24   *Ibid.*, 45.

25   Greenwood, T., *Public libraries: a history of the movement and a manual for the organization and management of rate-supported libraries*, London, Cassell, 1894, 456.

26   Thompson, A., *Library buildings of Britain and Europe*, London, Butterworths, 1963, 187.

27   Jenkins, O, M., *Conservation and modernization of British public library buildings of the 1930s with special reference to Greater London*, MLib thesis, University of Wales, 1990, 9.

28   Ashburner, E. H., *Modern public libraries: their planning and design*, London, Grafton, 1946, 45.

29   Thompson, A., *Library buildings of Britain and Europe*, London, Butterworths, 1963, 103.

30   Jast, L. S., *The planning of a great library*, London, Libraco, 1927.

31   For fuller details see Thompson, A., *Library buildings of Britain and Europe*, London, Butterworths, 1963, 114–17.

32   Jenkins, O, M., *Conservation and modernization of British public library buildings of the 1930s with special reference to Greater London*, MLib thesis, University of Wales, 21.

33   McColvin, L. R. (ed.), *A survey of libraries: reports on a survey made by the Library Association during 1936–1937*, London, Library Association, 1938.

34   Rae, W. S. C., *Public library administration*, London, Routledge, 1913, 54–6.

35   Whiteman, P., *Public libraries since 1945: the impact of the McColvin Report*, London, Bingley, 1986.

36 *Ibid.*, 45.

37 Ashburner, E. H., *Modern public libraries: their planning and design*, London, Grafton, 1946, 46–7.

38 Taylor J. N. and Johnson, I. A., *Public libraries and their use*, London, HMSO, 1973, 58.

39 For a full description of the building see, Thompson, A., *Library buildings of Britain and Europe*, London, Butterworths, 1963, 148–54.

40 *Public library buildings: the way ahead*, London, Library Association, 1960, [1].

41 Berriman, S. G. and Harrison, K. C., *British public library buildings*, London, Deutsch, 1966, 18.

42 *Ibid.*, 22.

43 Taylor J. N. and Johnson, I. A., *Public libraries and their use*, London, HMSO, 1973, 58.

44 Wilson, A., 'Public libraries and arts in Britain', *In*: Gerard, D. (ed.), *Libraries and the arts*, London, Bingley, 1970, 123.

45 Department of Education and Science, *Public libraries and cultural activities*, London, HMSO, 1975.

46 For details of this and other buildings of the period see Ward, H. (ed.), *New library buildings 1976 issue: years 1973–1974*, London, Library Association, 1976.

47 For details of Sutton, Dundee, 'Portsmouth and other buildings of the period' see Harrison, K. C. (ed.), *Public library buildings 1975–1983*, London, Library Services Ltd, 1987.

48 Department of Education and Science, *The libraries' choice*, London, HMSO, 1978, 8.

49 Martin, W. J., *Community librarianship: changing the face of public libraries*, London, Bingley, 1989, 165.

50 This section is a summary and revision of a published conference paper by the author: Dewe, M., 'Trends in UK public library buildings during the 1980s', In: *Petrification or flexibility, papers from the Anglo-Scandinavian Public Library Conference, Ronneby 1991*, Stockholm, Swedish National Council for Cultural Affairs, 1992, 31–7.

51 For fuller details of these and other libraries of the period, see Harrison, K. C. (ed.), *Public library buildings 1975–1983*, London, Library Services Ltd, 1987; *Library buildings 1984–1989*, London, Library Services Ltd, 1990.

52 Chartered Institute of Public Finance and Accountancy, *Public library statistics 1993/4 actuals*, London, CIPFA, 1994, 8.

6　The library and the rural community

❖　*John C. Crawford*

❖　*John C. Crawford*

SOCIAL BACKGROUND IN ENGLAND AND SCOTLAND

Britain is divided into two main geographical zones: Highland (Scotland, northern England, much of Wales and the Pennines), and Lowland (broadly central and southern England). In the Highland zone, agriculture is pastoral or mixed and largely concerned with sheep and cattle-rearing. In the Lowland zone agriculture is mainly arable.

The distinction is important because this basic fact of agricultural geography informed the historic social structure of rural Britain and influenced the debate about social change and innovation which was taking place a hundred years ago.

Champion England

In Lowland or Champion England, as it was often called, arable farming, which required a large labour force to tend the crops, conferred on rural society a rigid social hierarchy. Landowners and farmers comprised an identifiable rural ruling class which possessed a near-monopoly of employment opportunities and controlled most of the major institutions of rural society: housing, education, the Church, charity, the poor law and the administration of the law.

As administrators of charity (sometimes called 'prudential charity' because it aimed to reduce social unrest), they could be seen as administering a social structure which encouraged deference and gratitude and allowed the poor to identify with an oppressive system.[1] As library provision was sometimes seen as a form of charity, here was a possible trap for advocates of rural library provision.

Between 1875 and 1900, Champion England was devastated by agricultural crisis caused by falling grain prices and the failure of arable farmers to respond to a changed situation. The position of farm workers was poor. They received little more than half the average weekly wage and lived in bad housing. The result was a flight from the land. There were just over one million farm workers in 1861, a figure which had fallen to 609,000 by 1901. Linked to this was opposition among landowners and farmers to the spread of education because they feared social unrest as a consequence and an accelerating abandonment of the land.[2] Rider Haggard, the novelist, country squire and agricultural writer, met a farmer in Herefordshire who described farm labourers as 'a lot of shirkers', a defect which he attributed to the spread of state-sponsored, elementary education. A schoolmaster near Leominster told him that most boys and girls left the parish immediately on leaving school. Those who stayed were mostly 'dullards'.[3]

The crisis gave rise to a debate, during the final quarter of the nineteenth century, on what became known as the Land Question, which was about shifting the balance of the relationship between landlord and tenant and the social and political privileges which accompanied it. It was a debate into which rural library provision was inevitably drawn. In the 1880s and early 1890s, local government administration came to the countryside with the setting up of county councils in 1888, the Public Libraries Act of 1892, which permitted parishes to become library authorities, and the Local Government Act of 1894 which created parish and rural district councils in England and Wales. These developments were of great interest to professional librarians working in towns, because they seemed to offer an administrative base on which to build.

The north and west
In the pastoral north and west, the social distance between farmers and farm workers was less. Many farmers continued to be working (i.e. labouring) farmers, many labourers continued to 'live in' and, in many respects, their everyday lives were not dissimilar from those of their employers.[4] If, in England, town and country sharply diverged, this was less the case in Scotland. A hundred years ago, while most of Scotland was countryside, most Scots lived in towns and the most populous towns were mainly located in or near the Forth–Clyde valley. However, there were close links between town and country, both substantive and emotional, and the problems of the countryside engaged town dwellers, frequently in excess of the importance of the issues involved.

Rural Scotland suffered depopulation comparable to that of England. Between the mid-nineteenth and the early twentieth centuries the proportion of the population engaged in agriculture fell from 25% to 11%. However, there was no general crisis comparable to that which gripped Champion England. The Scottish countryside remained comparatively prosperous throughout the nineteenth century, partly because there was less marketing of arable produce and partly because the flexibility of agricultural production made the position of the labourer more secure.[5] As the historic base of Scottish community library provision was in market towns, serving a rural hinterland, and in villages, economic factors formed a basis for expansion of library provision on a declining population base.

In Scotland, however, there were major differences between rural regions, notably the Highlands and the Lowlands. In Lowland Scotland the foundations of rural library provision had been laid in the late eighteenth century, but in the Highlands poverty, ignorance, poor communications and the lack of books in the Gaelic language had inhibited development. However, two key pieces of legislation encouraged the development of library activity in the Highlands. In 1872 the Education (Scotland) Act introduced compulsory elementary education which made literacy in English universal in the Highlands by the end of the century. A network of elementary schools was built throughout the Highlands, providing many rural communities with their only public building where small libraries might be housed. Secondly, the Crofter Holdings Act of 1886, by guaranteeing security of tenure to crofters (small tenant farmers) had the indirect effect of creating settled communities in which community development of an educational and cultural nature might take place. Although rural Scotland was relatively prosperous and less socially divided than southern England at the period, there was growing social criticism of landowners, especially Highland ones, and the capacity of large estates to support the traditional way of life was in decline.[6] Nevertheless some landowners remained remarkably willing to support library activity.

Although very different in character, arable and pastoral Britain had two factors in common. Both regions suffered population decline which meant that the basic aim of rural library provision was to serve a diminishing user group. Secondly, the railway and the steamship brought about a great improvement in communication. Railways facilitated the integration of rural and urban society and brought cheaper coal and manufactured goods (including books and newspapers) into rural areas. In Scotland, railheads were established at Thurso (1874), Mallaig (1894) and Kyle of Lochalsh (1898). From there steamers linked the Western and Northern Isles with the mainland.[7]

One consequence of this was to reverse the economics of the rural community library. Community libraries were originally founded because books were expensive and distribution networks were poor. By the end of the nineteenth century books were cheap and communications were better than ever before, which helped old patterns of library use to survive in a different world. Newspapers too became a staple of the community library. In Scotland, for example, the first local newspapers to be published in small towns appeared in the 1840s and soon became ubiquitous. Until the beginning of this century print was the main medium of communication and data collection, for most people, a further source of strength for libraries. Competition from other forms of recreation was limited as mass working-class entertainment did not appear until the 1880s and was not, in any case, available in small communities.

The theorizing about rural library provision which took place in the 1880s and '90s was done largely in Lowland (Champion England) and was a by-product of the debate about the Land Question, itself a product of the great agricultural depression. The Land Question revolved round the issue of land reform and what could be done to improve conditions in the countryside. The decline in arable farming resulted in pressure to reduce rents, weakened the relationship between labourer and tenant farmer and led to new ideas about improving the wages and conditions of farm labourers.[8] Among the ideas proposed were allotments and smallholdings to create a new class of peasant proprietors, improved rural housing, better educational and recreational facilities and improved pay and conditions for agricultural labourers. Thanks to falling prices, the spread of education and improved communications, some progress was made in the 1890s.

Advocacy combined a mixture of amateur and professional standpoints. The amateur advocates were concerned about the state of rural society whose problems they thought libraries might alleviate. Their writings were often the product of localized experience and they were all English. The professional advocates, on the other hand, were interested in applying such legislation as existed to rural areas. They were also keen to test their new expertise, acquired in urban areas, to new circumstances.

The amateur advocates were either clergy or landowners. The earliest of these, F. W. Naylor, vicar of Upton in Nottinghamshire in the 1840s and '50s predates the era of agricultural decay but his ideas are worth summarizing because most of them recur later. He saw the library as a natural successor to the school as a means of providing the necessary intellectual stimulus to widen the narrow mental horizons of rural life. Libraries used by the adult rural working class would foster a respect for education which parents would pass on to their children and which would, in turn, lead to a mutually beneficial relationship between the school and the library. The importance of the link with education was insufficiently understood by later advocates and it is remarkable that Naylor should have emphasized it before elementary education had become free and compulsory.

Naylor's experience led him to believe that a number of factors contributed to failure: libraries with stocks restricted to religion or consisting of tract literature; libraries consisting only of donations; libraries selected by the rich for the poor and endowed libraries with stringent conditions of use. Libraries selected for the working classes without their approval were particularly suspect, especially if religion motivated book selection.

Having enumerated the reasons for failure he then gave tips for success. Rural libraries, to be successful, must be self-managed and self-supporting. Administrative units should be of an adequate size; if one parish was too small several should combine. Library formation should be suggested and led by the middle class but working-class participation was essential. Book selection should initially aim at popular material to ensure early success. The library should be administered by a properly chosen group of officers. Naylor thought it reasonable for a rural library to have small branches ('depots'). Book selection should cover history, science, political economy, farming, biography, geography, fiction, poetry and non-sectarian religion. Although Naylor was ready to expound matters of detail as well as general principles, two main themes stand out:

1. the need to avoid dominance by a closed elite;
2. the need to devise simple but effective methods of administration.

Much thought would be devoted to these two issues later in the century.[9]

To these themes Naylor added another in a subsequent pamphlet, namely the need to relate the library to programmes of adult and continuing education,[10] an issue not considered in detail again until it was taken up by R. D. Macleod, the ideologist of the county library movement, in the next century.

Although the 1850s was a period when much thought was given to rural library provision, it was also a period of rural prosperity. This explains the absence from Naylor's writings of the theme of the library as an agent of rural regeneration which dominated the thinking of the advocates of a later generation.

The one issue which Naylor had shirked, namely the role of the landed proprietor, was one on which Janetta Manners, second wife of the seventh Duke of Rutland, a leading Conservative politician, fell with naïve enthusiasm. Her writings are derivative without having the merit of useful synthesis but are worth mentioning because she saw the rural library as a form of prudential charity. The patriarchal relationship between squire and peasant, a pale reflection of the naïve political theories of her husband's youth, is everywhere implicit in her writings.[11]

Although she borrowed from others some sound basic principles – the need for careful book selection, the provision of newspapers for up-to-date information, the need to ensure that libraries and reading rooms are available to all and the desirability of lecture programmes to support systematic reading – her own thinking shines through in her book selection suggestions. Her list of recommended journals is based on religious belief and her choice of books includes late Victorian tracts and moralizing novels. Bishops and peers figure prominently among her recommended authors. The publications of tract societies, cheap reprint fiction, household economics, manuals of advice to working-class women and biographies of the worthy are her staples. Science and technology are briefly dealt with and social class attitudes dominate her book selection advice.

Because Lady Manners' use of terminology is imprecise it is not always clear what sort of institution she is actually promoting, but the model of a small reading room, taking a motley collection of innocuous popular daily, weekly and monthly periodicals and financed and/or controlled by a prosperous landowner appears to have dominated her thoughts. Contemporary observers agreed that the reading room was a reactionary phenomenon. Lady Margaret Verney recalled how a plan to adopt the Public Libraries Acts in an unnamed Buckinghamshire village was frustrated by local farmers who headed off the proposal by providing an inadequate reading room instead.[12] Her daughter, Ellin, librarian at Middle Claydon on the Verney estate, spoke scathingly of 'the spirit of patronage which generally prevails when a reading-room is condescendingly founded by some rich and philanthropic individual'.[13] Richard Jefferies, one of the most enduring commentators on the Victorian countryside, noted, 'Most of the reading rooms started in villages by well-meaning persons have failed from the introduction of goody-goody'.[14]

The landowner and the Verney family

Related to the issue of the paternalistically controlled reading room is the more general question of the role of the landowner. It was a widely discussed issue although amateur advocates (some of them landowners themselves) tended to see the squire as a threat rather than the 'boon' that Lady Manners identified.

The case for a positive role for the squirearchy was put by one of its most responsible members, W. E. Gladstone, who attempted to put his ideas into practice on his estate at Hawarden and who specifically repudiated the idea of Thomas Greenwood, the public libraries advocate, of government grants for rural libraries. English rural society, he believed, was still dominated by large landowners, wealthy men who recognized that the ownership of large estates entailed 'great social duties'. Greenwood considered that not only were the squires reactionary in principle, they were indifferent in practice.[15] In reality, although progressive landowners like the Verneys had an important role to play, the great majority were irrelevant. By 1914 the traditional bond between landlord and peasant had been broken. Many landowners, weakened by the agricultural depression, sold out to their tenant farmers and disappeared from the land. Others were replaced by businessmen who bought country estates for leisure purposes and did not see their new acquisition as a cause for socially responsible behaviour. Declining rents left small squires too poor to indulge in patronage. Furthermore, the squirearchy was losing its grip on the sources of power. By 1885 they had been eclipsed in parliament by professionals and businessmen. Although they found a temporary home in the newly created county councils (1888) and parish and district councils (1894), the growth in the number of trained administrators in county government eventually ousted them from their dominant position there.[16] While it is true, in principle, that the amateurish nature of rural library administration offered considerable scope for the amateur talents of the squirearchy, the practical reality was rather different. Although communities existed where the landowner interfered with tenants' affairs, either for their benefit or to exercise control over them, for most country people, landowners were remote figures who left them to fend for themselves.

An interesting exception to this rule was the Verney family, who owned a large estate in Buckinghamshire. The family's fortunes were revived in the early nineteenth century by Sir Harry Verney (1801–94), who modernized the estate, built labourers' cottages and schools, encouraged railway building through the estate and enforced the efficient administration of justice and the Poor Law. He bequeathed to his descendants a peculiar Liberal paternalism which encouraged its beneficiaries to be independent rather than subservient.[17]

The need to regenerate the English countryside underpinned the Verneys' thinking. Sir Harry Calvert Verney, Sir Edmund's son (and old Sir Harry's grandson), advocated land repopulation. A pamphlet written by his mother, Lady Margaret, *How to start a public library in a village,* was published by the National Land and Home League, which aimed to improve the quality of rural life by encouraging peasant proprietorship. They also aimed to improve rural housing, provide better educational and recreational facilities and improve pay and conditions for agricultural labourers. Although the Verneys were interested in promoting reading and intellectual activity, they saw village libraries primarily as a form of social cement for rural application, a view to which Thomas Greenwood also subscribed.[18]

As activists, their *modus operandi* is specified in Lady Margaret's pamphlet and her daughter Ellin's address to the Library Association's annual conference in 1895.[19]

Although the Acts were adopted without difficulty at Middle Claydon, the first village in England and Wales to do so, Lady Margaret conceded that considerable opposition might be expected, chiefly from ratepayers and those who opposed the spread of rural education. Lengthy and patient canvassing was recommended before risking a public meeting to discuss adoption. She believed that village libraries encouraged social mixing, something which was reflected in the composition of Middle Claydon's first library committee, although, as Naylor had predicted, leadership was provided by the middle class, the chairman being a local vicar. Unlike some advocates, the Verneys were not, on the whole, antagonistic to the clergy, although Sir Edmund did express criticism of the squirearchy and the Anglican clergy which undoubtedly reinforced Greenwood's Nonconformist prejudices.[20] The Verneys' emphasis on the pivotal role of the librarian illustrates the sophistication of their advocacy. Lady Margaret believed that, whether paid or not, the librarian should be a leader and an administrator, not a clerk and a caretaker, an idea admirably put into practice by her daughter. Ellin built up a useful little collection of 1033 volumes in two years, largely from donations. The Verneys were not opposed to donated material provided that it was suitable and fitted into a book selection policy which included scientific and technical books relating to rural life, popular fiction, children's books, good quality recreational non-fiction and a reference section which included maps, railway timetables and a file of the local newspaper. Various means were found to eke out the low bookfund. A grant of £5 was obtained from the County Council Technical Education Committee for buying technical books, and railway timetables were obtained, free of charge, from the railway companies. Lectures were given to encourage book use and a catalogue was printed to facilitate retrieval. Unlike earlier amateur advocates, the Verneys showed a real sense of professionalism and formed a link between the rural amateur and the urban professional, but their essential role was still as paternalistic landowners. Like other amateur advocates, they did not identify a major role for the school and the teacher.

Thomas Greenwood and the professional advocates

Thomas Greenwood was not merely an advocate of rural library provision but an advocate of public libraries in general. Although Greenwood did look forward to the day when county councils would be library authorities[21] he was mainly concerned to champion the parishes and districts as library authorities, a view which duly received legislative blessing in 1894. By 1892 he was doubtful about the possibility of adjoining rural parishes combining although in 1890 he had supported the idea in the third edition of *Public libraries*.[22] This idea, originally proposed by Naylor, was much paraded by professional advocates in the 1890s who showed a wonderful disregard for the particularist nature of parish politics. He did appreciate that the income of small authorities was inadequate and proposed that government grants of between £10 and £25 be given annually to individual libraries. For this modest proposal he was denounced by Gladstone, the champion of rural patronage, at the opening of the St. Martin-in-the-Fields library in 1891. In defending himself, Greenwood revealed his prejudices against the landed proprietors and the Church of England clergy. While the role of the landowner has already been discussed, the place of the Anglican clergy may be briefly mentioned.

The contribution of the Anglican clergy as a whole is ambiguous[23] but such clergymen as step from the primary sources usually appear as useful contributors to the village library movement. At Oakley, in Buckinghamshire, the vicar was the library's principal activist for the whole of its life[24] and Butler Wood, the first librarian of the City of Bradford, in his statistical study of Yorkshire village libraries, attached great importance to the role of the clergy.[25]

The professional advocates were not much concerned with the problems of rural decline and its alleviation and, indeed, the social role of rural library provision was insufficiently discussed by them although some perfunctory reference to the subject was usually made.[26] They were largely preoccupied with two issues: the search for the viable administrative unit and the form which administration within it would take.

The ultimate solution was spelt out in surprising detail as early as 1880 by John Maclauchlan, the librarian of Dundee, who suggested the creation of a library board for each county with powers to levy a 2d. rate. Schools would double as lending libraries and they could be fitted up as reading rooms which would include a few standard reference works as well as newspapers and magazines. All technical services would be centralized in a special headquarters building.[27] As the county councils were not created until 1888 this was very much a theoretical model, and thinking in the 1890s came to centre on the legislation of 1892 and 1894. The lack of legislation led professional advocates to consider further the idea, originally proposed by Naylor but rejected by Greenwood, of the voluntary association of parish and district councils to form a larger unit. Various schemes were proposed, the most sophisticated of which was that of W. R. Credland, the city librarian of Manchester, who proposed that all parishes in a county might combine to create a legally established library service.[28] Although commendable in theory, these schemes ignored the particularist nature of parish and district politics. They were never put into practice.

For administrative purposes, most professional advocates preferred the rotating stock model in which some or all of the stock would be divided into sections and rotate around each village within the county or smaller unit in turn. As Maclauchlan had originally suggested, there would be a central depot and reference library and reading room. As administrative models, these ideas were useful predictors of the amateur itinerating schemes of the early twentieth century and, in their most sophisticated forms, of the future county library service.

Scotland and the Ferguson Bequest

In Scotland, although advocacy was conspicuous mainly by its absence, some interesting ideas did exist in the shape of the rules of the Ferguson Bequest

Fund, an educational charity which was founded in about 1860 to give small annual grants to schools and rural community libraries in six counties in central and southwestern Scotland. After the passing of the Education (Scotland) Act in 1872, it ceased to give grants to schools but continued to patronize libraries. The fund normally gave grants of £5 to £10 per annum which had to be spent on the purchase or rebinding of books. Newly founded libraries received grants of up to £20. Between 1861 and 1881 the Fund gave regular grants to 62 small, non-rate-supported libraries.

The Ferguson Bequest Fund insisted on minimum standards, including an elected management committee, an appointed librarian, adequate shelf arrangement and cataloguing, stated opening hours, the keeping of proper issue and membership records and regular account keeping. This had the effect of raising standards as a whole in the favoured counties, and the trustees even claimed that it had led to the resuscitation of previously defunct libraries which had failed from lack of organization. This approach of supporting and developing a pre-existing community strategy on the basis of performance-related grants has interesting parallels with Scandinavia. The trustees had little faith in a rate-supported strategy, partly because they did not believe that the Acts could be properly applied in rural areas and partly because they felt that free libraries might lack popular support,[29] a contention which was quite correct. The promoters of the first Public Libraries Acts had gravely underestimated the continuing importance of the Scottish community tradition with the result that, by the mid-1890s, there had been only about 32 adoptions in Scotland.

THE SITUATION IN PRACTICE

Because of the inadequacy of legislation and countervailing ideological claims, a hundred years ago most rural libraries were not rate supported. The future lay with a legally established county library system. Attempts to promote legislation were made from 1904 onwards, but an Act did not reach the statute book until 1919 (1918 in Scotland). There were six locally promoted schemes, based on the periodic exchange of bookboxes: the Westmoreland Rural Libraries Scheme (f.1903), administered by Kendal Public Library Committee; Sir Charles Seely's scheme on the Isle of Wight (f.1904); the Suffolk scheme, run by a Village Clubs Association (fc. 1892); the Bishop's Book Boxes scheme in Herefordshire (f.1906); Sir Henry Peto's scheme in Dorset (f.1908); and, the most substantial of these schemes, the Yorkshire Village Library, founded as early as 1856.[30] Rate-supported parish council libraries were few. As late as 1927 the Kenyon Report recorded only 47 in all of England and Wales.[31]

In reality it probably did not make much difference whether a library was rate supported or not. The income from the 1d. rate ranged from £12 to £20 per annum[32] which was comparable to the income which an informally organized community library might raise. In such circumstances, rate-supported village libraries would also have to turn to informal fund-raising methods. Professional advocates emphasized the need for rural libraries to be democratically controlled and accountable to their users. They believed the adoption of the Acts would bring this about. The local Government Act of 1894, which created the new parish and district councils, did have the effect of bringing into local government new councillors with backgrounds in trade and industry,[33] but a study of one such group in action in rural Herefordshire presents a fairly conventional picture of continuing traditions of amateurish management.[34] Thomas Greenwood and some professional advocates published pamphlets on book selection and the management of village libraries, but all the evidence suggests that they were comprehensively ignored.[35]

Regional Studies
With the help of studies of two major regions – Yorkshire and Scotland – it is possible to get a fairly precise picture of rural library provision in these areas and to derive some general lessons.

Yorkshire
In September 1893 Butler Wood, the librarian of Bradford,[36] gave a presentation on Yorkshire village libraries to The Library Association's annual conference.[37] Using a questionnaire-based survey he identified 106 libraries, serving a total population of some 196,500 people. Stocks varied from 50 volumes to 11,000 at the old subscription library, founded in 1770 and run by the Settle Literary Society. The average stock size was 566 volumes. Issues ranged from 100 volumes a year to a suspiciously high 60,000 volumes at Hebden Bridge. In all cases, a lending service was provided and 44 libraries had reading rooms. In most cases the librarian was unpaid. Libraries were provided by Sunday schools, churches, Mechanics Institutes, mutual improvement societies, literary societies, schools, cooperative societies, Young Men's Christian Associations and unspecified local community groups. Income was derived from gifts and other contributions, subscriptions and fund-raising events like concerts. Opening hours were short and were usually in the evenings or afternoons.

Not surprisingly, Wood was horrified. The libraries were clearly entirely inadequate, most obviously because of the lack of funds and the large population they attempted to serve. Country people, he found, did want libraries but in poor areas they could not afford to join. Wood naïvely believed that adoption of the Acts, following their 'success' in urban areas and lobbying of the new county councils, would solve most of the problems he had identified.

Meanwhile, he felt more might be done by clergy and schoolmasters, although he acknowledged that active support by both occupational groups figured prominently in the returns. Wood appeared to find no evidence of manipulative strategies other than the existence of some collections of religious books which were of little practical use.

Scotland

Unlike England, rural library provision was central to Scotland's historic tradition. Britain's first subscription library had been founded in 1741 in rural Lanarkshire at Leadhills, and the market town and village came to be the natural home of the Scottish community library. The administrative model of the subscription library and the democratic ideology which accompanied it was the dominant philosophy of public library administration for over a hundred years. Library management was consensual and characterized by the participation of a wide range of social groups and individuals. Dominance, opinion forming and leadership by privileged elites was limited and transitory. These twin concepts of consensuality and wide-ranging public participation received some sort of legislative blessing in the Public Libraries (Scotland) Act 1867, which required library committees to contain equal numbers of elected members and householders.[38]

The rural tradition, which had achieved much, was not without its disadvantages. Although an understanding of the characteristics, value and management of libraries was widely diffused throughout the middle and upper working classes, management traditions were amateur and independent of a tradition of professional expertise. Furthermore, because library provision was historically based on small administrative units, it became hostile to bureaucratic organization and an ideology of professionalism. Leadhills Library, a hundred years ago, was still administered in much the same way as it had been in 1741. The basis of the library in the community unit, although a source of strength in the past, meant amalgamation to form larger units was out of the question. Leadhills Library would never have dreamed of amalgamating with its identical neighbour at Wanlockhead.

In the mid-1890s the community, non-rate-supported tradition still dominated. There were some 467 publicly available libraries of which only 32 were rate-supported and such rate supported libraries as existed were mainly concentrated in market towns and a few villages, the original home of the community library. Of these, 203 libraries (43%) served rural communities,[39] something which reflected a wider world of rural intellectual activity. Since the 1830s and '40s there had been a growth in the number of voluntary societies, and literary, historical and scientific societies, but this had been a characteristic of country districts rather than the new industrial towns. Theology, especially controversial theology, had promoted educational and intellectual values among the working classes.[40]

In rural areas, the weakness of legislation and the continuing strength of the community tradition ensured the continuance of traditional methods of funding and management. In Wigtownshire, for example, the Whithorn 'Public Library' (in reality a non-rate-supported library) was founded in 1896 and in 1911 opened a purpose-built library building, comprising a lending library, a reading room and a recreation room, which had been entirely funded from voluntary contributions.[41] Patronage was an important feature in funding. By the mid-nineteenth century it was clear that the future of publicly available library provision was dependent on greater investment than the independent subscription tradition could raise. The answer to this problem was the Second Endowment movement (publicly available, non-rate-supported libraries, founded by individuals, c. 1850–1927) which, although quantitatively important, did not change the picture qualitatively, for benefactors invariably confined their patronage to only one community, usually their own or one with which they were intimately or emotionally associated. The movement, rather than being one overarching manipulative strategy, was a great number of individual, small initiatives carried out by the old gentry or members of the new middle class, whose capacity for investment was limited.[42]

Although Andrew Carnegie is best known for his work in patronizing rate-supported libraries, just as important, and hitherto disregarded, is his patronage of non-rate-supported libraries and reading rooms. His grants, mainly small, were generally given to fund, partially or wholly, the erection and stocking of small village libraries and reading rooms. Some 118 of these grants were made, of which 88 (73%) went to Scotland.[43] This exercise was qualitatively identical to the patronage on a smaller scale undertaken by local benefactors and shows that Carnegie retained some links with the old community tradition.

A hundred years ago, public libraries in Scotland were still largely a voluntary operation. Their combined stocks totalled over 1.5 million volumes or about one volume for every three people The median size for all types of library at the period was 2539 volumes and the median size for village libraries was 600 volumes. Library users were overwhelmingly drawn from the middle and upper working classes and from geographical areas which were not densely populated.[44]

THE PICTURE OF RURAL PROVISION IN SCOTLAND
In the late nineteenth century, the distribution of rural libraries was beginning to change. Counties like Lanark, Berwick and Aberdeen had been important centres of library activity for many years, but peripheral counties like Moray,

Wigtown and Banff were becoming important. Here is evidence of the continuing vitality of Scottish rural library activity despite a decisive population shift away from rural areas. The *Report on the Ferguson Bequest Fund* noted that between 1861 and 1881 the total number of readers in the libraries it patronized had actually increased slightly by 34 to just under 6000. Significantly, it attributed this to a decline in library activity in industrial areas which had been rather more than counterbalanced by growth in more agricultural areas.[45] Confirmatory evidence comes from two different rural areas: Wigtownshire, and the southern shores of the Moray Firth. In the former county, activity between 1878 and 1906 was vigorous. Libraries were founded or proposed at Balmaclellan, Cairnryan and Garlieston. At the Isle of Whithorn a formerly defunct library was re-opened in 1895 and at other places (Glenluce, Kirkcowan and Port Logan) there are reports of the usual round of annual general meetings and fund-raising ventures.[46] Dunscore Library Institute, in Dumfriesshire, whose members believed it to have been founded by Robert Burns in 1790, was reorganized in 1889. It reached its highest point in 1906 when successful fund-raising permitted the buying of new books and the printing of a catalogue.[47] In Banff, Moray and Nairn, in the 1890s, two libraries (Aberdour Mutual Improvement Association and Boharm Mutual Improvement Association) were reopened and six new ones were founded at Buckie, Dyke, Findhorn, Garmouth and Kingston, Lossiemouth and Newmill. Elsewhere there is evidence of fund-raising and continuing activity. Library activity in Moray was greatly helped by the will of the Earl of Moray in 1896 for some legacies received. Alves Library received £100, for example.[48]

The most striking innovation in distribution, however, was in the Highlands, for here rural libraries made a decisive penetration. Argyllshire had as many village libraries as Berwickshire (nine each); Sutherland had five and Highland Perthshire, Ross and Cromarty and Highland Caithness each had two. There can be little doubt that libraries took their cue from contemporary educational policies and contributed to the decline of the Gaelic language. Such few printed catalogues as survive from the Highlands record few, if any, Gaelic titles. In 1887, Tongue Subscription Library, in Sutherland, had 14 Gaelic titles out of a stock of 2623 volumes.[49] Campbelltown (Ardesier) Public Library, near Inverness, had none at all,[50] nor did Salen Public Library on Mull[51] In the 1830s, 10% of the stock of Kilbride Public Library on Arran consisted of Gaelic books. By the end of the century it was indistinguishable from any Lowland village library.[52] Even the Coats libraries (see below) which stocked Gaelic books had no salutary effect. The writer and journalist, Finlay Macdonald, recalled that the Coats library in his school 'helped me on my weary journey towards literacy in English'.[53]

A computed median figure for the size of village libraries a hundred years ago is 600 volumes as against a general mean, for all types, of 2539 volumes. The largest village library at the time was the Corstorphine Library just outside Edinburgh (founded in 1856), with 4000 volumes. Second was the Eyemouth Public library in Berwickshire (founded in 1880), with 2400 volumes. The smallest was the Kerrera Parochial Lending Library, near Oban, with 54 volumes. Three libraries in Lanarkshire (Crawfordjohn Library, Abington Library and Culter Library) and one in Wigtownshire, which all had stocks of over 1000 volumes, received grants from the Ferguson Bequest, an indication of the importance of patronage. For Ferguson Bequest Fund libraries as a whole, the position had improved greatly between 1861 and 1881. The total number of volumes in all 62 libraries had increased from 52,631 to 85,156 volumes, an increase of 62%. A median figure for membership is 102, but evidence is limited. The smallest was the Cabrach Library on the remote Aberdeen/Banff border, with 25 members. Drumoak Public Library in rural Aberdeenshire, a rate-supported parish council library founded in 1893, had 145 users. The average membership figure for the Ferguson Bequest Trust libraries was 96. The limited evidence for loans suggest an average of about 2000 per annum. The median figure is 2,050 and the Ferguson Bequest Trust average annual issue for its 62 libraries was 1725.[54]

The Trust analysed its libraries' stocks by subject for 1881 with the following results:[55]

History	12,338
Biography	8973
Religious literature	8663
Philosophy, science and art	6952
Travels, geography etc.	6739
Poetry and general literature	19,819
Fiction	21,672
Total	85,156

These figures show a continuation of traditional Scottish reading tastes: history, biography, travels, geography 33%; philosophy, science and art 8%; fiction 25%, and religion 10%. The old Scottish enthusiasm for imaginative literature still survived with the combined totals for poetry, general literature and fiction scoring 49%.

Incomes were naturally low. Stow Reading Room and Library in Midlothian had one of the highest, with £37 per annum. Tarves Public Library in Aberdeenshire, a rate-supported parish library founded in 1883, had a rate income of £31. Carsethorn Library in Kirkcudbrightshire, which derived its income from subscriptions, was more typical, with £13. The Ferguson Bequest

Fund found that the average subscription in the libraries which they patronized was 2/6 a year, with many charging 6d. a quarter, an income 'seldom sufficient to maintain a library in a state of efficiency', the reporter noted. The Fund encouraged the organization of courses of lectures, seeing this as complementary to the work of the library and an encouragement to reading. The Fund normally gave grants of £5 to £10 per annum and, as comparable sums had to be raised locally in order to receive the grant, this was a spur to effective local fund-raising. In 1881, £251.4.9 was given in total,[56] which would probably have raised the average benefiting library's annual income to about £25 to £30.

In rural libraries, the lending service was the primary aspect and this was increasingly recreational. At Bonhill Parish Library in Dunbartonshire, the percentage of fiction issued was almost 80%. In rural areas, libraries played an essential role in the dissemination of information of all kinds, whether through the medium of books, periodicals or newspapers. Until the coming of the radio and the cinema there was no other means by which information could be disseminated. One nostalgic writer, describing life in the Lammermuir hills at the beginning of the century, noted that 'The small village libraries in those days contained the sort of books that men thus trained would read,[57] (i.e. those who had received a good parish school education). Those libraries which benefited from the Ferguson Bequest Fund could select books from a list provided by the Trustees which were intended to be 'solid and instructive', as it was the Trust's aim to promote qualitative developments in reading.[58] At Glenluce Public Library in Wigtownshire in 1907, 460 volumes of a stock total of 1142 had been given by the Trust and were listed separately in the catalogue and shelved separately.[59]

Sometimes a reading room was provided where the library was situated in suitable premises, as at Stow in Midlothian or at Leitholm Library and Reading Room in Berwickshire. In the smallest collections, as at Aberfoyle in Perthshire, the reading room was the primary element and the library was only a minor component.[60]

This comprehensive if small-scale network was greatly extended in the first decade of the present century by the work of James Coats Jr, (1841–1912), a Paisley thread millionaire, who, between 1903 and his death, gave some 4000 libraries to rural communities, mainly in the Highlands. About 1,200,000 volumes were distributed at a cost of some £150,000. Coats had close personal and emotional links with the West Highlands and this seems to have been the origin of his philanthropy. He began by giving small libraries of about 300 volumes each to individual local communities, the technical aspects of the work being done by the Gardner Press in Paisley, whose owner was a personal friend of Coats. The libraries were usually housed in the local school, with the

schoolmaster acting as librarian, a continuation of historic practices. This informal link with education encouraged Coats to link his work with education and
this was encouraged by government policy. In 1904, the Scotch Education
Department issued *Circular 374* which gave the requirements for educating
pupils between the ages of 12 and 14. This required the consultation of reference books and the reading of a number of useful books. The Coats libraries
were often used to meet these curriculum requirements and Coats took a close
interest in the work of individual schools. His other main policy initiative was
support for the Gaelic language. All the Coats libraries sent to the Highlands
contained 'a shelf of Gaelic books' and he even had some Gaelic books published by the Gardner Press to increase the limited number of titles available.
This support for the Gaelic language was highly unusual at a time when education in the Highlands was through the medium of English and, as has been
shown above, library stocks in the Highlands usually reflected educational
policy. Coats also arranged for lecturers to tour the communities he had benefited, giving lectures on literary topics to encourage book use. Unfortunately
he made no arrangement for his work to be continued after his death and the
libraries soon began to fossilize. However, many were taken over by the new
county library services or used in experimental schemes.[61]

CONCLUSIONS

The overall picture which emerges is of small, underfunded, independent
units run in an amateur fashion. Stocks averaged 500 to 600 volumes and
incomes from whatever source typically ranged from £10 to £20 per annum.
Legislation was inadequate and made relatively little difference either to
income, quality of stock or standards of management. Professional librarians'
faith in such legislation as existed was misplaced and they were naïve about
the particularism of local politics. A lending service was all that the majority of
rural libraries could aim to deliver.

The essential components of an ideology of rural library provision existed as
early as the 1850s and the preferred administrative model, the rotating stock
model, which survived in parts of rural Scotland until the 1960s, had been
invented in East Lothian in 1817.[62] Amateur advocacy had several serious
weaknesses. It overemphasized the role of the library as an agent of rural
regeneration. A study of Colwall, in the former county of Herefordshire,
shows that the founding of the library there was the consequence, not the
cause, of rural regeneration.[63] However, rural libraries did belatedly come to
participate in a policy of regeneration of the countryside by attempting to
reverse the drift of rural populations to the towns. The first Women's Institute
was formed in 1915 and Women's Institutes subsequently became active in the
promotion of county library services. The formation of the government-spon-

sored Village Clubs Association in 1918 was also part of this movement.[64] Secondly, librarians underestimated the role of the schoolteacher and the school in forming the basis of a possible network of provision, and thirdly they overemphasized the importance of the traditional, but declining rulers of Champion England, the landowners and the Anglican clergy. Because of this, the development of an ideology of rural library provision carried a good deal of irrelevant baggage.

It was only with the coming of the county library movement, whose ideology was so ably articulated by R. D. Macleod,[65] that the various threads were drawn together: regeneration of the countryside, the role of the school, the link with adult education and the administrative model foreshadowed by Maclauchlan. In Scotland, at least, the role of philanthropy was substantial and, on the whole, beneficial. Whatever the deficiencies of rural library provision a hundred years ago, it did at least form a basis for the county library service when it eventually began. The role of the teacher as voluntary librarian had long been rehearsed and the pioneer schemes formed a basis on which to build. In Scotland, the rural community libraries and the Coats libraries together formed nuclei for the county library services.

REFERENCES

1   Newby, H., *Country life: a social history of rural England*, London, Weidenfeld and Nicolson, 1987, 80–7.

2   *Ibid.*,106–35.

3   Haggard, H. R., *Rural England*, vol. 1, London, Longmans, 1902, 295, 305.

4   Newby, H., *Country life: a social history of rural England*, London, Weidenfeld and Nicolson, 1987, 141.

5   Campbell, R. H. and Devine, T. M., 'The rural experience', In: Fraser, W. H. and Morris, R. J., *People and society and in Scotland, 1830–1914*, Edinburgh, John Donald, 1990, 46–58.

6   *Ibid.*, 66.

7   Brander, M. ,*The making of the Highlands*, London, Constable, 1980, 196–7.

8   Newby, H., *Country life: a social history of rural England*, London, Weidenfeld and Nicolson, 1987, 138–40.

9   Naylor, F. W., *Popular libraries in rural districts*, London, Simpkin Marshall, [1855].

10 Naylor, F. W., *Continuous education*, 2nd edn, London, Bull and Hunton, 1858.

11 Manners, Lady J., *Some of the advantages of easily accessible reading and recreation rooms and free libraries*, Edinburgh, Blackwood, 1885; *Encouraging experiences of reading and recreation rooms*, Edinburgh, Blackwood, 1886.

12 Verney, Lady M., *How to start a public library in a village*, London, National Home and Land League, 1913, 4.

13 Verney, E., 'The Public Libraries Act of 1892 in a small country parish', *The library*, 7, 1895, 353–8.

14   Jefferies, R., *The life of the fields*, London, Chatto and Windus, 1889, 229.

15   Greenwood, T., *Sunday-school and village libraries*, London, Clarke, 1892, 44–7.

16   Ward, S., 'The landed interest', *In:* Ward, S. (ed.), *Seasons of change*, London, Book Club Associates, 1982, 17–24.

17   *The compact edition of the dictionary of national biography*, vol. 2, Oxford, Oxford University Press, 1975, 2153.

18   Greenwood, T., *Sunday-school and village libraries*, London, Clarke, 1892, 38–40.

19   Verney, E., 'The Public Libraries Act of 1892 in a small country parish', *The library*, 7, 1895, 353–8.

20   Greenwood, T., *Public libraries*, 3rd edn, London, Simpkin Marshall, 1890, 330.

21   Greenwood, T., *Public libraries*, 4th edn, London, Cassell, 1891, 438–47.

22   Greenwood, T., *Public libraries*, 3rd edn, London, Simpkin Marshall, 1890, 333.

23   Jones, G., *Political and social factors in the advocacy of 'free' libraries in the United Kingdom, 1801–1922*, 2 vols, PhD thesis, University of Strathclyde, 1971, Vol. 2, 486.

24   Lisher, L., 'Oakley, or the life and death of a public library', *Buccaneer*, 1968, 5–8.

25   Wood, B., 'Yorkshire village libraries', *The library*, 6, 1894, 37–41.

26   Brown, J. D., 'The village library problem', *The library*, 6, 1894, 99–105.

27   Kelly, T., *A history of public libraries in Great Britain, 1845–1965*, 2nd edn, London, Library Association, 1973, 209–10.

28   Credland, W R., 'County councils and village libraries', *Library Association record*, 1, 1899, 763–9.

29   Tait, M. S., *Report on the Ferguson Bequest Fund*, 1883, 168–83.

30   Kelly, T., *A history of public libraries in Great Britain, 1845–1975*, 2nd edn, London, Library Association, 1977, 137, 209–11. A good account of the progress of the early schemes to 1919 may be found in Ellis, A., 'Rural library services in England and Wales before 1919', *Library history*, 4 (3), 1977, 69–80.

31   Board of Education, Public Libraries Committee, *Report on public libraries in England and Wales*, Cmd.2868, London, Board of Education, 1927.

32   Baker, E. A., 'Rural public libraries', *The library*, 8, 1896, 298–303.

33   Horn, P., *The changing countryside in Victorian and Edwardian England and Wales*, London, Athlone Press, 1984, 191.

34   Crawford, J. C., 'Rural library provision in Herefordshire: the early twentieth century', *Library review*, 34 (4), 1985, 181–94.

35   See for example, Greenwood, T., *Sunday-school and village libraries*, London, Clarke, 1892; Burgoyne, F. J. and, Ballinger, J., *Books for village libraries*, London, Simpkin Marshall, 1895, *Library Association series*, no. 6.

36   Duckett, B., 'Standing on forgotten shoulders: who was Butler Wood?', *Library review*, 44 (2), 1995, 6–27.

37   Wood, B., 'Yorkshire village libraries', *The library*, 6, 1894. His survey did not include the Yorkshire Union of Mechanics' Institutes' travelling library scheme.

38   Aitken, W. R., *A history of the public library movement in Scotland to 1955*, Glasgow, Scottish Library Association, 1971, 240.

39   Crawford, J. C., *Historical models of library provision: the example of Scotland*, PhD

thesis, Glasgow Caledonian University, 1993, 103, 248.

40   Harvie, C. and Walker, G., 'Community and culture', *In:* Fraser, W. H. and Morris, R. J., *People and society in Scotland, 1830–1914*, Edinburgh, John Donald, 1990, 348, 350.

41   *Wigtownshire Free Press*, 30 November 1911, 5.

42   Crawford, J. C., *Historical models of library provision: the example of Scotland*, PhD thesis, Glasgow Caledonian University, 1993, 269–70.

43   Smith, A. J., *Carnegie library buildings in Great Britain: an account, evaluation and survey*, FLA thesis, 1974, Vol. 1: *Account and evaluation*, 65, 107–21.

44   Crawford, J. C., *Historical models of library provision: the example of Scotland*, PhD thesis, Glasgow Caledonian University, 1993, 250, 260.

45   Tait, M. S., *Report on the Ferguson Bequest Fund*, 1883, 181.

46   Data drawn from reports in the *Wigtownshire free press , 1887–97* and indexed in the *Wigtownshire free press index*.

47   *Dumfries and Galloway Standard*, 17 January 1931.

48   Data drawn from the newpaper indexes held by Moray District Libraries.

49   *Catalogue with rules and regulations of the Tongue Subscription Library*, Hereford, Adams, 1887.

50   Ardesier Public Library. *Reference catalogue, c.*1920.

51   *Catalogue of books belonging to the public library*, Salen, Mull, *c.*1890.

52   Crawford, J. C., 'Books, libraries and the decline of Gaelic on the island of Arran', *Library review*, **36** (2), 1987, 92.

53   MacDonald, F. J., *Crotal and white*, London, Futura, 1986, 119.

54   Data drawn from Crawford, J. C., *Historical models of library provision: the example of Scotland*, PhD thesis, Glasgow Caledonian University, 1993, 179–82.

55   Tait, M. S., *Report on the Ferguson Bequest Fund*, 1883, 181.

56   *Ibid*, 170, 178, 183.

57   Bradley, A. G., *When squires and farmers thrived*, London, Methuen, 1927, 164.

58   Tait, M. S., *Report on the Ferguson Bequest Fund*, 1883, 168.

59   Glenluce Public Library, *Catalogue of books (inclusive of Ferguson Bequest)*, Newton Stewart, Galloway Gazette, 1907.

60   Data drawn from Crawford, J. C., *Historical models of library provision: the example of Scotland*, PhD thesis, Glasgow Caledonian University, 1993, 183–4.

61   Crawford, J. C., 'The library policies of James Coats in early twentieth century Scotland', *Journal of library history*, **22** (2), 1987, 117–46.

62   Aitken, W. R., *A history of the public library movement in Scotland to 1955*, Glasgow, Scottish Library Association, 1971, 30–9.

63   Crawford, J. C., 'Rural library provision in Herefordshire: the early twentieth century', *Library review*, **34** (4), 1985, 181–93.

64   Ellis, A., 'Rural library services in England and Wales before 1919', *Library history*, **4** (3), 1977, 73–4.

65   Macleod, R. D., *Rural libraries and rural education*, London, Grafton, 1921; *County rural libraries: their policy and organizaiton*, London, Grafton, 1923.

7   Services to schools

❖   *Peggy Heeks*

NTRODUCTION

Three themes run through this chapter: the educational role of the public library, the wide disparity in library services to schools throughout the country, and their resilience in the face of change.

The first section examines the relationship of public libraries and education, and this is followed by a historical review of school library services (SLS) covering nearly 150 years. The remaining sections consider specific aspects of service until a final section of conclusions is reached.

AN EDUCATIONAL ROLE FOR PUBLIC LIBRARIES?

In considering the educational commitment of the public library in this country, one can point to its origins in the Mechanics Institutes, and the many aims which these two institutions had in common. Although acknowledging the mixed motives of those supporting the first Public Libraries Act, one can find evidence in the debates surrounding it to support Thomas Kelly's view that the establishment of public libraries was part of the forward movement in mass education in the nineteenth century.[1] The very fact that library legislation was 20 years ahead of the Education Act of 1870, which accepted the principle of universal elementary education, gave added impetus to educational programmes by libraries.

Initially, public libraries manifested their interest in education mainly by organization of lectures. As Greenwood noted in the 1891 revision of his *Public libraries*, 'no Public Library will be considered to have a complete record unless it has within its ramification of work winter lectures and, in one way or another, science and art classes associated with its efforts'.[2] Such enthusiasm did not last. As a theory of librarianship developed and libraries expanded, so early activities were reassessed. In his influential *Manual of library economy* of 1903, James Duff Brown stressed that book provision was the first call on library budgets, commenting that arranging courses of lectures was 'no part of a librarian's work'.[3]

The support of adult education through supply of materials was identified as the core library role in the 1923 report of a joint committee of the Library Association and the British Institute of Adult Education. Its opening observation was that the public library 'occupies a special place in relation to the adult education movement in that it provides the material on which the mind of the student may work . . . '.[4] This view was confirmed in The Library Association's *Proposals for the post-war development of the public library service* in 1943: 'It is the function of the public library to provide books; the adult education it provides will be mainly in the informal and unregulated study of these books'.[5]

The library extension work which occurred in the 1950s and 1960s, exemplified by Harold Jolliffe's programmes at Swindon, came less from an education commitment than a pragmatic response to the 1948 Local Government Act which enabled local authorities to spend up to a 6d. rate on cultural activities. Such work really belongs to the history of arts development and libraries, and is explored in *Public libraries and the arts: an evolving partnership.*[6] Adult education work in public libraries continues to be equated largely with provision of stock, even though the nature of the materials may change. For example, the initiative described in *Opening learning in public libraries* centred on supply of packs to adult learners. Most libraries (significantly) deliberately chose stock that could be used without a tutor, as the authors noted: 'Librarians rarely found themselves in the role some feared – that of advisor/counsellor'.[7]

A study of the public library's educational role shows a division of opinion among librarians, once outside provision of stock, and, as Kelly put it, a 'curious kind of love–hate relationship' existing between public libraries and education.[8] Perhaps, even more important, is the lack of a policy. The approach has been partly political – with considerable suspicion of the greater power of formal education agencies – and partly pragmatic – a series of individual responses to specific situations or opportunities, largely conditioned by personal enthusiasm. The report *The public libraries and adult education* ended with the admission that 'No attempt has been made to go very deeply into first principles'.[9] While public libraries have seen some connection between their work and education from the outset, this has demonstrated itself largely in a number of add-on activities, and has not been integrated into a philosophy of purpose. Among the libraries taking part in the 1991–2 open learning initiative noted above, only Birmingham showed a commitment to life-long learning, manifested in policies, staffing structures and programmes. One can even detect a distancing from education in recent library history, for example in the move in many counties to independence for the library committee from its previous position as a sub-committee of education, and in the growing alliance of libraries, arts and leisure services. This is the background against which we should consider the history of library services to schools.

HISTORICAL SURVEY

Early services

The early services to schools were conditioned by two factors: the situation of public libraries and that of school libraries.

Some description of the first has been outlined above. From this we can see the ambivalence of the public library's attitude to education, and the opportunism rather than principle which has characterized its educational activities. The development of children's libraries is also relevant here. Provision for children was clearly not in the minds of those pressing for the establishment of public libraries: the emphasis in the parliamentary debates was on the education and moral improvement of adults. However, the demand from children soon became apparent, and a range of responses began to be made. In some cases, reading halls were opened for children; in others, older children were permitted to borrow books, but with little specially bought stock and selection being made via indicators, the suitability of the books borrowed must be questionable. In a paper given at the 1917 Library Association Conference, John Ballinger commented that 'The progress of the children's movement is a record of development slow at first . . . seeking a solution of the difficult problem of how best to carry on the education begun in the schools'.[10] It was expansion of the service to children which was frequently sought in early cooperation with schools. For example, the reading rooms set up in schools in 1888 by W. H. K. Wright at Plymouth were, in effect, branch libraries.[11] This point is underlined by the scheme established at Bootle in 1894, where the public library placed in schools a *Catalogue of books for the young*, from which children selected titles which were then delivered by handcart.[12]

As for school libraries, a report of 1861 suggests that in London they are 'so rare as almost to be unknown',[13] and put much of the blame on the negative effects of the 'payment by results' system. Some years later, the Committee of Council on Education's Report for 1895–6 found both the state of school libraries and the use made of them unsatisfactory, and recommended that a system of circulating libraries should be established by urban School Boards.[14] These were, indeed, the kind of services offered in the closing years of the nineteenth century. The system established by Ballinger is frequently cited in histories of librarianship, and is described by Emery as the one 'adopted very generally by British libraries',[15] but Plymouth (1888) and Reading (1900) were also among the pioneers, while Hereford (1906) and Cumberland (1909) were leaders in providing for rural areas. Important points to note are the relationship between the state of school libraries and the need for outside help, and the emphasis on circulation of stock – both themes which have continued through the history of SLS.

It would be wrong to impose a pattern of steady progress on the history of

SLS. The actual record is much more uneven. L.S. Jast, for example, comment-ing on Ballinger's 1917 paper, suggested that the work with schools in Cardiff had misled him about the general picture.[16] Several of the early schemes col-lapsed after a few years, usually because of financial problems, as Ballinger admits: 'In much the same manner, the supply of books to schools out of the limited library rate has broken down. The strain on the funds of the library was such as could only be borne by curtailing the amount expended on books for the older reader'.[17]

Direct lending of books to schools was a matter of controversy, not least when the cost was borne by the public library. It was, though, widely accepted that public libraries should encourage visits from school classes. In a pamphlet of 1898, Ballinger described sessions offered to school groups, where 'A defi-nite lesson, fully illustrated with pictures, diagrams, models . . . is given by the Librarian or one of his staff. The same lesson is repeated to each of the schools'. There is an ambivalence here which still continues. While delivering books to schools might be questionable, it was considered part of the public library's business to offer schools services from within the library: 'it was of the utmost importance to put children into close touch with the Public Library before they left school – in order that they might move easily, and as a matter of course, from the one to the other'.[18]

The beginning of a specialism
Moving to the 1920s, we find some advance in school libraries. Ethel Fegan wrote her *School libraries, practical hints on management* because 'so many schools are now able to set up libraries, however small'.[19] The *Year's work in librarianship* of 1928 reported that, in respect of schools, 'The general opinion is evidently in favour of cooperation with public libraries'.[20] The disparity in expenditure on school libraries was considerable,[21] as were the funding sys-tems in operation for their support services, but the Kenyon Report recorded 113 public libraries as lending collections of books to schools.[22] By now, the rationale for the system was economy: 'General co-operation between urban and county libraries and public elementary schools is the most economic and effective method of increasing within the near future the total supply of books available for scholars in such schools'.[23]

The Kenyon Report generated interest in school libraries, a momentum maintained by the 1936 report of the Carnegie United Kingdom Trust[24] and advanced by the formation of the School Library Association in the same year. In 1946, the Schools Section of The Library Association amalgamated with the School Library Association, in a move which could be seen as enriching both, or as an abdication of interest by The Library Association.

The years surrounding the Second World War were, not unexpectedly, years of reassessment and new planning. The County Libraries Section of the Library Association edged towards standards, with recommendations that loans should provide 1½ books per child aged over eight years, and that 50% of SLS costs should be borne by Education Committees.[25] Reports emanating from education sources praised the goodwill of public libraries – witness a 1952 Ministry of Education report: 'Much may be learnt from . . . personal contact with the librarians of public libraries, to whose generous and able cooperation a large number of teachers are deeply indebted'.[26]

Librarians, however, were increasingly pressing for reimbursement of the cost of services to schools, with Lionel McColvin raising many questions on finance and service basis in his 1942 report.[27]

The variation in funding continued into the next decade, as H.C. Dent noted in his 1955 survey. He found no uniformity of practice on funding 'nor any consistency in the basis of calculation. In some county boroughs the School Library Service was administered either entirely or partially by the public library, but in other cases it was quite independent'.[28]

While the number of services increased during the 1950s, less than 50% of the library systems responding to a 1958–9 Library Association survey had a service to schools.[29] The school perspective was given in a 1952 pamphlet from the Ministry of Education: 'The idea of a school library is only now making its way into our system of education at large and progress is, therefore, very uneven'.[30] One illustration of the primitive state of school libraries is provided by Berkshire. Here, in the late 1950s, a 'standard library' was provided for each primary school, consisting of 50 books. The collection consisted of approximately half fiction, predominantly children's classics, and half information books, for example bird and flower identification guides. The purpose of the scheme was to ensure that certain core books were available in each school, and its enthusiastic reception by teachers is an indication of the paucity of school stocks.

The Berkshire initiative also shows a movement in attitude to the SLS. Ethel Fegan's last chapter, headed '*external aids*', suggested that schools could use postal services such as The Central Library for Students, as well as noting that in most public libraries 'special and sympathetic help is always extended to teachers and pupils'. Of formal services to schools she merely comments that 'they are becoming increasingly available'.[31] Expectation of the SLS had changed considerably by the 1950s. Faced with a shortage of books in schools, the Berkshire Education Committee turned to the library service as the obvious agent for helping remedy the situation. It was the SLS which had the necessary expertise in stock selection, distribution and promotion, and could ensure that the collections were soundly chosen, and that pupils and teachers were encouraged to use them.

The increasing activity of the Youth Libraries Group is also noticeable in this period. The 1958–9 survey has already been mentioned, but there were also initiatives in the training of specialists. Chief among these were the six-week courses held at the North-West London Polytechnic on work with young people which began in 1954. Among the organizers were people whose names are still known: Joan Butler, Eileen Colwell and Richard Mainwood, for example. The movement forward in services to schools owes much to such outstanding librarians.

The years of growth
The years between 1960 and 1988 brought SLS to a new stage of confidence and growth. The early part of the period was one of economic prosperity and a general growth in public services. It brought a flowering of children's literature which has led to the period being called a 'second golden age'. Along with writers and illustrators of distinction, there were talented editors to support their work, and review space to spread news of it. This was also a time of curriculum innovation, encouraged by the establishment of the Schools Council. The trend in these initiatives was towards resource-based learning, and this had obvious implications for libraries. The Youth Libraries Group continued to advance professional development. These were some of the external factors conducive to growth.

Fresh recognition of SLS was given in the 1962 report of a working party appointed by the Minister of Education to study public library standards. In a section on 'Service to schools' it was noted that 'most of the larger municipal libraries and all the county libraries in our survey provided books for schools on behalf of the education authority'. The service was described as going beyond the supply of books to include their promotion through book lists, instruction in book use, provision of exhibition collections to help book selection, and special loans of material (including illustrations) for school projects. It was concluded that 'both schools and public libraries stand to gain if there is effective liaison between the two services, whether or not the public library acts as an agency for the provision of school books. This agency service, which normally supplements books held permanently by schools, seems to us an administratively useful arrangement'.[32]

Such comments reinforced those of the earlier Roberts Report which had defended the economy of SLS. Just as helpfully, the Roberts Report had identified the need for more specialist posts in public librarianship, and so encouraged a more specialist approach to work with schools.[33] These moves came at a time when considerable improvement in school libraries was taking place, which, in turn, altered the emphasis of their support services. A sign of the change was apparent in *The use of books* of 1964. The introduction noted the improvements since *The school library* was published in 1952. That pamphlet had put forward a case to justify the existence of school libraries. The practical problems then 'were the basic ones of gaining recognition for the need to make physical provision for a library in terms of space, equipment and furniture in every secondary school and to ensure that library books were regarded as essential in all schools'.

By 1964 priorities had changed: 'Books are now coming into schools in growing numbers; their quality, and the manner of their use, are now the matters calling for attention'. In its description of the nature of knowledge and learning, this pamphlet foreshadowed both the 1975 Bullock Report and the information skills movement: 'Knowledge is indeed the raw material, but it is how pupils acquire their knowledge, what they do with it and the effect that it has on them that mark the difference between uninspired instruction and true education'.[34]

The task envisaged here is one of greater depth and complexity than the aims earlier in the century of just giving children access to books. SLS responded by leading in-service training for teachers on such matters as topic work and library induction programmes. Many SLS staff participated in courses for the newly instituted Certificate for Teacher-librarians, which was sponsored jointly by the Library Association and the School Library Association. Alec Ellis, in his standard history, saw this as a period in which 'The situation was one of almost complete coverage and the target in the 1960s was to achieve one of coverage in depth'. It is significant that the examples Ellis gives to illustrate his point are drawn almost entirely from county libraries, while he notes that 'In numerous boroughs services to schools of varying standards were provided'.[35]

As the next decade dawned the matter of local government reorganization became a major preoccupation. This took place for England and Wales in 1974, and reduced library authorities in the two countries from 383 to 115. A similar reorganization in Scotland resulted in larger education authorities and paved the way to the establishment of SLS at regional level.

What amounts to a blue-print for school support was provided in *The public library: reorganization and after*, produced by the Libraries Division of the Department of Education and Science (DES). This set out the services commonly offered:

A loan collection of books . . . a proportion usually being exchanged termly or annually;
Collections on specific topics to help with 'project work';
The exhibition collection;
Publication of book lists and other bibliographical aids;

Centralized facilities for book ordering and processing;
The integration of the bookstocks of school and public libraries;
Services to teachers.

It was recommended that 'A comprehensive service to schools, which is highly desirable, should embrace them all'.

Most of the services listed are self-explanatory, but two may need clarification today. 'Integration of bookstocks' enabled schools to exchange books purchased from the SLS for other stock. Under 'Services to teachers' some specific examples are given:

> Any school . . . should be able to call upon suitably qualified and experienced librarians in the public library service for advice and assistance on any aspect of the organization of libraries . . . Other services . . . may include training courses and talks for teachers and teacher-librarians, advice on arrangements and routine procedures and practical assistance in exceptional circumstances – for example in the initial establishment of a library . . . There is need for help not only in regard to the organization of libraries, but also in regard to their use.[36]

Overall, this report was positive about the advantages of larger units in providing a greater range of stock and enabling deployment of specialist staff.

The beneficial effect of the 1974 reorganization and of SLS received acknowledgement from a different direction when the major education report, *A language for life*, was published: 'Used properly, the School Library Service is an excellent aid and is one of the most valuable developments of recent years'. However, the importance of an active role for schools was emphasized: 'The important thing is that such an aid should not be used passively. Its advantages are diminished if schools lean on it as a prop and their own self-reliance is diminished'. Teachers and librarians were seen as engaged in the same enterprise: 'We found evidence of a growing sense of partnership and an increasing range of joint activities'.[37]

The Library Association was active in promoting school libraries throughout the 1970s, producing standards for school libraries which *inter alia* recognized the growing use of non-book materials.[38] By now, the number of professional librarians in schools had grown considerably, led by practice in the Inner London Education Authority and in Scotland. Such was the strength of interest in this field that in 1979 a School Libraries Group of the Library Association was formed. Standards were also seen as the province of SLS, as Sheila Ray noted in 1972, commenting that 'the existence of a school library service . . . should ensure a reasonable standard of library provision throughout all the authority's schools'. Yet, while effort was focused on achieving some uniformity in standard of school library provision, there was great disparity in the level of support available. Ray emphasized that 'the school library services in this country represent nearly as many variations as there are services'.[39] This was apparent in budgets, support emphasis and relationships with education agencies: further attention will be paid to these in later sections of this chapter.

It has been suggested that in the 1980s SLS began to move into a new service dimension, taking a more proactive role in school library development. Hitherto, partly in response to the growth of project work and partly because of the language-based initiatives springing from the Bullock Report, SLS had concentrated much of their resources and activities on primary schools. However, a 1981 survey from the DES drew attention to the poor state of secondary school libraries. Only 75% of the sample had a library; of these 33% were open for only ten hours or less a week. In 69% of schools, the library was staffed by a teacher with no library qualification: most were allocated 3.5 hours weekly for their library duties.[40]

Several local authorities began to institute their own surveys, and awareness grew of both the overall inadequacy of secondary school libraries and the disparity in their funding. In a discussion paper to the Library and Information Services Council (LISC), urging establishment of a working party, Max Broome drew on the 1981 survey and other official figures to reinforce these points. For SLS, expenditure on materials per 1000 of school population ranged from £134.70 to £1,915.50, and on staff from £134.70 to £2,767.40. The proposed working party was set up and reported in *School libraries: the foundations of the curriculum* which, in summary, found firstly that 'school libraries and school library services have a vital role to play in educating children . . . Secondly that school libraries are under used and thirdly that they are under funded'.[41] This report had a great effect. Research carried out 1985–7 found a great growth in SLS activities, reaching far beyond the traditional resourcing role, with 54% of SLS in England acknowledging the 1984 LISC report as an influence on subsequent development.[42]

The LISC report ended with a series of recommendations, and The British Library supported one authority, Berkshire, in a piece of action-research built around Recommendation 13.3.1: 'To clarify the objectives of school libraries and the school library service and to establish a policy framework for them'.[43] It is significant that, although Berkshire's Education Committee accepted policy statements on school libraries, the most that was achieved in terms of SLS policy was a statement agreed by the BELL (Berkshire Libraries for Learning) Project Consultative Working Party entitled *Implications for the education library service of the Berkshire secondary school library survey and policy.*[44]

It is, perhaps, an indication of the service orientation of librarians that more attention was paid in the 1980s to helping formulation of library policies for schools, and less on SLS policy formulation. It is interesting that a 1985 report from the Library and Information Services Committee (Scotland) contained similar recommendations to those of LISC (England): 'the development of a policy on the regional organization and provision of library resources for schools'.[45] In his paper to LISC, already noted, Max Broome identified some of the causes in the variation in SLS support:

> The restricted perception of school library services as resource and information providers;
> Lack of adequate national guidance – no statutory requirement, no recognized standards and an imperfect inspection programme;
> Lack of knowledge – no comprehensive statistics and no overall monitoring of the situation.[46]

These observations were corroborated by James Herring in 1988,

> In the UK there is a great disparity in the provision of school library services. In some areas where there are few professional librarians in schools, school library services are often under funded and under staffed and have to spread meagre financial resources across a wide spectrum of primary and secondary schools.[47]

So, we find low levels of service in some places, set against a national impetus to school library improvement, with *School libraries on the move* charting some of these in England, and the Scottish Library Association commenting on the way SLS 'have gained in confidence in their role and have become an accepted part of Regional services to education'.[48]

The curriculum development characteristic of the 1980s, such as the General Certificate of Secondary Education (GCSE) and the Technical and Vocational Education Initiative (TVEI) brought greater demands on SLS The 1981 book, *Extending beginning reading*, found evidence that schools were making increasing use of SLS[49] and Jennie Ingham, reporting in 1986 in *The state of reading*, perceived that conditions were good for library development. Schools were having their expectations widened, through in-service courses, advice from Her Majesty's Inspectors of Schools, and other advising staff. At the same time, new curriculum materials were stimulating the demands for supplementary resources, while falling rolls freed space for a designated library room:

> It is not surprising, then, that teachers are turning increasingly for support to the school library services, the public libraries and museum services . . . In some areas they have been under-used in the past. Today the situation is very different. The school library service is no longer supplementing . . . it

is providing the lion's share of books, even to the extent of supplying most of the fiction stock. Not surprisingly, the service is finally feeling the strain.[50]

A new strand in SLS work began in 1981, following publication of *Information skills in the secondary curriculum*[51] and a range of associated initiatives and research, documented in *Perspectives on a partnership: information skills and school libraries, 1983–1988*.[52] The interest in information skills was reflected in in-service sessions arranged by the SLS, and in development programmes in individual schools.

In connection with the 1984 LISC report, the Office of Arts and Libraries gathered information from English and Welsh authorities which formed a unique archive. Although never published, some of the data were included in *School librarianship in the United Kingdom*[53] and the papers, submitted by 96 local authorities, were analysed by Linda Hopkins in a 1987 article.[54] This material presents a snapshot of SLS in the mid-1980s, and has many familiar aspects, for example the variation in funding arrangements and funding levels. Hopkins perceived 'some correlation between the position of the Principal Librarian with responsibility for Services to Education and the levels of staffing and funding'.

The need for continued monitoring of service levels was emphasized, for at that time the annual statistics compiled by SOCCEL (Society of County Children's and Education Librarians) and AMDECL (Association of Metropolitan District Education and Children's Librarians) were unpublished and available only to members. This need was, in fact, soon addressed as the Library and Information Statistics Unit (LISU) at Loughborough University produced, in 1989, *Schools' and children's libraries in England and Wales 1987–88*.[55]

The LISU survey reinforced earlier perturbation: 19 services were operating with fewer than two members of staff, and a ratio of 50,000 pupils to one librarian was not uncommon. At a time when a children's book cost around £5, 66 SLS were spending under £2.50 per pupil on resources and 14 were spending less than £1.25. It was clear that in some areas the impact of the SLS on curriculum delivery could only be slight.

This period ends then, with some SLS – probably just under 50%[56] – moving to a different evolutionary stage, working as service organizations to help both local education authorities and individual schools develop the educational role of libraries. Most SLS had, though, moved beyond the original role of provider of materials to offer add-on activities such as displays, book weeks and other promotional activities.

After the Education Reform Act
The feeling that SLS had entered a new phase was strong in the years imme-

diately following the LISC Report of 1984. Although, as has been indicated, much needed to be done, there was a fairly clear view of what should be done, and a number of role models. Such certainty of direction came to an end with the passing of the 1988 Education Reform Act. This important Act strengthened the role of central education, introduced limitations on the functions of Local Education Authorities (LEAs) and gave greater autonomy to schools and governing bodies. Provisions of particular significance to SLS were the introduction of a National Curriculum for pupils aged 5–16 years, and local management of schools, under which a high proportion of funds previously held centrally by LEAs was delegated to schools. Greater competition between schools was introduced through a policy of open enrolment. The Act also created a new category of school: grant-maintained, financed directly by central government and, as later emerged, on advantageous terms. The Inner London Education Authority (ILEA) was abolished and the inner London boroughs took on an education responsibility. The Act covered England and Wales, and similar legislation was brought in for Northern Ireland.

It is interesting to note the early professional reaction to the Education Reform Act. Proceedings of two seminars on the subject held in 1988 show a wariness justifiable in the later history. It was called 'a bad and flawed Act' by Gordon Cunningham of the Association of County Councils, and Virginia Berkeley rightly perceived that 'Far from supporting the significant steps taken by many LEAs in recent years to improve their school libraries, the Act could make some of the LEA initiatives difficult, and in some cases, impossible . . . '.[57] LEAs would be unable to ensure minimum standards or equality of provision. It is interesting to recall here that Ray, nearly two decades earlier, had given this as a major justification of an SLS.[58] Many of the suggestions put forward at the 1988 seminars for minimizing the problems which would face SLS are no longer applicable, as the DES, in the succeeding years, tightened procedures and reduced flexibility.

Views of a much larger group of librarians were obtained from a questionnaire distributed as part of the Supports to Learning Project, based at Loughborough University during 1989–91. While LMS came second in response to the question 'What are the main current problems for SLS?', top was the problem of balancing increased demands against a standstill budget. Only 6% expected cuts in the first stage of local management of schools but most felt uncertain about their longer-term financial situation. The questionnaire replies indicate that SLS were still more concerned about improvement of libraries in schools than about their own survival. Of the development areas which SLS listed, in-service training of teachers and advisory work came top. Marketing and producing SLS policies and costings were mentioned less frequently. Only 32% of respondents had actually produced a policy statement on the SLS, and in only 9% of these had that policy been ratified by both Education and Library Committees. In summary, most SLS at this time (March 1990) were still concentrating on the needs of the schools; only a minority had taken Ross Shimmon's view: 'The major challenge in front of us is to try to secure the future of schools library services . . . '.[59] We can also see that the strains on the SLS which had become apparent earlier in the decade not only continued but increased, as the advent of the National Curriculum in primary schools brought heavy demands, especially for science books.

Survival was linked in the minds of many librarians with the question of delegation of SLS budgets to schools. A statistical survey from LISU for 1991–2 found that 'the majority of authorities have neither implemented or planned delegation'.[60] However, it described the situation as 'complex and changeable'.

Some of the tensions observable in England and Wales were less apparent elsewhere in the United Kingdom, for Scotland had no comparable legislation, and Northern Ireland had decided to delay decisions on local management for schools for a year, in view of the vast amount of change schools were facing.

The early statistical publications from LISU gave no indication of trends, but this was remedied in later surveys. The 1990–1 report contained graphs showing spending per capita by SLS from 1987–8 until 1990–1. For this period, despite the anxiety prevalent, modest growth was the general pattern, with any cuts most frequent among Metropolitan Districts.[61] Later editions built in comparison with the previous year, and reveal a growing expenditure problem. For 1992–3, budgets of SLS showed an increase over the previous year in 68% of authorities, and falls in 27%.[62] The situation worsened for 1993–4, with only 37% of authorities recording an increase on the previous year, and falls recorded in 57%. These figures, though, should be read in the light of local management of schools: 'Most of the falls are due to moving expenditure out of the SLS through delegation'.[63] By the time of the 1993–4 edition, patterns of service had become so varied and complex that the whole LISU report (despite its title) was devoted to SLS. Delegation of budgets had begun in 49% of authorities in England and Wales. No delegation of budgets was occurring in Northern Ireland or Scotland. Summaries of total expenditure for the UK showed a decrease for 1994–5 against 1993–4 in all UK countries except Scotland. All countries showed a decrease in materials, which amounted overall to 8.5%. Total expenditure was down 4.7%. Taking the period 1990–1 until 1993–94 for England and Wales, a similar pattern appears: of particular concern is the decline of 15.7% in staffing.[64]

The history of SLS since 1988 was conditioned by wider movements, such as departmental restructuring in LEAs or pressure for a market-led approach in national and local public services. The rapid shifts in DES requirements and budget restrictions consequent on the community charge complicated an already complex environment for SLS. The extent of the changes over just a five-year period can be judged by the report of a 1993 seminar, *The 'business' of schools library services*. However, the seminar chair, Max Broome, was able to say 'Despite the turmoil of changing policies and parameters which would have taxed the most adventurous and entrepreneurial of private businesses, schools library services have succeeded in selling their services'. The case studies from Cambridgeshire and Leicestershire at the seminar illustrated the point, yet, as Margaret Smith said, 'We are successful, but at a price'. The concept of the SLS as a business 'brought to the surface doubts and difficulties, rather than eager, entrepreneurial enthusiasm'.[65]

A 1994 report for the Department of National Heritage acknowledged the problems for SLS in trying to adapt easily to sharp changes in demand, and concluded: 'There are operational features of SLSs which support partial delegation of budgets only, and a higher proportion of central hold back than for other educational support services'.[66]

This history of SLS since the Education Reform Act ends with great variation in their status – business unit or protected service – but a record of survival. On the horizon for many was a new threat: the reorganization of local government.

SERVICE PARAMETERS AND PURPOSE

Throughout their history, SLS have had loans of materials as an important component. We can see them as having the benefits of cooperatives, giving access to a wide range of materials in an efficient way. The system begun nearly a century ago in Cardiff by John Ballinger incorporated annual exchanges, and the SLS described in *The 'business' of school library services* of 1993 still retained that element. The innovation is that wholesale exchange has now been replaced by exchanges of part of the collection, the titles for return being decided by school staff, and usually chosen by them from a mobile library or SLS base.

As primary schools, in particular, moved to topic work in the 1960s the need for a short-term loan of material on special subjects grew up, and project loans developed. By the late 1980s these were so popular that many SLS were finding it difficult to keep up with demand. The value of the loans service began to be questioned. Doubts were raised about both the cost and appropriateness of bulk loans, and about the use made of project loans.[67] By this time a purchasing scheme, enabling schools to buy books through the SLS, was an accepted part of service and its provision diminished the importance of loan collections, especially at secondary school level.

The interests of SLS heads lay principally in in-service training of teachers (INSET) and advisory work, according to a 1990 survey.[68] Indeed, from the

1960s onwards, and especially following the 1984 LISC report, SLS moved far beyond their original role of resource providers to activities such as development of authority-wide policies on school libraries, design of challenge-funding schemes, and participation in collaborative pilot projects. The role of SLS head as adviser to the LEA grew, and manifested itself also in the planning and refurbishment of school libraries. Statements of SLS purpose at this time from the School Library Association and Library Association[69] are all-embracing, but the Berkshire policy statement of 1987 shows clearly the new thrust of SLS as service organizations helping develop the educational role of school libraries.[70]

As new responsibilities were taken up, some earlier services fell away. With the rapid increase in the number of titles published, exhibition collections of 'the best books' began to be seen as not practicable. Production of local booklists diminished, except in Northern Ireland, and passed to national agencies. Some forms of materials, such as filmstrips, were dropped from stock, and newer forms of media such as computer software, were added. In all this one can see the flexibility which has characterized SLS from the outset, and stood them in good stead in the years following the Education Reform Act.

While the range of services provided may, as Hopkins suggested in 1987, has been fairly consistent,[71] different authorities chose a different mix, and the extent of service clearly varied: witness the great disparity in budgets reported by Hopkins and apparent in successive LISU surveys. Behind such variations lie different LEA cultures and situations, yet, even allowing for these, one sees the same uncertainty about purpose which McColvin perceived in 1942.[72]

The great change in purpose and service parameters has come in the aftermath of the Education Reform Act. The purpose now is to meet customers' needs, and the service parameters are judged by a careful balancing of demands from schools and the economic viability of specific services. Both customer satisfaction and the income/expenditure balance have to be monitored on a continuing basis. Shepherd gives examples of services dropped because not viable,[73] and the Coopers and Lybrand report for the Department of National Heritage lists fresh services coming in, such as pre-OFSTED (Office for Standards in Education) advice.[74] The need to demonstrate value for money motivates SLS whether their budgets are delegated or not. The National Curriculum has enabled staff to target stock more closely to the curriculum, and this has had a considerable effect on project loans, where there has been a general move from 1989 to use of pre-packed subject boxes. There is a view that, in the longer term, schools will wish to have these materials permanently in stock, and some SLS are now offering a purchase option.

The keynote in service design was caution rather than innovation, as staff carried out costings, undertook some market research, sharpened the SLS image, presented the service menu, and hoped. New service models have reflected schools' suggestions, but also had to take into account a complex of political and practical factors.

RELATIONSHIPS

'Setting out to make readers is our only duty, and we should fasten on that.'[75] L. S. Jast made the task seem so simple, but his words came in the context of an argument with John Ballinger on the extent of public library involvement with schools. They are a reminder of the uneasy relationship between public libraries and formal education which has existed since 1850.

At national level there was a short period when, following the Public Libraries and Museums Act of 1964, public libraries became the responsibility of the Secretary of State for Education, but this ended in 1979 when a separate Office of Arts and Libraries was established. The division continues today through the Department of National Heritage. It is significant that the 1984 LISC report on school libraries came from a library rather than an education department, and that the DES did not openly follow up its recommendations.

Next, at national level, we have two major agencies with an interest in school libraries: the Library Association and School Library Association. The relationship between the two has waxed and waned, with particular differences about the qualifications of school librarians. The two came together in the 1960s to administer a Certificate in School Library Studies, and now have a continuing cooperative relationship through the Library Association/School Library Association Joint Standing Committee.

Reading publications over three decades, one sees growing affirmation by Her Majesty's Inspectors of Schools of the value of SLS. In *The use of books* (1964), it is assumed that the library will be staffed by a teacher-librarian rather than a professional librarian. There is no mention of the SLS and of the recently instituted Library Association/School Library Association certificate there is the comment: 'It is arguable, however, whether such a degree of specialized training and expertise is essential.'[76]

The 1985 report by Her Majesty's Inspectors on secondary school libraries looks first for leadership to LEA advisors: 'In those LEAs where a member of the advisory service carried responsibility for school libraries and was active in exercising this responsibility schools benefited considerably in material terms and in advice, especially where this coincided with a substantial and active schools library service.'[77] By 1990 there is clear praise for the informed guidance and curricular support of SLS.[78]

The relationship between local education and library committees has a complex history. The usual pattern in England and Wales is for the Education Department to fund an SLS operated on an agency basis by the Library

Department. Yet, for years, most education departments took no part in deciding SLS policy. In other authorities, however, a mixed economy grew up with, as Hopkins points out, no apparent rationale for the division of costs. Occasionally, the total cost of the SLS was borne by the Library Department.[79] The lack of a teaching background made it difficult for Education Department staff to accept the Head of SLS as an adviser. The Education Reform Act, local management of schools and restructuring of LEA departments brought a shift in some of these attitudes. About half the SLS established in inner London were based in Education Departments, in some other areas, Bradford and Cambridgeshire, for example, the service moved from a library to an education base. An education base for an education support service does seem the logical location, although DES changes in regulations for local management of schools made it gradually a less safe place.

Even where SLS remained with the public library, there was greater distinction between service to children and service to schools – a great change from the integration of the two advocated in the early 1980s. Concern grew that when schools were required to pay for the SLS, they would turn instead to the free children's library, and radical changes were suggested, such as making children's stock purely recreational. Although these fears do not appear to have been realized, the relationship between the two services has changed. The comments below illustrate the range of views: 'The SLS could be our flagship. It could teach other parts of the library service a lesson and provide a model to be followed elsewhere'; 'How will the library department react to having a commercial unit – School Library Service PLC – in its midst? We are moving from the cocoon of a traditional service to the cold wind of market forces, but leaving the rest behind, engaged in completely different problems.'[80]

Another major change in relationship is that between the SLS and individual schools. Before the Education Reform Act, many references were made to the generosity and goodwill of SLS to schools: there was an element of the Lady Bountiful approach. With the National Curriculum the concepts of entitlement and equality of opportunity come to the fore. With local management, schools became the clients or customers of the SLS as providers, whether that provision was materials or advice. SLS began to survey customer needs and gave high priority to marketing. The targeting of stock to National Curriculum topics made the SLS appear more relevant to teachers' needs, and the drawing up of service levels and contracts further improved relationships. This change took place irrespective of the question of budget delegation. As one Head of SLS put it, 'It's not just about budgets and costings: it's about ownership'.[81]

RESPONDING TO CHANGE

The history of SLS shows a continuing ability to respond to change. Examples include the INSET programmes to encourage language development which followed the Bullock Report, *A language for life*, the information skills work in schools spreading from the move to foster independent learning in the early 1980s, and the early support for computerized systems for school libraries. The concern for equal opportunities and the building of a multicultural society was reflected in stock selection and supporting programmes. From the 1960s there was a growing awareness of educational issues.

Ellen Dickie has written of the close involvement which 'has ensured the embedding of the work of the School Library Service into the fabric of the delivery of education'.[82] Local government structures in Scotland have encouraged this involvement, as have the Northern Ireland Education and Library Boards, but one can point to many examples in England and Wales also where SLS staff have worked hard to ensure credibility in an education environment.

At some stages we can see change which sought to restore balance. An example is the move to integrate all library services to young people, which occurred in the early 1980s as a reaction against the separation of work with schools from mainstream public librarianship characteristic of the 1960s and 1970s. At other times, SLS saw the need for action-research. Examples are the challenge-funding scheme in Essex,[83] the BELL Project in Berkshire[84] and Norfolk's experiment in testing the effectiveness of a devolved SLS.[85]

Such a background proved valuable in dealing with the unprecedented changes consequent on the Education Reform Act, and other central government measures to extend the market economy to public services, and reduce financial support to local authorities. Heads of SLS found themselves caught up in a complex of decisions as they adapted to new departmental structures, promoted the LEA culture, designed client-led services and began detailed service costings. They learnt to recognize that core strategic decisions affecting SLS were frequently made at higher levels within the LEA, and that careful plans might be overturned by some new government instruction. New skills in marketing and financial management were called for. The case studies of Cambridgeshire and Leicestershire reveal how well some SLS responded to these new challenges. Max Broome described the history as remarkable.[86]

CONCLUSION

It is appropriate in this conclusion to return to the three themes identified at the opening of this chapter. After surveying the history of SLS, the question of the extent of the public library's educational role still seems ambiguous. The concept of education being the primary purpose of the public library probably commands less support than it did in 1850. Now it may conflict with the affiliation of libraries with leisure and recreational facilities and, in any case, must compete with business information services, arts activities and a community development commitment. Services to schools arose from expediency rather than policy; they remained as offering economy in circulation of stock. How far the SLS is an agency service perched at the edge of the public library system, and how far it is a focus for a library system permeated with an educational purpose, depends largely on local culture. One innovation in the period under review has been the establishment of some SLS in Education Departments. An education base had much to commend it on logical and operational grounds, but in many cases it has seemed political to remain in the less-threatened Library Department. There was even a suggestion at the 1993 Stamford seminar that public libraries should seriously consider whether they should shed what is often no more than an auxiliary service.[87]

Reports on both school libraries and SLS over the decades have pointed out the wide variations in budgets, stock and staffing. This is a continuing theme and the likelihood is that local management of schools – which gives schools greater choice in disposal of funds – will lead to greater variations in school library provision. How far OFSTED inspections will lead to a levelling-up is uncertain, but at least there are both standards to inform inspectors and technical guidance.[88] Throughout this century the state of school libraries and their support services have been closely linked. At first, SLS were needed to remedy the deficiencies of the schools' book supply. By now school libraries have improved dramatically, but even (or perhaps, especially) good libraries recognize the need for external services as Loughborough research has shown.[89] The big change in the situation now is that SLS budgets are increasingly dependent on customer use. So far, those with delegated budgets have attracted sufficient income, but, as the Coopers and Lybrand report shows, their future is far from secure.[90]

The record of SLS has shown their resilience and capacity to adopt to new circumstances, with a history which spans the basic book delivery service of the nineteenth century and the present curricular support services. Pressures on SLS during the late 1980s were such that some reassessment was due, and the Education Reform Act has been valuable in leading to new measures of SLS effectiveness. Those identified by the Supports to Learning Project included:

- committed and politically skilled leadership;
- customer focus;
- dependable service of high quality.[91]

The terminology is new, but these factors are not vastly different from those given by the Scottish Library Association in 1985: '[the] quality of the Library Resource Service staff, their interpretation of educational requirements, and the efficiency of the organization and communication'.[92] The experience of the years between these two statements is that SLS do have a marketable product as they seek to play a part in the development of quality education.

REFERENCES

1 Kelly, T. and E., *Books for the people*, London, Deutsch, 1977, 10.

2 Greenwood, T., *Public libraries*, 4th edn, London, Cassell, 1891, 471.

3 Brown, J. D., *Manual of library economy*, London, Grafton, 1903, 441.

4 Library Association and British Institute of Adult Education, *The public libraries and adult education*, 1923. London, Library Association, 1923, 4.

5 Library Association, *Proposals for the post-war development of the public library service*, London, Library Association, 1943, 14–15.

6 Heeks, P., *Public libraries and the arts: an evolving partnership*, London, Library Association, 1989.

7 Allred, J. and Heeks, P., *Open learning in public libraries*, revised edn, Sheffield, Employment Department, 1992, 20.

8 Kelly, T., 'Public libraries in adult education', *Journal of librarianship*, July 1970, 145–59.

9 Library Association and British Institute of Adult Education, *The public libraries and adult education*, 1923. London, Library Association, 1923, 14.

10 Ballinger, J., 'Work with children', *In: Library Assoociation Conference proceedings 1917*, London, Library Association, 1918, 29–38.

11 Willcock, W. J., 'Are children's reading-rooms necessary?', *Library Association record*, (9), 1907, 184–5.

12 Emery, J. W., *The library, school and child*, Toronto, Macmillan, 1918, 179–80.

13 *Report of the Commissioners appointed to inquire into the State of Popular Education in England*, London, 1861, Vol. 3, 315 (Newcastle Report).

14 Committee of Council on Education, *Report 1895–6*, 443.

15 Emery, J. W., *The library, school and child*, Toronto, Macmillan, 1918, 176.

16 Ballinger, J.. 'Work with children', *In: Library Assoociation Conference proceedings 1917*, London, Library Association, 1918, 10.

17 *Ibid.*

18 Ballinger, J., *School children in the public library*, Cardiff, William Lewis, 1898, 3, 5.

19 Fegan, E., *School libraries: practical hints on management*, Cambridge, Heffer, 1928, 1.

20 Rees, G., 'Libraries for the young; school and public libraries', *In: Esdaile, A. (ed.), The year's work in librarianship 1928*, London, Library Association, 1929, 93–114.

21 Board of Education, *Memorandum on libraries in state-aided secondary schools in England*, London, HMSO, 1928.

22 Board of Education Public Libraries Committee, *Report on public libraries in England and Wales*, London, HMSO, 1927, 45 (Kenyon Report).

23 Board of Education: Consultative Committee on Books in Public Libraries, *Report*, London, HMSO, 1928, 84.

24 Carnegie United Kingdom Trust, *Libraries in secondary schools*, Edinburgh, CUKT, 1936.

25 Library Association: County Libraries Section, *Memorandum on the provision of libraries in elementary schools*, London, Library Association, 1939.

26 Ministry of Education, *The school library*, London, Ministry of Education and Central Office of Education, 1952.

27 McColvin, L., *The public library system of Great Britain*, London, Library Association, 1942.

28 Dent, H. C., *Books in your school*, London, National Book League, 1955, 109.

29 Library Association: Youth Libraries Section, *Public library service for children, 1958–1959: a survey*, London, Library Association, 1960.

30 Ministry of Education, *The school library*, London, Ministry of Education and Central Office of Education, 1952, 5.

31 Fegan, E., *School libraries: practical hints on management*, Cambridge, Heffer, 1928, 97.

32 Ministry of Education, *Standards of public library service in England and Wales*, London, HMSO, 1962, 24–5 (Bourdillon Report).

33 Ministry of Education, *The structure of the public library service in England and Wales*, London, HMSO, 1959 (Roberts Report).

34 Department of Education and Science, *The use of books*, London, HMSO, 1964, 1–2 (Education Pamphlet 45).

35 Ellis, A., *Library services for young people in England and Wales, 1830–1970*, Oxford, Pergamon Press, 1971, 150–2.

36 Department of Education and Science, *The public library service: reorganization and after*, London, HMSO, 1973, 13–17 (Library Information Series 2).

37 Department of Education and Science, *A language for life*, London, HMSO, 1975, 302–3 (Bullock Report).

38 Library Association, *School library resource centres: recommended standards for policy and provision*, London, Library Association, 1970. *Supplement on non-book materials*, London, Library Association, 1977.

39 Ray, S., *Library service to schools*, 2nd edn, London, Library Association, 1972, 32, 53.

40 Department of Education and Science, *Secondary school library survey*, London, Department of Education and Science, 1981 (Statistical Bulletin 7/81).

41 Office of Arts and Libraries, *School libraries: the foundations of the curriculum*, London, HMSO, 1984.

42 Heeks, P., *School libraries on the move*, London, British Library, 1988, 3 (Library and Information Research Report 69).

43 Office of Arts and Libraries, *School libraries: the foundations of the curriculum*, London, HMSO, 1984, 25.

44 Heeks, P., *School libraries on the move*, London, British Library, 1988, 54–8 (Library and Information Research Report 69).

45 Library and Information Services Committee (Scotland), *Library services and resources for schools and education in Scotland: report of a working party on current provision*, Edinburgh, National Library of Scotland, 1985, 58.

46 Office of Arts and Libraries, *School libraries: the foundations of the curriculum*,

London, HMSO, 1984, 28.

47 Herring, J., *School librarianship*, 2nd edn, London, Clive Bingley, 1988, 66.

48 Scottish Library Association, *The school library resource service and the curriculum 'before five' to 'sixteen plus'*, Motherwell, Scottish Library Association, 1985, ii.

49 Southgate, V., Arnold, H. and Johnson, J., *Extending beginning reading*, London, Heinemann Educational Books, 1981, 77–9.

50 Ingham, J., *The state of reading*, London, Publishers Association, 1986, 49–56.

51 Marland, M., *Information skills in the secondary curriculum*, London, Methuen, 1981.

52 Heeks, P., *Perspectives on a partnership: information skills and school libraries, 1983–1988*, London, British Library, 1989 (British Library Research Review 13).

53 Pain, H., *School librarianship in the United Kingdom*, London, British Library, 1987 (British Library Information Guide 4).

54 Hopkins, L., 'School library services in England and Wales: a review of the current position', *International review of children's literature and librarianship*, **2** (3), Winter 1987, 137–60.

55 Donoghue, M., *Schools' and children's libraries in England and Wales, 1987–88*, Loughborough, Loughborough University, LISU, 1989.

56 Heeks, P. and Kinnell, M., *Managing change for school library services*, London, British Library, 1992, 14 (Library and Information Research Report 89).

57 Brown, R. and Spiers, H., *The Education Reform Act and its implications for library services*, Stamford, Capital Planning Information, 1988, 9, 21.

58 Ray, S., *Library service to schools*, 2nd edn, London, Library Association, 1972, 32.

59 Brown, R. and Spiers, H., *The Education Reform Act and its implications for library services*, Stamford, Capital Planning Information, 1988, 48.

60 Fossey, D., Marriott, R. and Sumsion, J., *A survey of library services to schools and children in the UK, 1991–92*, Loughborough, Loughborough University, LISU, 1992, 146.

61 Fossey, D., *A survey of public library services to schools and children in England and Wales, 1990–91*, Loughborough, Loughborough University, LISU, 1992.

62 Fossey, D., Marriott, R. and Sumsion, J., *A survey of library services to schools and children in the UK, 1991–92*, Loughborough, Loughborough University, LISU, 1992, 114.

63 Pickering, H. and Sumsion, J., *A survey of library services to schools and children in the UK, 1992–93*, Loughborough, Loughborough University, LISU, 1993, 133.

64 Creaser, C., *A survey of library services to schools and children in the UK, 1993–94*, Loughborough, Loughborough University, 1994, 3, 71.

65 Ashcroft, M. and Broome, M. (eds.), *The 'business' of schools library services*, Stamford, Capital Planning Information, 1993, 2, 39, 49.

66 Department of National Heritage, *Schools library services and financial delegation to schools*, London, HMSO, 1994, 1 (Library information Series 21).

67 Heeks, P. and Kinnell, M., *Managing change for school library services*, London, British Library, 1992, 86 (Library and Information Research Report 89).

68 *Ibid.*, 66.

69 School Library Association, *School libraries: steps in the right direction*, Swindon,

School Library Association, 1989, 13; Kinnell, M. (ed.), *Learning resources in schools*, edited by Margaret Kinnell, London, Library Association, 1992.

70   Heeks, P., *School libraries on the move*, London, British Library, 1988, 55 (Library and Information Research Report 69).

71   Hopkins, L., 'School library services in England and Wales: a review of the current position', *International review of children's literature and librarianship*, **2** (3), Winter 1987, 137–60.

72   McColvin, L., *The public library system of Great Britain*, London, Library Association, 1942, 73–80.

73   Ashcroft, M. and Broome, M. (eds.), *The 'business' of schools library services*, Stamford, Capital Planning Information, 1993, 33.

74   Department of National Heritage, *Schools library services and financial delegation to schools*, London, HMSO, 1994, 1 (Library information Series 21), E1.

75   Ballinger, J., 'Work with children', *In: Library Assoociation Ccnference proceedings 1917*, London, Library Association, 1918, 29–38.

76   Department of Education and Science, *The use of books*, London, HMSO, 1964, 24 (Education Pamphlet 45).

77   Department of Education and Science, *A survey of secondary school libraries in six local education authorities: report by HM Inspectors*, London, Department of Education and Science, 1985, 20.

78   Department of Education and Science, *A survey of secondary school libraries in six local education authorities:* report by HM Inspectorate, London, Department of Education and Science, 1990, 1, 11.

79   Hopkins, L., 'School library services in England and Wales: a review of the current position', *International review of children's literature and librarianship*, **2** (3), Winter 1987, 137–60.

80   Heeks, P., The effect of the Education Reform Act on public library services to children, *Journal of librarianship and Information Science*, **24** (4), December 1992, 195–201.

81   Heeks, P. and Kinnell, M., *Managing change for school library services*, London, British Library, 1992, 99–100 (Library and Information Research Report 89).

82   Dickie, E., 'School library service provision', *In:* Kinnell, M. (ed.), *Managing library resources in schools*, London, Library Asssociation Publishing, 1994, 222–37.

83   Best, R., Heyes, S. A, and Taylor, M., *Library provision and curriculum planning: an evaluation of the Essex Secondary Schools Education/Library Project*, London, British Library, 1988 (Library and Information Research Report 61).

84   Heeks, P., *School libraries on the move*, London, British Library, 1988, 3 (Library and Information Research Report 69).

85   Valentine, P., *Bridging the gap*, Norfolk, Norfolk County Council, 1993.

86   Ashcroft, M. and Broome, M. (eds.), *The 'business' of schools library services*, Stamford, Capital Planning Information, 1993, 31–8, 39–47, 2.

87   Ashcroft, M. and Broome, M. (eds.), *The 'business' of schools library services*, Stamford, Capital Planning Information, 1993, 7.

88   Alexander, S. *et al.*, *Inspecting school libraries: technical guidelines to support the*

OFSTED handbook, Loughborough, Loughborough University, Department of Information and Library Studies, 1995.

89 Heeks, P. and Kinnell, M., *School libraries at work*, London, British Library, 1994 (Library and Information Research Report 96).

90 Department of National Heritage, *Schools library services and financial delegation to schools*, London, HMSO, 1994, 1 (Library information Series 21).

91 Heeks, P. and Kinnell, M., *Managing change for school library services*, London, British Library, 1992, 141–4 (Library and Information Research Report 89).

92 Scottish Library Association, *The school library resource service and the curriculum 'before five' to 'sixteen plus'*, Motherwell, Scottish Library Association, 1985, 11.

8 Reaching out

❖ *Alan C. Hasson*

❖ *Alan C. Hasson*

INTRODUCTION

In 1988, Joe Hendry, giving his presidential address to the Scottish Library Association, argued strongly for the continuing need for libraries to reach out to those who did not use their services. As part of his argument he quoted an editorial from the *North British Daily Mail* for April 1888: 'Half the education of the children of the masses, which has been provided at such a heavy cost, is being absolutely wasted because they cannot get books to sustain or extend their knowledge, to enable them to put education to its most delightful uses and to help them from the idleness and evils of the streets and public houses.'[1] In 1991, the need for the establishment of a new library project in Hamilton was given as: '(providing a facility) . . . where people of all ages can meet and develop learning, leisure, education and community skills and reduce to minimum levels problems of vandalism, illiteracy, parenting skills and lack of educational, informational and social and inter personal skills.'[2] The language may change, but the underlying justification for the provision of libraries would seem to remain very similar. However, in the same way as society has evolved, the influences which govern the provision of services have changed. In the period from 1975, which forms the focus for this chapter, three overlapping factors have governed the context in which most Scottish libraries operate.

SOCIAL CRISIS, CULTURE AND POLITICAL WILL

Firstly, there is an acute and developing social crisis, centring around unemployment, low pay and the development of areas of extreme deprivation. Multiculturalism in Britain has come to mean factors deriving from race. This is legitimate, but not exclusively so. In significant areas of Scotland the defining cultural factors, the factors which affect the quality of peoples lives, are based on access or rather a lack of access to employment. Where unemployment, low pay and insecure employment are the dominant and limiting facts of life, it would seem legitimate that services which seek to be relevant must adapt in the same manner as it assumed they would adapt in a multiracial area.

The effect of the current economic situation, and government policy, has been to maintain relative poverty and create areas where absolute deprivation is the norm. Thus, in Strathclyde Region, which includes the traditional powerhouses of the Scottish economy – Clydeside, Lanarkshire and their hinterlands – the overall unemployment rate is 16%, with 23% of families on income support and 44% of children receiving clothing grants.[3] Yet the situation is worse than this because such deprivation is not spread evenly. For instance, whilst in 1992-3 just under one in eight of the Region's school leavers went straight into unemployment, more than one in five did so in Glasgow, whilst in those areas of Glasgow designated as areas of acute deprivation, one in three went from school to unemployment.[4]

Secondly, there are cultural changes which match anything previously existing. In addition to cultural attitudes deriving from the economic factors laid out above, Scotland has participated in the growth of leisure time, whether enforced or not, technological change and a mushrooming of alternatives to library use.

Thirdly, there is the question of the political will to acknowledge and address these realities. The will to face changing needs has been shown in a spectrum of ways. Most basically this is exemplified in the comparatively high levels of financial support which local authorities in Scotland have supplied. For instance, in 1994-5 the total amount spent per thousand of population in Scotland on library services was £17,525, whilst £12,658 was the equivalent figure for England and Wales.[5]

In addition, Scottish local authorities have invested time and effort in suggesting agreed levels of provision for library services, most clearly shown in the production by the Convention of Scottish Local Authorities (COSLA) of *Standards for the public library service in Scotland*. This represented a sharpening of outlook, in response to changes in society. The COSLA report of 1986, with a new version produced in 1995, followed the Robertson Report of 1969. But whereas Robertson concentrated on minimum stock standards per thousand of population, the 1986 report took a much wider, less quantitative outlook. This attitude was summarized in the opening statement of the *Standards*:

> We believe that any assessment of, and recommendations on, standards for the public library service made in 1986 must, in their approach and format, reflect past changes and those likely to occur prior to the turn of the century. Among these changes are the growing, and consistently maintained levels of unemployment; the greater amount of leisure time available to members of the community, whether on a voluntary or involuntary basis,

the developments which are occurring in the new technologies . . . the growing needs for and interest in adult and continuing education; . . . the growing awareness of the needs of the disabled; the needs of ethnic minorities.[6]

Interestingly, this willingness to address social issues has been shared, at least to some extent, by central government's agents in Scotland, the Scottish Office, through the supply of funding by Urban Aid Grants. These grants are made to projects targeting areas of socio-economic need, and provide a proportion, often 75%, of initial capital costs and revenue funding for a set period, usually three years. Many of the initiatives mentioned below could not have been established without funding provided by this central government source.

In essence, then, library services have been faced with a situation where a recognized need has existed for services akin to traditional provision but different from it, in the context of a political will to address such needs. The actualizing factors have been the ability of senior managers to identify an evolving role for libraries and, crucially, the skills of front-line staff in delivering and evolving services effectively.

REACHING OUT

The attempt to reach out, to make services more accessible, is long standing: one only has to cite the change from closed to open access as an obvious example. But, for the reasons outlined above, this attempt has taken on a new edge in the period under review. As in all such processes, the development of services has proceeded along different, if sometimes parallel, tracks. One constant theme, however, has been the attempt to bring traditional core services to people who, for a variety of reasons, have been cut off from them.

For instance, the Western Isles as an authority is faced with serving a population of under 30,000 spread over 14 inhabited islands which stretch more than 130 miles from north to south. With mobiles and book boxes not being a complete answer, the authority has sought partners for a cooperative use of resources. One such project is situated at Linaclaite on the island of Benbecula: Margaret Sked, then president of the School Library Association, described it as a 'superbly designed complex, blended together as school, community centre, museum and dual-purpose library'.[7] Similar patterns exist or have existed elsewhere, as in Erskine, west of Glasgow, where a library open to the public was provided in a school in the early 1980s when such a service would not otherwise have existed. Again, in 1990, the North East of Scotland Library Service (NESLS) entered into a cooperative project with the school in one of its communities, Alford. This allowed a branch library, which had been open 10 hours a week, to increase its hours to 48.5 each week and thus increase its issues by

485%. Similarly, where no funding partner was available, collections run by local voluntary or community groups have been established. Examples of such projects are situated in Glasgow, Renfrew and Cumbernauld and Kilsyth. Perhaps no more unusual vehicle for the provision of library services was Clydebank's use in 1984 of a mobile fish-and-chip shop to supply local history publications: 600 copies were sold in a month.

In a slightly different context, other authorities have sought to provide services to the isolated within their communities by supplying traditional services to institutions. Thus, to mention only two, from 1977 Dundee supplied material and expertise to Ninewells Hospital, with Perth and Kinross giving a similar service by the 1990s. Additionally, this latter authority has established a service, including author visits, to a local prison.

Again, activity has been directed at those with a physical disability which has historically prevented or lessened their access to library stock. As an example, in the case of visually impaired people, the scale of services has developed from the simple provision of large-print books through the free provision of page magnifiers by, for example, East Lothian in 1977, to Cunninghame's production of a weekly talking newspaper by 1990 and Dundee's use of Braille guides to their spoken word collection by 1992. By the early 1990s both Edinburgh and Glasgow had a sophisticated matrix of provision for the visually impaired, including Kurzweill machines, on-line daily newspapers and print-to-voice facilities, with other authorities, such as Renfrew, having similar, if less integrated, provision.

In addition, throughout the period from 1975, collections of materials for ethnic minorities were increasingly established: Edinburgh, for instance, launched its collection in 1979, while that of Dundee, after taking advice from members of the target communities, was established by 1992. Glasgow's provision was perhaps the most comprehensive. It was based on an Urban Aid Grant over five years of £110,000 for material, with personnel back-up, and involved both Urdu- and Punjabi-speaking members of staff and the community, on much the same basis as Dundee's scheme. Glasgow's service, which is actively promoted via community venues such as mosques and Sikh temples, acts as a resource for other authorities throughout the west of Scotland.

The provision of information, particularly community information, in a more readily accessible form has been an area of significant activity. In essence the process here has been one of taking existing scattered facts, contacts and local knowledge, and collecting, organizing and presenting it in a form that is useful to potential clients. Thus, in 1985, Aberdeen published a directory of clubs, charities and voluntary services and provided the work without charge. By 1987, Falkirk, amongst others such as West Lothian, had established an on-line local information database to all of its libraries. In 1986–7, Perth and

Kinross produced a factbank of contact addresses for voluntary groups in the district; Stirling, having taken out newspaper advertisements seeking input, produced a nearly comprehensive local guide. These initiatives represent a real and sustained effort to open up services. However, they remain firmly wedded to the established role of libraries: the organization and provision of lending and information services in a traditional manner. This tradition is characterized by the library's provision of the resources in an essentially passive manner, with the potential user being presented with the basic resources in a neutral form.

Linfo

The reaching out process was taken a stage further with the establishment of Linfo, the Linwood Information Project. While other projects, and indeed library services in general, concentrated on the provision of existing information, Linfo was focused on the active *interpretation* of information: making information accessible to individuals through the mediation of properly trained and focused staff.

Linfo, which opened in August 1981, was situated in an area where male unemployment stood at 40%, owing to the closure in the same year of the Talbot Car Plant. Although the project was established only a matter of yards from a well-used library, its purpose was different. It was to provide a one-door approach to local services and information sources: 'The place to go when you don't know where to go.'

The staffing of Linfo reflected this need. Interestingly, although the officer in charge was a qualified librarian, his two principal assistants, titled 'Information Officers', were not, but were people with experience of local government administration, social work and Citizens' Advice Bureaux operations. These three and a further two members of staff were supported on a sessional basis by a Welfare Rights Officer provided by Strathclyde Social Work Department, and lawyers from a local firm. Similar sessions were offered by an alcohol advice organization and the Glasgow Marriage Guidance Council.

With up to 1000 enquiries a month, including queries on noise pollution, domestic waste collection, financial investment, warrant sales, and state benefit, Linfo was, and is, obviously fulfilling a need. A key point here is that queries are dealt with on a one-to-one basis, with the interpretative skills of staff being fully utilized. A passive 'Here's the relevant law/leaflet/chapter', is replaced by 'This means that . . .'. Linfo represented a shift from a concentration on the easier access to material to a focusing on the enablement of the knowledge which the material contained.

Linfo's success provided some obvious lessons, outstandingly that targeted, relevant services provided in a library setting could fill an unarticulated need within a community. Equally, it raised a number of questions. If such a specialized information service could be successful, were there ways in which other mainstream library provisions could be made relevant in similarly deprived communities? How were non-users to be attracted into libraries in such areas? Again, the answer has evolved slowly, but can be summed up in two words: community librarianship.

COMMUNITY SERVICES

In seeking to make libraries effective in this role there were two major conditioning factors, one a disadvantage and one a potential opportunity. The disadvantage was the transformation in the image of the library service which has occurred in the last 50 years, pointed out by Ann Saunders at the launch of the Community Services Group in Scotland: 'After the second world war, middle class use of the public library service increased exponentially . . . By the time the provision of library services had become statutory, the libraries' emphasis had changed to satisfying middle-class demands and not serving the needs of the less advantaged or disadvantaged in society, its original intention'.[8] The advantage was the maintenance, through the Thatcher years, of the library as a free public service with minimal institutional barriers to use. As one of the Comedia Working Papers put it: 'The essential ethos of the public library system derives from the fact that it is *public*. It is not like the private library of a gentleman's club or an educational institution which requires qualifications to join, or a commercial library. It is open to anyone'.[9] In essence, this could be taken to mean that the library service coming into a community is essentially a *tabula rasa*. Although it carries with it overtones of a middle-class institution, where the norms of behaviour and the services offered are 'worthwhile', there is nothing intrinsic to the service to direct its actual operations into such a channel. It can, and arguably should, reflect in the manner in which it carries out its core functions and in the evolution of its services the values and priorities of the community in which it is situated.

Community projects

Three out of the current range of projects operating are of particular interest in this context: Whitehill Resource Centre in Hamilton which opened in 1992, Ferguslie Park Community Library in Renfrew District, opened in 1983, and Monklands' Petersburn Community Library and Youth Drop-In Centre which opened in 1991. All of these projects operate in communities defined as 'areas of priority treatment', meaning that they are clearly defined as having serious socio-economic problems. Whilst the services offered by these libraries are in themselves of interest, the process of change they have undergone to produce a 'fit' to their communities is of equal importance. This evolution is only possible because of a higher management which at the very least encourages change or, as in the case of the projects cited above, actively encourages it, coupled to a political leadership which supports the philosophy underpinning the initiatives.

It should be pointed out that both the resources provided and the need to become effective in their host areas were perhaps sharpened because of the source of funding. The dependence of these projects on central government money, through the Urban Aid Fund, meant that a clear purpose had to be delineated to the fund providers, with definite, if somewhat difficult-to-measure, benchmarks for success spelled out, which were subject to evaluation during the life of the projects by external review. For instance, the submission for Urban Aid funding for the Whitehill Community Resource Unit states that the justification for the project was: '. . . evidence in the area of low literacy levels, anti-social behaviour amongst young people, lack of communication between youth and the other sections of the community and poor use of existing library facilities'.[10]

Amongst the stated aims of the project were:

> To provide a meeting place for all age groups within Whitehill A.P.T. which could be used as a planning and co-ordinating base for existing and new groups.
>
> To establish a community resource base for activities in the centre of Whitehill which would be welcoming to people and where they could develop activity and interest groups which would be welcoming . . . and where constructive aspects of leisure and education can be provided.
>
> To encourage community involvement with problems of vandalism, illiteracy . . . and through parental involvement (encourage) a more constructive and educational input to their child's learning . . .'.[11]

As Ferguslie Park Library is the longest established, having opened in 1983, it can perhaps be taken as a benchmark for the other projects. Housed in two converted shop units, the project at its inception was generously staffed, with three professional librarians, three para-professional staff and a cleaner, to serve the population of around 8000. The librarians were a Community Librarian, in charge of the project, and two Assistant Librarians, with individual responsibility for community information and services to children. Similar heavy investment of resources was made in the other two projects; Whitehill, for instance, in addition to its existing library staff, had three individuals specifically allocated to open up the service to the community: a Project Leader, an Outreach /Research Worker and a Library Assistant.

Whilst changes in service provision had been worked out before the opening in Ferguslie, e.g. the level of staffing and a complete categorization of stock (rather than a Dewey/alphabetical arrangement), it soon became apparent that this in itself was not enough. Over the course of two years, and in direct response to the demands which were put on the library as an open-door facility, significant changes had to be made. Owing to the level of demand, two full-time youth workers were employed, the categorization system was radically modified, time-divisions for 'noisy' and 'quiet' periods were established, and a fundamental change in the nature of duties of the professional staff was introduced. The Community Librarian found that most of her time became devoted to liaison outside the library building; the Assistant in charge of information found his time taken up by getting information out of the library and into the hands of people who needed it; the Children's' Librarian moved from the traditional library role of selecting and presenting stock to organizing events for groups and clubs, both library initiated and pre-existing, both to harness the interest of the clientele, who came almost completely from a non-book culture, and to encourage more individuals in to the facilities.

In an internal 1991 document defining staff duties, the basic roles of the three professional librarians were defined as:

> Community Librarian: Promoting library within/outwith area . . . general management, attendance at meetings, support to staff . . .
> Assistant Librarian, Adult: Book selection . . . community information, adult activities, promotion of library . . .
> Assistant Librarian, Young People: Book selection . . . school visits, story times, work with youth workers, relationship building with kids . . . .[12]

Ferguslie, as the first of these projects, was on a learning curve from which both it and the projects established later benefited. However, not only did the manner in which traditional services were presented change, but the actual content and emphasis of the library's activities evolved as the project became established. This change was predicated on the willingness of senior management to allow and support change, coupled to the ability of front-line staff to delineate and fit their services ever closer to the demands of the host community. Effectively, this equates to a recognition and legitimization of what the Comedia Working Papers call 'cultural pluralism'. In the current context, this means an effective rejection of the cultural norms equated with mainstream library provision as existing and deriving from the change in the make-up of users, pointed out above by Ann Saunders. In reality, whilst the ostensible purpose of the changes in service provision carried out by these libraries was to make the library more efficient in pursuing the type of goals recognized as legitimate in mainstream provision, and defined in their Urban Aid submissions, a reciprocal process was underway: an acculturalization to the norms of the host community.

The process of attracting and holding local people as users of the library involved a closer and closer identification with the priorities of that community. Much of this fit to the host community is achieved by the provision of services which are not radical in themselves, although some certainly are. Rather, it is a refining, a tangential emphasis on methods and content of provision which are recognized as appropriate by the host community and which cumulatively give a service far removed from what would be recognized as mainstream provision. The manner in which this process has affected provision to date can be summed up under four broad areas: activation, cooperation, empowerment and legitimization.

Most clearly related to traditional or core library functions is activation. By this is meant the presentation of core services in a way which results in traditional resources actually being used rather than simply being held. A prime example of this is in the field of community information. All of these projects had a commitment to the collection and organization of information of interest to the local population. However, although significant effort was put into compiling community files, organization lists, club indexes and so on, the anecdotal feedback from staff was that the use made of these holdings did not, at least in numerical terms, justify the effort needed to collect and maintain them.

Expanding the role of the library

The result, in both Whitehill and Ferguslie, was a decision to present this information differently, making it available to the community. In Ferguslie's case, a 60-page brochure of local contacts for District and Regional Council services, Department of Social Security (DSS) telephone numbers, and community organizations was provided and hand-delivered to every household in the library's catchment area. The result, as shown in a joint Regional/District Council survey, was that 90% of people had seen the brochure and about 80% had used it. Whitehill adopted a different strategy, gathering the same sort of information but organizing it via a PC, and later marrying it online to wider information holdings provided by Strathclyde Region.

As in the provision of a database, many other services on offer in these projects have been used in long-established libraries. For instance, a free telephone link to a daily selection of job vacancies, provided by the local Job Centre, is provided by West Lothian, and other regions have established toy libraries. Provision of these services and others, located in one building situated in the heart of the community, gives an over-all resource which greatly expands the traditional role and relevance of the library.

Similarly, effort in most of these projects has been directed at making stock 'live' by indirect promotion. For instance, significant work with young people is a feature of all these projects. In Petersburn, for instance, theme events, lasting from a day to a week, have been held on subjects as diverse as circus work-shops, women's events and computer skills. In Whitehill, activity has included a youth festival, 'taster sessions' on environmental issues, and puppet shows. Ferguslie has run Burns nights, theme weeks on different countries, drama sessions and video workshops. Because of the staff resources available, these can be intensively organized with the result that previously dead stock is brought into focus and activated. Similar events for adults have been held, including Elvis nights, instruction in story-telling, car repair workshops, home wine-making and DIY sessions. A key point here is that such activities are not irregular or one-off, but represent a sustained and central part of the service.

This sort of provision forms the basis from which an increased emphasis on cooperative work has grown. Such work has involved, for instance, the library service working in multidisciplinary teams made up of local activists, social workers, community education staff, educationalists and careers officers. Such cross-disciplinary working has included the targeting of services on young people by both Whitehill and Ferguslie staff, in pursuit of defined youth action plans, whilst amongst its activities Petersburn has run job search workshops with a local organization and is central to the production and editing of a community newsletter, supported by all local agencies.

The neutral, undefined image of the library has arguably been an advantage in this area of activity. As the image of a library reaching out, being proactive, is as foreign to local professional providers as it is to the local community, a role for libraries can largely be self-defined. It depends on the energy, imagination and ability of staff and the resources available. Indeed, one agency in Petersburn made exactly this point in justifying their use of the library, stating that 'The Drop-in staff have initiated and supported the development of the Community Mediation Scheme . . . The Drop-in and Library are ideal as neutral places for the local people (to meet) . . .'.[13] Similarly, Strathclyde Social Work Department used Ferguslie Library as a contact point with a group of alienated young men, on the basis that it was neutral ground but also a recognized meeting place which could form the basis for relationship building and positive work

As in the case of Linfo, or indeed traditional services, empowerment can be derived simply from the activation of the traditional resources of the library. On a basic level, this process can be worked out by the straightforward transfer of material held by the library to an autonomous community-based group which could not otherwise have the resource, such as Ferguslie's provision of the DSS Brown Book to a welfare rights group. Similarly, the use of photo-copiers and desk-top publishing resources to support community-based organizations can make their operations that much more effective, as in the case of Petersburn's involvement in the community newsletter mentioned above.

LEGITIMIZING THE COMMUNITY

On a different plane, the involvement of local people in the decision-making processes of the library arguably transforms the idea of community librarianship into a reality. Whilst the limits of such influence are obviously crucial, for instance in matters of stock selection, the right of local people to have an advisory role, for instance in the timing and content of children's activities or in acceptable levels of behaviour, is of benefit both to them and to the efficient functioning of the service. As an example, in Ferguslie, the library's youth workers wished to withdraw from full involvement in the library playscheme, which was run each summer. The playscheme consisted of two two-hour sessions each day, five days a week for six weeks. The quite legitimate argument was that such a heavy involvement precluded them from working on developmental issues when it could be run by other agencies. This wish to withdraw was not acted on following representations by local parents.

Closely allied to the previous concept is that of legitimization, by which is meant the presentation to a peripheralized and often stigmatized community and the individuals who make up that community, of a sense of individual and collective worth. In Whitehill this was partially achieved by the formation of a local reminiscences group, producing an oral history of the experience of local individuals. In Ferguslie, excerpts from 'The Slab Boys', a play dealing with life in a local carpet factory, were staged in the library by a group of professional actors. The Community Librarian reported that the excerpts, and the question-and-answer session which followed it, elicited the liveliest response for any 'cultural' provision that had ever been provided in the area. In Petersburn, a video of a community event, the Spring Fling, was made with a voice-over provided by a local young person. In a letter to the project, a worker with the Home School Community Partnership thanked the staff for their efforts and noted that the confidence of the young person involved 'had taken a tremendous boost'.[14] In the same context, the mere possession of a building in the community, which is made available at no cost to groups, can encourage the building of feelings of self-worth, as in the case of Petersburn, where a lone-parents group was given use of the building for ten weekly sessions.

Similarly, both Whitehill and Ferguslie have run girls' groups, which seek to confront issues of personal development and choice, providing the young women involved with a sense of their own worth through discussion, theme orientated work and practical projects. A focused series of activities for one of these groups was the fund-raising for, and organization of, a group trip to Greece. This involved autonomous decision making, the generation of ideas for fund-raising, contact with official bodies and the practicalities of the logistics involved in finally setting up and running the trip successfully. Such work also points out the limits of the acculturalization process: the library, in this context, is working as an effective vehicle in its traditional role of offering individuals the knowledge and right to question the accepted givens of their lives.

This last example could be seen as educative in the broadest sense, but the power of more formalized education in the empowerment of people is not ignored in these projects. Whitehill has hosted taster sessions and formal courses to introduce its clients to new skills. These have included Scotvec modules in basic computer skills, which resulted in six people gaining this formal qualification. Petersburn has hosted classes leading to the Scottish Education Department's Higher English qualification. In the same context, both Whitehill and Ferguslie have hosted sessions with the Careers Service, providing people with information on qualifications available to upgrade their skills, and Petersburn has run a wide variety of sessions enskilling people in subjects ranging from aromatherapy to self-defence.

The success of these projects is not susceptible to quantitative measurement, but an indication can be seen in that three years after opening, 67% of local residents were members of Ferguslie's library, Petersburn's Drop-in Centre was being used by over 1200 per month and Whitehill, in its second year of opening, had already attained a membership of 40% of the community.

SERVICES TO CHILDREN AND YOUNG PEOPLE

Whilst this reaching-out process towards economically deprived communities proceeds, other groups have been targeted throughout this period, most noticeably those defined by age.

Services to young people, particularly those between roughly 14 and 25, have always been problematical for library services; in the period under review, pioneering work was carried out by Dundee District. Although their project culminated in 1980 with a 'teenage' area within the Central Library, their background research had included cooperative work with students of Duncan of Jordanstone Art College, who provided a design and layout for a purpose-built facility for young people, and gave significant information and anecdote gathering.

This research work was taken up, utilized and added to by Renfrew District in their Johnstone Information and Leisure Library (JILL) and, by derivation, in Glasgow's Castlemilk and Yoker Youth Libraries. JILL was established in 1984, following a user and non-user survey carried out by the library service to see what young people thought of libraries, what they would use libraries for and what stopped them from using such facilities. Like Yoker, established in 1988, and Castlemilk, in 1985, JILL was set up using funding from central government's Urban Aid Fund.

Whilst JILL was the first of these libraries, their service offerings and ambience are very similar. Most obviously, the physical type and stock of these libraries differed greatly from what one would expect in a traditional library. Audio collections and software took a large, if shifting, percentage of stock, with graphic novels, comics and periodicals making up a high proportion of the printed material on offer. Access to computer resources was given, which was not quite the normal state of affairs in the early 1980s. Additionally, as in some of the projects mentioned above, innovations in the arrangement of the stock were made: Dewey was largely abandoned, face-forward display was prominent, and furniture and fittings were chosen which sought to get away from the institutional feel of traditional libraries. Again, as in the projects mentioned above, the lending of stock was only the core of these libraries' business, with significant resources being invested in other activities. These have ranged from the organization of discos, trips and visits, the production of (theatrical) reviews, camping trips, quiz nights, T-shirt printing sessions, participation in sports, courses and local history activities.

But whilst this effort is important in setting the scene, it is not the core of the success of these projects. On a first visit, the aspect that immediately comes to attention in these libraries, as it often does in the other projects mentioned above, is the feeling of suppressed energy which permeates the buildings. In the case of these 'teenage' libraries, this points out their success. The success is that young people are actually in a library setting and using it: in Yoker's case a membership in 1990 of over 2000 young people was reported, approximately 70% of local people in the 12-25 age group. This success is built on the feeling of ownership which all these projects give to their users. Both Yoker and JILL have User Committees which have a direct input into the functioning of the libraries. Whilst these committees cannot make rules or select stock they can and do advise or suggest in these areas. Additionally, the relationship between staff and users is on a basis of near-equality, with the behavioural norms which are acceptable to users and to staff worked out on a mutual basis.

In effect, what has happened in these libraries is that the process of acculturalization, which evolved slowly in the more successful of the urban aided projects mentioned previously, was planned for and integrated into their set-up. The fit of project to target group was achieved via a direct and purposeful strategy. As Joe Hendry put it: 'The whole purpose of this project is to give working class kids – who have left school and may never work – the chance to listen to 'their' music, read 'their' kinds of books. And in the long term, to think, ask questions and to get information they need for their lives and on their terms'.[15]

It should be noted that this success is not simply a question of providing clients who are potentially disruptive in a mainstream setting with a diversion, although even that minimal outcome might be useful. Rather, it is about the feelings of legitimacy and of self-worth which are encouraged, having beneficial effects outside the artificial setting of the library. In 1990 an evaluation group visited Yoker to report on the degree to which the project had fulfilled its remit. A police representative told the group:

> . . . better links have been formed with the youth of the area and without this facility [the library] it was more than likely that the majority of young-sters would either fall into a life of crime or indulge in drug abuse. Now, by focusing their attentions on the library it gave them the opportunity to ben-efit in terms of education and learning new skills.[16]

The role of staff

All of the above projects share a common factor: the importance of staff. Where the diversity of on-the-ground demands and the need for innovative approaches are a prerequisite, special sets of skills and approaches to the task are necessary. During the period under review, two projects operating in areas of multiple deprivation, and attempting to fulfil the same role as outlined above, were forced to close temporarily. In assessing the reasons for closure, both projects identified management failures and staff deficiencies as key to the problem. Whilst both of these projects successfully reopened, they did so with a significant change in staff and managerial practice. The pressures placed on staff in an attempt to provide a proactive service, in an open-door facility, can perhaps be seen in that Ferguslie had a total of over 20 staff changes, out of a full-time staff of seven, in the first three years of its operation.

The managerial, interpersonal and innovative skills to maximize the library's role in these areas are not inculcated at library schools nor necessarily in 'traditional' library settings. All of these projects, when operating at their most effective, have adopted a team approach to service provision, on a scale not usual in the traditional library setting. This largely derives from the fact that innovation, change and potential crisis, for instance in the imposition of behavioural standards, are constant. An organic approach to the management of these projects seems to be a prerequisite, allied to specific qualities needed by the staff. The managerial style generally utilized involves a matrix approach to functions, a non-hierarchical flow of ideas, a high level of responsibility for ostensibly junior staff and the reality of leadership deriving from functional experience rather than official position. Such an approach is very different from that traditionally demanded, and arguably for which library schools pre-pare their students. This fact, which has serious implications for the profession, is recognized by some of the authorities that run these projects. For instance, John Fox, Chief Librarian in Petersburn's authority, is adamant that the pos-session of enthusiasm, commitment and an attitude that will fit the aims of these projects are more important than the specific professional qualification held. Thus the drop-in section of Petersburn Library is currently led by an individual with a community education background. Similarly, at the date of writing, Ferguslie Park Library is more active and arguably more successful than it has ever been: it is led by a non-librarian. It would appear that a multidisciplinary approach to service provision is evolving in these libraries, almost by default. Important questions arise from these facts, concerning both the type of people being attracted into librarianship and the kind of professional framework provided by library schools.

SERVICES TO SENIOR CITIZENS

At the other end of the age scale, services targeted at senior citizens have expanded greatly throughout the period under review. As in provision to any group as broadly defined as this, services have been varied, but a strong theme has been a concentration on services to the physically, and hence socially, isolated. Such provision has included the widespread provision of housebound services to those incapable of using the traditional service, such as that provided by Dunfermline. But it has also involved an investment in staff, with Hamilton and Renfrew, for example, appointing individuals and teams whose central remit includes services to older people. Additionally, at least one authority (Dundee) has redirected resources from general use to target the elderly. In Dundee's case this involved the decision to redirect a mobile away from outlying communities specifically to target this age group. In Cumbernauld and Kilsyth, a pilot project to transport housebound individuals to their local library was established in 1995, with the stated objective of not only increasing accessibility to the library service but also giving users the chance to interact socially with their peers. In purely information services, Glasgow produced a series of six guides on activities, clubs and contacts of potential interest to this age group. These examples of reach-out efforts based on age could be termed by a marketing professional as segmentation and market-targeting, deriving from a purposeful process of delineation. This process is obviously not only applicable to the economically deprived or to age categories.

MARKETING AND SERVICE DEVELOPMENT

A general and increasing interest in marketing activities, ranging from basic publicity campaigns to integrated marketing strategies has been a marked theme of the period since 1974. The need for this concentration on marketing is shown by the steady decline in libraries' core activity, book lending. For instance, between 1984–5 and 1993–4 loans of book material fell by a total of around 5,000,000 throughout Scotland. The reasons for this decline are obviously varied, but at least one anecdote points to a major source: the existence of other ways to spend leisure time. In 1984 the local ITV station in Aberdeen temporarily ceased transmission. Aberdeen Library Service seized an opportunity and advertised on local radio. The result was an increase in book issues of 15,000 in a week.

With the increasing leisure alternatives available, such as satellite TV, increasing accessibility to sports centres, the growth of previously fringe activities and the relative decline in the price of books compared to average wages, libraries have been forced, in the parlance of the day, to fight for market share. The scale of such activities, their width and variety, points to a managerial realization of the need to attract, not to passively wait: 80% of authorities in Scotland who replied to a letter asking for information on their activities specifically mentioned publicity events as an area which was important to them. Involvement in such events has ranged from one-offs to what amounts to a concentrated effort to keep the profile of libraries high. Stirling District can stand as an example of this latter approach.

Stirling's involvement in promotional efforts has covered a wide spectrum of activities, from participation in national events, such as Children's Book Weeks, to specifically local initiatives such as involvement with disablement weeks and with the local talking newspaper. In the purely local context, their organization, of a Santa's grotto between 1986 and 1988, may seem a minor matter. However, in the three working weeks each year in which this facility was provided, between 10,000 and 11,000 people attended out of a District population of 81,000.

A basic principle of marketing is knowing what your users and potential users want. Many authorities, including Cumnock and Doon Valley, Kyle and Carrick, Cumbernauld and Kilsyth, Stirling, Renfrew and Strathkelvin, have carried out exercises to gain just such information. As an example, a user and non-user survey carried out in 1994 by Cumbernauld and Kilsyth resulted in the District Council approving fairly basic changes to its service provision. Examples of these changes included: opening all but its smallest library on Saturdays, due to an expressed wish by non-users for such opening hours; the provision of baby-changing facilities; a commitment to more activities for young people; and an expansion of public access to personal computers. Similarly, this authority invested in a publicity campaign involving advertising on buses, leafleting and posters to counteract an image of libraries as staid and old-fashioned, revealed by the non-user survey, which was felt by councillors and service management not to reflect the actual provision. Such activity in purely publicity matters is of course not radical, as shown in Aberdeen's actions mentioned above.

A further strand in the reaching-out process has been a movement from the passive collection and display of material to the active targeting of potential users of specialized services and the highlighting of mainstream services to specific groups. Thus, Aberdeen Libraries hosted a three-day Women's Fair in 1990, Kirkcaldy held a two-day event in 1991 to encourage physically disabled people to use the library service, attracting over 200 such individuals, and Dundee has regular involvement in the local Women's Health Fair. The justification for this sort of activity could not be clearer and was neatly summed up by Dundee: 'Events such as the above lend themselves to promoting library services. They allow the library to access potential customers who do not regularly use the library. Events such as this allow certain services to be given a higher profile within the community'.[17]

Health education

A specific example of niche marketing of services is in health education, which is especially relevant in Scotland where the incidence of chronic heart disease is the highest in the world. Thus East Kilbride ran a 'Health Yourself' campaign, which focused on collecting and displaying a wide-ranging set of material on healthy living practices. Whilst the provision of such a collection in itself is not a reaching-out process, the project was accompanied by high quality printed publicity material and a local media campaign, aimed at bringing to the library people who would otherwise have been non-users. A related project, provided by Motherwell District in its Craigneuk Library, involved cooperation with Sports Development staff who gave advice on healthy living habits.

Open learning

A major area of success in the reaching-out process, and a specific example of niche marketing, has been in library authority involvement in open learning. Interestingly, a major source of funding for this area has been Scottish Enterprise, the quango responsible for a wide range of economic matters in Scotland. The Scottish Enterprise involvement has been to provide grants of three-quarters of set-up costs to successfully applying authorities. To receive a grant the authority must provide the remainder of the finance, produce a detailed outline of the proposed service and, through the Scottish Library and Information Council, supply monthly reports on use of the service. The mere fact that libraries were selected to receive this funding perhaps says much for the continuing perception of them as a natural place for self-motivated learning. The scale of use of such resources would seem to justify this belief with, for instance, Highland Region reporting more than 50% of its open-learning stock on loan at any one time, and the Whiffet Open Learning Centre in Monklands having over 730 registered users in 1994.

An integral part of each project, as laid down by Scottish Enterprise, is the marketing of the service and again this has provided a vehicle for libraries to bring knowledge of their services out to the wider community. Thus the Whifflet Centre in Monklands has, like projects in Strathkelvin and other authorities, produced what amounts to a targeted publicity and promotion campaign specifically aimed at non-users of other library services. This has included local media support, positioning of displays and promotional material in community venues, and active promotion by staff members to relevant groups.

CONCLUSION

The attempt by Scottish libraries to reach out has, then, been of long standing. It derives its legitimacy both from the very reasons that public libraries were set up in the first place and from the difference that effective library services can and do make in the quality of people's lives. The methods by which effective services can be delivered vary greatly, as they should in a service that in its central ethos is local, but a number of common threads exist.

The provision of effective services is fundamentally a question of political will and support: high quality public services are no longer a given. All of the examples of excellence provided in this chapter require that the use of scarce resources be allocated to the library service. Similarly, all of these projects have, in the context of a free public service, adopted best practices which have their origin in the private sector. Such best practice includes the adoption of techniques derived from marketing to find out what potential clients need and want. It includes the use, in practice if not always on paper, of flatter management frameworks, of team approaches, of organic responsibility rather than mechanistic duties, and of working practices that give precedence to flexibility. It does not include the worn-out ideology of contracting out. Where such support and strategies are integrated, success has been assured. How many other local libraries have the scale of membership of Whitehill, Ferguslie or Yoker?

These indicators of success, in addition to the less quar.difiable improvements in the day-to-day experience of people outlined above, point to a fundamental need for a reappraisal of what libraries and librarians are about. The skills needed to produce effective library services are no longer only to select and organize material. The necessary skills needed are those which allow each library to take a proactive role within its community. They require the skills to define need, to listen to potential users, to enter into cooperative work both with the local community and colleagues from other disciplines, and to provide the services that are needed in a manner which ensures that they are used. Above all it requires the recognition that whilst the provision of books and information is central to our role, it is only a part of the arsenal which we can, and should, employ.

166   *Continuity and innovation in the public library*

REFERENCES

1   Hendry, J. D., 'Caring libraries in a caring society', *In: Progress through partnership proceedings of the, Scottish Library Association Conference, Glasgow*, Scottish Library Association 1988, 1.

2   Hamilton District Council, *Urban programme application form*, Hamilton, unpublished internal document, 1991.

3   *The Herald*, 1 May 1995, 7.

4   Strathclyde Regional Council, *Moving on*, Glasgow, Strathclyde Regional Council, 1994, 4–15.

5   Chartered Institute of Public Finance and Accountancy, *Public library statistics 1994–95 estimates*, London, Chartered Institute of Public Finance and Accountancy, 1994, 3.

6   Convention of Scottish Local Authorities, *Standards for the public library service in Scotland*, COSLA, Edinburgh, 1986, 10.

7   Sked, M,, 'Presidential report', *In: Annual report of the Scottish Library Association*, Glasgow, Scottish Library Association, 1991, 3.

8   Saunders, A., 'Community services: the future of public libraries', *In: Scottish Library Association news*, **175**, 1983, 11.
Mulgan, G., *The future of public library services. Working paper 6: The public ethos and public libraries*, Bournes Green, Comedia, 1993, 3.

10 Hamilton District Council, *Urban programme application form*, Hamilton, unpublished internal document, 1991.

11 *Ibid.*

12 Renfrew District Council, *Ferguslie Park Community Library staff development/training days* (report), Paisley, unpublished internal document, 1991.

13 Monklands District Council, *Petersburn project review*, Coatbridge, unpublished internal document, 1994.

14 *Ibid.*

15 Renfrew District Council, *Response of the library service to the district council's community development strategy*, Paisley, unpublished internal document, 1984.

16 Yoker Youth Library, *Yoker Youth Library: project review and annual report*, Glasgow, Yoker Youth Library, 1992, Appendix II, 2.

17 City of Dundee District Council, *Community librarianship initiatives*, Dundee, unpublished, internal document, 1995.

9 Managing in a corporate culture: the role of the chief librarian

❖ Margaret Kinnell

INTRODUCTION

Public librarians have developed their services within distinctive local authority cultures, cultures which have shifted over the last hundred years as roles, structures and management styles have changed. Librarians have also contributed their own particular management philosophies and practices and these, in turn, have helped to shape the specific local contexts for services. However, distinctive professional skills have sometimes seemed at odds with those management techniques which local government has increasingly adopted from the private sector. The story of the chief librarian's role in local authorities parallels the adoption of those techniques.

Reconciling the professionalism of librarianship and that of the business manager is not always easy. The two roles have been regarded as, if not incompatible, at best uneasily linked.

'Should a library head be a manager or a librarian?', Ernest Savage asked in 1952 at the end of a long career as a public library manager,[1] posing a question which has continued to be a fundamental issue at the heart of the chief librarian's function. The head of a service has a considerable variety of management tasks to fulfil as part of developing a library service – tasks which include developing a vision of the way ahead. This will require senior librarians to possess a wide and deep understanding of their specialism and how libraries can meet the needs of the community being served.

Where the emphasis is placed on the strategic management of a service within a corporate culture which values primarily financial control, there may, however, be more need for an effective generalist manager who can draw upon vision and expertise from lower down the organization, rather than an executive who is more of a hands-on specialist with service-specific knowledge. There is some evidence that this point has become increasingly relevant to public libraries, as it has to other local authority services. Today, the 'chiefs' of public library services might additionally be responsible for leisure, arts and amenities, and are therefore managing a diverse portfolio of programmes beyond the library sector. Conversely, the person appointed to run the public library service, as just one of several programme areas, could hold professional qualifications in an unrelated field – perhaps social studies or recreation management. The head of a service increasingly appears to require interchangeable, transportable knowledge and skills relevant to the corporate culture. These may be more significant than a first specialism.

Flexibility in career development between local authority senior managers has become more common in recent years in some authorities, which indicates the rising importance of such core management competence. These examples point up the rising influence of managerialism as a support to professionalism within local authorities. They also highlight how the role of the chief of a library service has changed to take account of the more intense demands on senior management expertise in running a large service enterprise. Until recently, the Head of Library Services in East Sussex was a social services professional, whilst the Head of Social Services was a chartered librarian, and in Birmingham the former Director of Library Services has moved to head up social services. The job of library chief is no longer just the preserve of the professional librarian. Senior librarians are valued as local authority managers and may move on to other programme areas. Management skills are now being recognized in local authorities as having at least as much significance as a professional specialism.

Changing expectations and challenges
The evolution of the librarian's role in local authority corporate cultures will be explored in this chapter against a background of these changing expectations and the challenges to chief librarians. In particular, relationships between professionalism and management practice will be considered. From specialist keeper of the library service to today's local authority senior manager takes in the whole gamut of changes encountered as local authorities have been restructured and revamped to take account of shifting functions. Changes in the relationship between central and local government during the term of the present Conservative government have been responsible for some of the most dramatic of these. However, there have also been continuities.

The need for chief librarians to be effective as leaders as well as administrators, to be adroit in managing committees and relationships with members, to have a detailed awareness of the local community and its library needs, and at the same time to be in touch with developments in the wider library and information profession is as essential today as it was in the nineteenth century. Public librarianship has always demanded the management of resources and of people within the wider political and social context. Early public libraries grew on careful administration and the clarification of professional roles. The managerialism of the 1990s, which is so significant a part of local government culture, and the public sector, therefore has strong links with the history of public libraries and those who led its development. A profession may be defined through the qualities of its leadership. What part have the chief public librarians of this country played in the development of public libraries within a changing local government context?

LEADERSHIP

From the very beginnings of public libraries, the joint contribution of civic leaders and librarians was important, but the balance of influence was very much with local political leaders whose prestige and philanthropy initiated adoption of the early Library Acts. Librarians needed credibility and considerable perseverance in establishing their claims to leadership, as one of the best known examples testifies.

The Manchester experience

In Manchester – the first of the major public libraries to be opened under the 1850 Act – Edward Edwards, the founding librarian who began his long relationship with libraries first as a user of the British Museum Reading Room and then as a cataloguer, was involved in the fund-raising for the Free Library. However, even before his arrival in the city in December 1850, the Mayor, John Potter, had collected funds and secured Robert Owen's Hall of Science as the new library building.[2]

As explored in Chapter Two, Edwards had been much involved with William Ewart in setting the national agenda for public libraries; in 1849 he provided answers to 459 questions of the Select Committee. He had generalized about the impact that a lack of libraries was having on the education of society from the London experience.[3] Despite these national credentials as a library campaigner, when he reached Manchester the local political pressures were uppermost and his powers, like those of other local officers, were very limited. The Committee appointed to oversee the new library had wide authority: to authorize the alterations to the building, prepare rules and regulations, appoint a librarian and 'generally to promote the speedy establishment of a free library and museum'. As new librarian he had to equip the building, select the bookstock and organize it ready for use, appoint staff and control relationships with readers, but all under the watchful eye of the Committee. Book selection, for example, was supervized by a books sub-committee and Edwards had to submit his lists of suggested titles for scrutiny. The Chair of the sub-committee even accompanied Edwards on book-buying expeditions to London and the provinces. The cataloguing methods for the new library were similarly subject to careful Committee scrutiny, although Edwards was at least able to begin developing his ideas on classification, which were revolutionary for the period. The story of Edwards' relationship with his Committee at Manchester was one of continuing attrition in order to implement new ideas. That he largely succeeded in building a foundation for later collections was due, in large measure, to his clear sense of purpose and a vision for the future. He focused resources on a few chosen subject fields – history, politics and commerce – and recommended this to others establishing new library services.[4] Undoubtedly, though, his continuing difficulties with the Committee constrained him in implementing new ideas even before they summarily dismissed him.

The kind of lead given by the Manchester Committee was common elsewhere. But without the services of a forward-looking and forceful librarian to provide the necessary impetus, however generous the benefactions, there was not the innovative development seen there.

Municipal development

In Salford, as in Manchester, the creation of the library was driven by local philanthropists. As a result of bequests and the development of branches, the stock reached a respectable total of 81,000 volumes by 1886 but, as Kelly has judged, the library 'never attained the size or importance of its wealthier neighbour in Manchester'.[5] It lacked an Edwards. By contrast, Leeds had achieved only 37,000 volumes by 1886 but its lending libraries had grown rapidly, with many of the branches being provided cheaply through using the city's Board Schools, all under the leadership of James Yates. Yates did not achieve the prominence of higher profile contemporaries like Edwards; he was ill-served by the Council, which turned down a salary rise recommended by his Committee to reward his efforts. Despite this half-hearted support, his record on school library provision, reference library promotion, subscription departments, branch libraries and library publicity was outstanding. He also financed himself to attend the 1876 US Bureau of Education Conference of Librarians in Philadelphia; he was the sole British representative and the only foreign librarian there.[6] Even with collections more modest than those of Manchester, a librarian with Yates' outward-looking professionalism and understanding of his community's needs could lay the foundations of excellence.

At the beginning of the nineteenth century, these large municipal library services were therefore still dependent on the calibre of their chief librarians, as much as on their committees. Librarians in the smaller authorities were of a very different stamp; being little more than municipal caretakers in many instances. This situation continued even after the First World War. The Kenyon Report of 1927 was particularly concerned at the salaries and conditions of service of staff, and concluded that 'owing to the unsatisfactory conditions of the profession, there are too many librarians holding posts for which they are unfitted'.[7] Similar concern had been voiced in the earlier Mitchell Report, when salaries and status had also been identified as a bar to library development: 'It would seem to be clear that ratepayers in very few towns are paying salaries such as are likely to attract men and women who are competent to guide the great mass of the reading public'.[8] One librarian was receiving less than a groundsman at the council's tennis courts.

County library leadership

Inevitably, the larger library services in centres like Manchester and Leeds were the ones providing chief librarians of quality to lead not only in their own services, but also the profession at large. Kelly has identified Pitt in Glasgow, Savage in Edinburgh, Jast in Manchester, Powell in Birmingham, Sayers in Croydon and Pacy in Westminster as particularly distinguished,[9] but there were also significant contributions at the beginning of the twentieth century from the new county libraries, which were established up to and following the 1919 Public Libraries Act. Kent, one of the most forward-looking of the new services, had as its librarian A. S. Cooke, who took up office in 1918 at the early age of 22 and continued as County Librarian until 1943. 'Enthusiasm, inspiration, insight and energy' were qualities ascribed to her. She certainly had considerable influence on professional development, as at one time 12 chief librarians in English counties had worked in Kent.[10] Another influential librarian was Raymond Irwin, who became the first Professor of Library Studies at University College, London, and author of *Origins of the English library*.[11] He drew his practical experience from posts as County Librarian of Northamptonshire and then of Lancashire.

Establishing theory and principles

There are numerous examples from the early decades of public library provision. These were individuals who led within the profession as well as heading up the new library services in the municipalities and counties. Their contribution went beyond that of implementing specific services. Building a new profession was an essential element in their work and included the development of theory and its application, books and articles in the growing professional press, and harnessing professional energies via the Library Association. Editions of Brown's *Manual of library economy*, first published by James Duff Brown in 1903, indicate something of the progression of ideas and developments in techniques and also in the range of library equipment being acquired. Nothing serves better to show how far public library management has come since the nineteenth century than comparisons between the tedious routines for recording borrowing then and today: from ledgers, tickets with book cards to 'photocharging' and, finally, after the *Manual*'s time, computerized library housekeeping systems. Brown was librarian of Clerkenwell from 1888 to 1905, where he pioneered open access to library collections, and then of Islington up to 1914.[12] Usefully, the editions of the *Manual* (still being recommended in the training of librarians into the 1960s) indicate the preoccupations of chief librarians who had to build services from virtually nothing. In the early editions there was great emphasis on developing these basic management techniques within severe financial limitations.

Establishing routines for the classification, cataloguing and issuing of books, and for systematizing 'library economy' (Brown's telling term for library management), was the prime task. Motivating and managing staff, considered now to be a core function of management, was much less of a concern. By the time of the seventh edition of the *Manual* in 1961, completely rewritten by Northwood Lock, there was beginning to be more recognition of the chief librarian's complex role as executive manager, with the role of figurehead and representative as well as administrator becoming prominent. But policy formulation and developing a longer term vision for the service was still being laid at the door of local politicians: 'Primarily, he [sic] is an administrator and an educationalist and he should be able to make a public speech, to conduct meetings of any kind and have a strong sense of systematic organization . . . his authority – committee, board or council – is reponsible for the policy to be pursued and he for the manner in which it is done'.

Staff selection, although not always their appointment, was also in the chief librarian's remit, with staff management at last recognized as 'his chief privilege and his most difficult task'. There is also some insight into the increasing demands on senior managers: 'The main requirement is system, in order that he may cover the whole of his reponsibilities without undue nervous and physical strain'.[13] The importance of an effective manager, able to relate well to a committee and with the necessary professional skills, became a growing concern as expectations of public libraries increased.

The McColvin Report
The most significant of the reports on public libraries following Kenyon was written by Lionel McColvin, City Librarian of Westminster. Produced during the Second World War and looking forward to post-war reconstruction, it laid great emphasis on the need for better management. McColvin, described by a contemporary as 'the outstanding librarian of his generation and one of the great figures produced by public libraries since 1850',[14] surveyed singlehandedly, through visits, a remarkable 350 central and branch libraries and saw 'something' of 130 library systems in order to offer his recommendations. He

was realistically critical of the disparities of provision across the country, disparities which meant that a 'chief librarian' meant very different things according to the size and resources of a library authority. Above all, though, he felt that 'for the future development of the service we must employ the right leadership . . . the value of library provision will depend almost entirely upon the ability and suitability of library staff'.[15] In particular, 'every chief librarian must be experienced, qualified, capable, impartial and keenly interested in his work'.[16]

While McColvin was ahead of his time in recommending much larger units of library provision – local government reorganization on the scale he envisaged did not happen until 1974 – his proposals on the training and pay of staff and on professional education did make an impact. The distinction between professional and non-professional grades became even more firmly established, with entry to the profession through education and training in a library school becoming the norm by the 1960s. McColvin's preoccupation with the training and qualities of senior librarians has, however, continued to be relevant up to the present.

Where are senior managers to acquire the wide range of knowledge and skills now required for managing what are, in effect, large not-for-profit 'businesses'? The consultants undertaking the Department of Heritage's Review of Public Library Services arrived at broadly similar conclusions to McColvin. They found a need for high-level management training, in order to offer 'a challenging and opportunity-rich career' within public libraries. The establishment of a new 'staff college' 'to identify, attract and develop future leaders for the public library service' was one option. Another was the use of secondment.[17] The calibre of senior managers, seen as a problem from the early years of the century, was still a live issue.

Changing concepts
Despite these continuing concerns over the training of managers, concepts of leadership in relation to library services have undoubtedly changed over the past century, due directly to the context in which particular library authorities have operated. The size of the library authority has been a crucial factor. The 'chief' of a small urban district council, even just before the 1974 reorganization in England and Wales, had a very different task from that of the director of a major municipal authority. The range of tasks facing chief librarians today is also much wider. Heads of library services are expected to provide a lead for their committees on policy as well as operational issues. Despite the variability of library authority size, some other core factors, in addition to that of training, have remained constant up to the present. Involvement of committees in the management of services still remains significant, even with the enhanced

expectations of a chief librarian's role. The intensity of committee engagement no longer reaches the level of some of the smaller Scottish authorities as late as the 1970s, when old practices were still in evidence. Alice Mackenzie recalled that when she was librarian of the small authority of Paisley: 'I had the Chairman with me when I went to select books – he didn't interfere, but he came and sat and puffed his pipe at my side'.[18] Still, the input of members to policy implementation, as well as to policy development, remains considerable in some authorities. In a recent study of quality management practices in public libraries, for example, it was found that one-third of elected members had a direct input to developing a quality management approach, with three out of six case studies describing their role as 'pivotal'.[19] As quality systems involve considerable changes to management techniques, especially in the collecting and analysing of performance data, this continuing engagement with library management on the part of members demonstrates more than token interest. A further indicator of politicians' commitment and support is the continuing popularity of the annual public library authority conference, which some members and their chiefs attend together.

The chief librarian's leadership role therefore still demands an ability to work closely with politicians and to manage the political as well as operational aspects of their job. Members are forces to be reckoned with and can also provide welcome advice and support. At a time of uncertainty, such as that facing managers in the public sector, leadership of this kind at the political level and the ability to negotiate in a political context are important attributes of chief librarians. Public libraries are facing similar political and economic turbulence to other public services and, as Stewart found in analysing Natonal Health Service changes, 'in difficult times people need leadership as well as management'.[20]

THE POLITICAL ENVIRONMENT

Experience from the nineteenth century to the present shows that this local political context has been a central feature of public library development – until recent times, the overriding feature. Chief librarians have always had to sustain sometimes uneasy relationships with committees: Edwards' battles for resourcing and a free hand were not unusual. Even then, there were also more positive aspects to members' involvement, as Charles Sutton, Librarian of Manchester at the beginning of this century, exemplified. He visited nearly 70 of the large library services in the USA and Canada with two of his aldermen, so that all of them could advise the Committee on lending policies and he kept his councillors on side through this kind of close consultation. Neither was he afraid to speak his own mind in winning a point.[21] Librarians of Sutton's eminence and experience ensured that they negotiated with members as well as deferring to them. However, they needed both credibility and political skills.

Over recent decades, local politicians have been less directly involved with their librarians in the type of hands-on decision over matters like book or newspaper selection (although *causes célèbres* like the Wapping dispute with *The Sunday Times*, the *Satanic verses* case, or even Enid Blyton have proved exceptional). Even if they have insight into the management problems of libraries and can be supportive of their chief librarian, members' depth of knowledge is likely to be limited. Librarianship, like other service areas, has become more complex and less easy for laypersons to penetrate at operational levels. Relationships between officers and members have also eased, along with the enhancement of professionalism in librarianship. The need for librarians to have a firm grasp of all of the management issues – especially those relating to information technology – and to be able to relate them to their services, has increased as members' ability to encompass the range of technology-related aspects of librarianship and information work has diminished. Relations between chief officers and their committees throughout local government have shifted in similar ways. The patriarchalism of the nineteenth century has largely gone, due mainly to the rise of managerial specialisms across all programme areas.

Paradoxically, and despite this, local politicians' ability to shape service priorities according to a particular viewpoint remains significant.[22] The intensification of party politics at the local level was one of the main features of local government throughout the late 1970s and 1980s, and there is no sign of this slackening. However, a new dimension has been more dominant: the imposition of central government policies on local communities.

Centralizing power

As one of the higher-spending areas, education services, with which many library services were linked through committee structures, were particularly prone to the impact of this kind of politicization.[23] The 1988 Education Reform Act and consequent implementation of local management of schools, with its impact on schools library services, has been one of the most fundamental engines of change for library services.[24] (Schools library services were previously funded largely by education departments and delivered by public library authorities.) To a considerable extent, the political attitudes which have affected developments since the Education Reform Act, and subsequent legislation, were formed as part of the Conservative government's radical agenda during the Thatcher years. Value for money, a belief in the market economy's role within public sector services and the customer consciousness which led to the Citizen's Charter initiative[25] have all dominated the local government arena. As well as local management of schools, this has led to compulsory competitive tendering for many services and the movement of jobs from the public to the private sector. Local government review is also creating new structures, with library services in some areas being repositioned in smaller unitary authorities. Significantly, these ideas have been dictated from the centre, with local priorities becoming much less important. Party politics within local government have been increasingly subsumed within national political agendas.

Tom Featherstone, Chief Librarian of Tameside from 1970 to 1994 and Library Association President in 1991, anticipated real dangers for public libraries within the new ethos for public services: 'If the present [Conservative] government retains control, things are going to continue as they are but even more so and . . . the process of reducing freedom in local government and farming as much as possible out to the private sector will continue. I am sure the next time round the library service will go'.[26]

Chief librarians today are therefore faced with centralist political pressures which have to be negotiated at local level, while the allegiance of local members is ultimately determined by their party's national postition. As Usherwood has noted, the members' role is complex. Chief librarians have only two considerations: their own service and their role in managing within the local authority as a whole. Members, though, have to fulfil many more roles – certainly more than their nineteenth century counterparts: 'They are representative of the electorate, their party, their community and the committee on which they serve. They may see themselves as watchdogs, managers, policy makers and/or problem solvers'.[27]

Political change, even more than technological change, has become the overriding factor in the professional lives of chief librarians. Politics differ, according to the level of the local authority, the culture of a particular service and the committee to which a chief librarian reports, so local contexts do still have meaning. But, as the very fact of the Department of Heritage's Review indicates, government is now intent on setting a new national agenda for library services, to take account of changes in the political and operating environment for public libraries since the defining 1964 Public Libraries and Museums Act.

Challenges to corporate management

There are considerable implications for chief librarians of this delocalization of political decision-making and the changes in local government. Their role as corporate managers within a public service tradition has been challenged in fundamental ways. Before the last major reorganization of local government in 1974, chief librarians were part of a vertical structure, with responsibility solely for their own service. Then, they were invariably heads of their own department, reporting directly, politically, to a Library Committee and to the Town

Clerk for administrative purposes. Communication and management horizontally between service areas was limited. The concept of corporate, local-authority-wide management, which was developed in the Bains Report and embodied in the 1974 restructuring as a means of ensuring that resources were used most effectively, radically changed this.[28] From this period up to the more recent era of competitive tendering – and more stringent centralized financial controls through rate and then council tax capping – corporatism was pre-eminent. A local authority corporate approach meant that local services were seen within the local authority as part of a unified public service, challenging the assumptions behind the previous specialized committees and professional systems. Chief librarians, together with directors of education, recreation services, social services and other service areas, became much more entwined with each other through new committee structures and the sharing of corporate responsibilities. This even resulted in some tensions between public libraries – like education, a statutory service – and other services.[29] It also resulted in the kinds of wide-ranging responsibilities and career flexibility for chief librarians/directors of library services noted in the Introduction to this chapter.

Local government review

Local government review – which will entail the re-engineering of relationships and the placing of some library services in smaller authorities, or ensuring cooperative arrangements between authorities – is liable to put back the clock to the pre-1974 situation in some parts of the country. Services will be jostling for position and there is a possibility in the new authorities of a return to library committees, potentially resulting in a lower status for libraries. Reporting to leisure, arts and amenities or education committees (by far the most likely reporting mechanism for library services from the 1980s to the present[30,31]), has meant that libraries have been increasingly linked with prestigious programme areas that attract interested and knowledgeable members to their committees. Apathetic library committees have been criticized – by McColvin, for example – as an important cause of poor library services.[32]

There is an alternative view that a move back to more library committees will facilitate a focus purely on the library service and that decision-making will be better informed as a result. The Northern Ireland Education and Library Boards have been highly regarded by their chief librarians as instruments of policy direction because of their clear remit. This capacity of committees to devote time and expertise to a specific service has had to be balanced, though, by arguments in favour of libraries being placed within directorates which allow libraries to develop new functions that are more in line with the changing demands of communities. This has been the view of those who see leisure directorates as the natural home for library services at the end of the twentieth century, when libraries' leisure roles are more pronounced.[33]

Competitive tendering

A further challenge to the role of the chief as a corporate manager is being posed by the impetus to competitive tendering. This has already been implemented for leisure services, with which many public libraries are linked through committee structures. (A 1991 study found that just over half of the 143 UK library authorities responding to a survey reported to leisure or recreation committees[34]). The full implications of the split between 'purchasers' and 'providers' of services are not yet clear. The consultants' report to the Department of National Heritage on tendering for public libraries is, at the time of writing, still with the Minister for consideration.[35] However, the experience of the leisure sector provides some pointers to its likely impact on senior managers.

The Local Government Act of 1988 extended compulsory competitive tendering to the management of sports and recreation facilities. All of these facilities had to be put out to tender by January 1993. While local authorities retained their statutory powers over pricing and programming, many of the functions that were previously part of the local authority remit were delegated to contractors. These might be the authority's own successful 'in-house' team or a private contractor. The split in responsibilities between the purchaser – the local authority – and the provider – the contractor – caused considerable practical problems where in-house teams won the contract. Ensuring a coherent, strategic vision of the overall direction of the service was made more difficult, especially in the area of marketing, by the two 'hats' which the director of services had to wear. On the other hand, there were positive aspects to competitive tendering. There was some evidence that management practices had been tightened and that a more customer-driven and business-led approach to services was being developed by senior managers.[36] The problem remains that there is no conclusive evidence to suggest that relying on service contracts is more cost effective than providing services by the previous, traditional means. The role of the local authority as an employer has been increasingly shifting to that of an 'enabler' of service provision, but this is not a comfortable function for chief officers who previously have known precisely their reponsibilities and whose line of democratic accountability to their members and the community has been clear. Contract specification is often mechanistic and lacking in flexibility; it lacks the strategic element which is vital for service development in a democratic context.[37] The human resource issues for local authorities are also problematic and are now being reconsidered following court judgments about the equity of contracting out a whole range of services – which frequently means paying the same staff less under a tendered out contract than they previously received from the local authority.[38]

Continuing changes

Perhaps the most telling impact of the political environment on managers, however, has been simply the amount of change to which they have had to respond in recent years. As well as the legislation and consequent organizational and cultural changes referred to already, there has been a veritable avalanche of other significant regulation. Local government and housing legislation not only brought in competitive tendering, it also placed restrictions on the raising of capital for new building projects. The introduction of the Library Charges (England and Wales) Regulations, following the 1989 Act, required all chief librarians to reassess, often with their committees, their policy on charging and their approach to 'free' access to information. Copyright legislation has been similarly important. A difficulty, therefore, is the apparently constantly changing situation across many of those significant aspects for which chief librarians bear responsibility, including the statutory role of the public library, relationships with local and central government, the basis on which the service is provided ('fee or free'), and the longer-term strategic role of the library in its community. All of this is set in a context of dwindling resources and cash limited budgets.

LIBRARY ORGANIZATIONAL STRUCTURES

One response of chief librarians, like that of managers in business and other not-for-profit sectors, has been to restructure their service as a means of implementing change and controlling its impact. The size of a local authority has been an important determinant of structure throughout the history of public libraries, and a constraining factor for chief librarians. What constitutes the 'right' size of an authority to provide the optimum library service has continued to be debated as part of the discussions on the recent local government review.

Size and its impact on authority development

The 1850 Act allowed authorities in England and Wales with over 10,000 population to levy a rate for public libraries; the 1853 Acts for Scotland and Ireland allowed even smaller populations of 5000 and above to have a public library service. The resulting mix of library authorities, from the small services served by mere caretakers to the larger municipal libraries run, like Manchester, by professional librarians of the highest repute, inevitably meant a wide variation in quality. McColvin suggested sweeping reforms to regularize this, though the Kenyon Report in 1927[39] had also seen size as a key to further development.

Populations between 300,000 and 1,000,000 were seen by McColvin as the ideal,[40] an issue that was not resolved until the proposals which formed the basis of the 1964 Act set 40,000 as the minimum population to be served. This lasted until the reorganization of local government in England and Wales in 1974 following the conclusions of the Redcliffe-Maud report that the old authorities were too small and that public libraries should lie mainly within county councils. Whereas in England and Wales the lowest figure of population served after restructuring was around 100,000, in Scotland the smallest of the new districts served populations of 40,000 to 50,000. However, experience since then has meant that the view that larger authorities provide better opportunities for public libraries has now become part of the professional orthodoxy. Midwinter and McVicar affirmed this in their recent study of size and efficiency in the context of local government review and also competitive tendering.[41] Although there now appears to be little likelihood that very many small authorities will be created in England and Wales, the question remains as to how services which were once part of a larger, better-resourced unit will now be organized and, conversely, how smaller units, which are to be merged, will be managed. How will senior managers respond?

Clues can be found in the post-1974 restructuring, when the move was all one way and smaller authorities merged. Then, local loyalties and jealousies were a problem for chiefs. Peter Labdon, speaking of his experience in West Suffolk at the time, noted how difficult it was to develop a cooperative relationship with the Borough of Bury St Edmunds: 'There was considerable resistance to that . . . if you tried to do anything that wasn't in the national cooperative picture. Local jealousies, rivalries between county and borough councillors and, more than anything, the continued practice of cross-charging for library use, made life pretty difficult'.[42]

Dealing with the 'downsizing' of the merged authorities was also a difficulty; redundant chief librarians were retired, or offered deputy posts or associate head-of-service reponsibilities. For the new chief librarians it meant dealing with strained relationships and a level of bitterness in some individuals. Leadership qualities were essential to sustain them, as one Welsh chief noted: 'There we were trying to unite, within one Library department, three county libraries and four borough libraries. Note also that I had been appointed not only from the smallest authority, but also as younger than some of my new colleagues who had already been chiefs in their own right. I expect resilience was what saved me'.[43]

Merging senior management teams, or creating new ones, was essential. The collective expertise of senior managers and the success with which they were motivated by the chief played an important part in the development of services at this time.[44] The Bains Report had emphasized that local authorities needed to look again at their personnel practices, which were found to be generally inadequate. It was felt that more training was needed to fit people for their new roles.[45] The Local Government Training Board provided national courses to support restructuring, but the take-up was variable and authorities who did use these courses often failed to follow up with in-house training.

Size and organizational structures

Size played a very practical part in determining structure. A simple hierarchical model – with the chief librarian at the top, and then principal librarians in charge of specialist functions, for example, children's services, bibliographical services, reference and local history, and lending – would comprise a typical senior management team prior to 1974. As soon as authorities covered larger geographical areas, decentralization became more necessary, which affected the relationship between chiefs and their staffs. Delegation to middle and junior managers became essential, with effective communication needed at all levels. A preoccupation with structure in public libraries became more prevalent as library authorities grew in size and complexity. Importantly, library authorities grew at about the same time as their functions expanded. *The libraries choice*, an influential report from the Department of Education and Science, identified many of the areas of disadvantage that libraries had failed to support sufficiently.[46] Services to hospital patients, the housebound and handicapped, ethnic minorities, prisoners, adult learners and 'deprived areas' were developed by many authorities following the good practice described by the Library Advisory Council (England) in this analysis.

Since 1974, the structures of public library services have, then, been determined not only by the size of authorities. Providing more extensive services to groups within the community has been significant. The need to economize on staffing has been a further important factor. Chief librarians have had to maximize the impact of their professional staff and spread them ever more thinly across the increasingly varied functions. The result has been a move to 'matrix' and team structures, with ad hoc project groups sometimes being used for specific purposes and then disbanded when these are fulfilled. 'Restructuring' has therefore become a euphemism for coping with the loss of professional posts and the need to cover service specialisms with fewer librarians. The Department of Heritage Review was concerned at some of the results of these often dramatic changes, which have placed chief librarians in a position at the apex of organizations that are undergoing upheavals to meet economic realities: 'The management climate is changing as the top jobs become downgraded and the position of the Chief Librarian in many authorities is no longer attractive in terms of either salary or prestige. If this is happening to a substantial extent, then it must have important implications for the whole service'.[47]

Despite this, staff in the authorities studied for the Review were often positive about the organizations' structures and their internal communications were seen as a strength. An emphasis on employee participation, seen as a hallmark of successful organizations across all sectors, was being developed by many chief librarians.[48]

SERVICE DEVELOPMENT

A major determinant of structure has undoubtedly been the changes in the range and depth of public library services since the nineteenth century. There has been a shift from a service meeting those social and educational needs identified by an elite, to one focused firmly on the 'customer' within their community and the library and information needs which arise from that relationship. These have been expounded in the Department of Education and Science and later the Office of Arts and Libraries publications from the 1970s up to the present, as well as in a wide-ranging professional literature. The 1995 Department of Heritage Review therefore follows on from a considerable body of professional analysis of the desired roles and functions of libraries in society.

Children's services

The pattern of service development can be seen, perhaps most dramatically of all, in services for children and young people. From services which many nineteenth century committees and chief librarians saw as secondary to their main purpose, children's services have become central to the public library's role. Library services for children began relatively slowly, as was described in Chapter Two. There were sporadic early developments in those library authorities where chief librarians had some understanding of the real needs of children, and the 1870 Education Act was a spur to actions. In Nottingham, for example, Potter Briscoe, who became librarian there in 1869, opened a children's library with the help of a donation of £500 from a local manufacturer. By 1898, however, there were only 108 libraries out of the 300 in England and Wales making provision for children and young people.[49]

There was a role for visionary chief librarians in developing services. McColvin was once more important in drawing attention to the continuing lack of services up to the Second World War, and the need for the profession to lobby for more and better children's books.[50] The advent of county libraries and the development of school library services, which served children in schools whilst the children's services met their recreational needs at home, were supported by far-sighted chiefs who responded to McColvin and others. Authorities like Hertfordshire, Nottinghamshire and Lancashire led the way in provision for schools and to individual children. These authorities were managed by chief librarians who appointed some of the most influential children's librarians of this century: Eileen Colwell, Joan Butler, Esme Green and Nancy Dale. By the 1960s, children's work was firmly established as one of the most important of all services and premises were being improved, with services to young adults beginning to be addressed as a further specialist area. The expansion of children's library services – which are now available to some extent in every branch library – and services to schools – which are still significant despite the impact of the Education Reform Act – testify to the growth in this more child-centred approach to library provision. The importance of children as users of today's services can be seen from the dramatic recent increase in books and other items borrowed by children from their public library: from 82 million in 1990–1 to 101 million in 1992–3.[51] The growth in children's use of libraries for computer use, homework and the range of promotional activities now routinely provided by libraries, also indicates the shift from a solely book-centred service to one which offers wider opportunities to users.

Problems of diversity

The success story of children's services is in some ways, however, in sharp contrast to other areas of service development. Precisely because children and young people are a clearly differentiated sector of the community, their needs could be identified and resources targeted on them. The difficulty for senior managers in looking at the range of other community and individual needs for library services has been simply the diversity of the task facing them. In a 1993 study of the marketing practices of library services, a questionnaire survey of chief librarians found that public libraries were spreading their resources across a huge range: from the core book-lending and reference services to outreach for the elderly and housebound, hospital and prison services, film shows, lectures, writers in residence and other literature promotion activities, open learning, business and tourist information, and even a funeral service in one authority (presumably as part of an amenities directorate).[52] Public libraries have promoted the arts since before the Second World War; equally, they have had a long-standing role in business information provision. The breadth, variability and overlap of provision evident today between libraries and other local authority and voluntary sector services does now raise important questions about the extent to which managers need to prioritize the 'comprehensive' and largely free service demanded by the 1964 Act. Questions also have to be asked about how the undoubted needs of communities for a comprehensive public library service should be funded for the future.

Unambiguous definitions of the 'core' functions of a public library have become the holy grail for chief librarians, their committees and the government. An attempt was made to achieve this by the Office of Arts and Libraries report on public library objectives, but it failed to provide much support for senior managers in their difficult task of prioritizing the core and add-on functions of public libraries, and also failed to provide a more rational basis for charging than that eventually arrived at in the Library Charges Regulations.[53] The *Review of the public library service* largely avoided the issue, coming up instead with 13 broad areas which, as the review team admitted, 'reveal a great deal about the common purpose of the public library for the community as a whole, yet tell us less about the service needs of groups or individuals within that community'.[54] The Comedia report had similarly stressed the importance of the library as a community resource, but had also not provided any new thinking on how library authorities should set about defining what precisely their communities needed from a public library service for the future and how it should be funded.[55]

It could appear that some of the certainties which librarians and their committees developed in the nineteenth century have been replaced by a lack of vision and purpose, other than in clearly defined service sectors with a readily accessible clientele and where there are few dissensions from the principle of a free service at the point of delivery. Children and young people's services fall neatly into this category. However, perhaps an alternative scenario is simply that local authorities have been feeling their way to the services that best meet local needs, i.e. that a local public library service is just that – local. While national standards or norms are useful for comparing services and performance criteria have real merit in sharpening management practices, they cannot capture the variability of a local service. The need to exploit information highways through the networking of public libraries, and to offer communities wider information opportunities at local, national and even international levels is even now changing the concept of what is 'local'. 'Local' increasingly means providing immediate access to information at a convenient service point for the library customer. Connecting public libraries to the Internet and exploiting its huge potential for communities is a logical step forward.[56] But still the question of prioritizing and funding remains unanswered, making the task of senior managers well nigh impossible without clearer political direction.

CONCLUSION

From this overview, it can be seen that the role of chief librarians as both professional librarians and managers of diverse and important public services has changed immeasurably since the implementation of the 1850 Act. Their contribution to local authority corporate cultures has depended largely on combining these twin responsibilities. They have had to balance meeting the needs of their communities and serving their committees with managing a cost-effective organization. To answer Ernest Savage's opening question, they have had to be both librarians *and* managers. They have also needed considerable political insight. The emphasis has, however, shifted over time as imperatives have changed. At present, managerialism is highly significant in meeting the challenges being posed by the various stakeholders. Public librarians are seen to require an understanding of business and a range of management skills. Strategic and human resource management, marketing, and financial management have become important in order to ensure the survival of services within a threatening local and central government environment.

Chief librarians have also needed, and generally won, the support of professionals in other sectors; both within their own local authority and also from the wider information community. Local Library and Information Plans have helped them to develop a much more regionally focused strategic approach and have provided much-welcomed professional support, as have national groupings of chief librarians. FOLACL (the Federation of Local Authority Chief Librarians) has been influential in developing a common response to major issues and providing a point of contact. It is this wider influencing role, within and beyond their own organizations, that now waits to be addressed. Recent research into the role of managers has suggested that the notion of 'competences' and skills in traditional management specialisms like marketing or finance is no longer an adequate explanation of success, and a lack of them may not indicate failure. Interpersonal and other skills have, instead, to be contextualized: 'A manager's competence is as much a matter of the structural and cultural context in which they are operating as it is of their personal qualities'.[57]

In assessing the part played by librarians in their corporate culture, the sheer difficulty of the task they have faced ought to be acknowledged. Perhaps it is time to celebrate their successes as well as the work still needing to be done and to view their roles more realistically within the complexity of local authority cultures and community information needs for the next century.

REFERENCES

1 Savage, E. A., *A librarian's memories: portraits and reflections*, London, Grafton, 1952, 143.

2 Munford, W. A., *Edward Edwards 1812–1866: portrait of a librarian*, London, Library Association, 1963, 81–99.

3 *Ibid.*, 62–3.

4 Edwards, E., *Memoirs of libraries*, 2 vols., 2nd edn, Newport, Isle of Wight, Brannon & Fradd, 1885, Vol. 2, 574–5.

5 Kelly, T., *A history of public libraries in Great Britain*, 2nd ed, London, Library Association, 1977, 51.

6 Macleod, R. D., 'Who was James Yates?', *Library review*, XVII, 1959–60, 250–7.

7   Board of Education, Public Libraries Committee, *Report on public libraries in England and Wales* (Kenyon Report), London, Board of Education, 1927, 78.

8   Mitchell, J. M., *The public library system of Great Britain and Ireland 1921–1923: A report prepared for the Carnegie United Kingdom Trustees*, Edinburgh, T. and A. Constable, 1924, 29.

9   Kelly, T., *A history of public libraries in Great Britain 1845–1975*, 2nd edn, London, The Library Association, 1977, 251.

10 Stockham, K. A. (ed.), *British county libraries: 1919–1969*, London, Deutsch, 1969, 29.

11 Irwin, R., *The origins of the English library*, London, Allen and Unwin, 1958.

12 Munford, W. A., *James Duff Brown 1862–1914*, London, Library Association, 1968.

13 Northwood Lock, R., *James Duff Brown's manual of library economy*, 7th edn, London, Grafton, 1961, 33–4.

14 Munford, W. A., *Penny rate: aspects of British public library history, 1850–1950*, London, Library Association, 1951, 54.

15 McColvin, L. R., *The public library system of Great Britain: a report on its present condition with proposals for post–war reorganization*, London, Library Association, 1942, 107, 169.

16 *Ibid.*, 114.

17 Aslib, *Review of the public library service in England and Wales for the Department of National Heritage*, London, Aslib, 1995, 255–6.

18 Kinnell Evans, M., *All change? Public library management strategies for the 1990's*, London, Taylor Graham, 1991, 17.

19 Milner, E., Kinnell, M., and Usherwood, R., *Public library services and quality management: the right approach?* British Library, 1995 (in press).

20 Stewart, R., *Leading in the NHS*, London, Macmillan, 1989, 3.

21 Savage, E. A., *A librarian's memories: portraits and reflections*, London, Grafton, 1952, 153–6.

22 Usherwood, B., *Public library politics*, London, Library Association Publishing, 1993.

23 Bush, T., Kogan, M. and Lenney, T., *Directors of education – facing reform*, London, Jessica Kingsley, 1989, 45.

24 Heeks, P. and Kinnell, M., *Managing change for school library services*, London, The British Library, 1992.

25 *The Citizen's charter: raising the standard*, London, HMSO, 1991, Cmnd 1599.

26 Kinnell Evans, M., *All change? Public library management strategies for the 1990's*, London, Taylor Graham, 1991, 66.

27 Usherwood, B., *The public library as public knowledge*, London, Library Association, 1989, 37.

28 Study Group on Local Authority Management Structures, *The new local authorities: management and structure* (The Bains Report) London, HMSO, 1972.

29 Lomer, M. and Rogers, S., *The public library and the local authority – organisation and management*, Birmingham, Institute of Local Government Studies, 1983.

30 Rogers, S., 'Local authority management structures and the public library service',

Library review, **33** (1), 1984, 6–13.

31 Kinnell Evans, M., *All change? Public library management strategies for the 1990's*, London, Taylor Graham, 1991, 33–34.

32 *The public library system of Great Britain: a report on its present condition with proposals for post–war reorganization*, London, Library Association, 1942, 106.

33 Lovell, G., 'The leisure services context', *Library review*, **33** (1) 1984, 14–21.

34 Kinnell Evans, M., *All change? Public library management strategies for the 1990's*, London, Taylor Graham, 1991, 34.

35 KPMG and Capital Planning Information, *DNH Study: contracting out in public libraries*, London, KPMG, 1995.

36 Kinnell, M. and MacDougall, J., *Meeting the marketing challenge: strategies for public libraries and leisure services*, London, Taylor Graham, 1994.

37 Pollitt, C., *Managerialism and the public services*, 2nd ed, Oxford, Blackwell, 1993.

38 *The Daily Telegraph*, 7 July 1995, 13.

39 Board of Education, *Public Libraries Committee, Report on public libraries in England and Wales* (Kenyon Report), London, Board of Education, 1927, 78.

40 McColvin, L. R., *The public library system of Great Britain: a report on its present condition with proposals for post–war reorganization*, London, Library Association, 1942.

41 Midwinter, A. and McVicar, M., *The size and efficiency debate: public library authorities in a time of change*, London, Library Association Publishing, 1994. (British Library Research and Development Report 6143).

42 Kinnell Evans, M., *All change? Public library management strategies for the 1990's*, London, Taylor Graham, 1991, 19.

43 Kinnell Evans, M., *All change? Public library management strategies for the 1990's*, London, Taylor Graham, 1991, 21.

44 Lomer, M. and Rogers, S., *The public library and the local authority – organisation and management*, Birmingham, Institute of Local Government Studies, 1983, 125–6.

45 Study Group on Local Authority Management Structures, *The new local authorities: management and structure* (The Bains Report) London, HMSO, 1972, 67.

46 Department of Education and Science, *The libraries' choice*, London, HMSO, 1978.

47 Aslib, *Review of the public library service in England and Wales for the Department of National Heritage*, London, Aslib, 1995, 253.

48 Tylczak, L., *Effective employee participation*, London, Kogan Page, 1990.

49 Ellis, A., *Library services for young people in England and Wales, 1830–1970*, Oxford, Pergamon Press, 1971, 14–15.

50 McColvin, L. R., *The public library system of Great Britain: a report on its present condition with proposals for post–war reorganization*, London, Library Association, 1942, 72.

51 Library and Information Services Council (England) Working Party on Library Services for Children and Young People, *Investing in children: the future of library services for children and young people*, London, HMSO, 1995, 15 (Library Information Series 22).

52 Kinnell, M. and MacDougall, J., *Meeting the marketing challenge: strategies for public libraries and leisure services*, London, Taylor Graham, 1994, 17–18.

53 Office of Arts and Libraries, *Setting objectives for public library services*, London, HMSO, 1991 (Library Information Series 19).
54 Aslib, *Review of the public library service in England and Wales for the Department of National Heritage*, London, Aslib, 1995, 172.
55 Comedia, *Borrowed time*, Stroud, Comedia, 1993.
56 Dick, J., *Croydon Libraries' Internet project: connecting public libraries to the Internet. A progress report to British Library Research and Development Department*, Croydon, Croydon Libraries, Museum and Arts, 1995.
57 Watson, T. J., *In search of management: culture, chaos and control in managerial work*, London, Routledge, 1994, 222.

10 Public libraries and political purpose

❖ *Bob Usherwood*

Politics is still crucially important. Our choices are vital . . . Dennis Potter [1]

INTRODUCTION

The public library is a product of history. It exemplifies a set of values and reflects our different views of culture and class. Like other public institutions, it functions within the context of different political systems and because of this there are many different views as to its political purpose. Politicians, professionals and, to a lesser extent, the public have reached divergent conclusions on the basis of different ideological, professional and political perspectives.

Over the years, the political purpose of the public library has been denied, decried and celebrated. Thus in a work designed to help new local councillors a British County Librarian expressed the view that 'public libraries . . . should be free from political issues'.[2] Less than ten years ago a notice from the Press Office of the then Office of Arts and Libraries declared that 'libraries must not become an ideological battleground'.[3] Others, however, refer to 'the myth that public libraries must be kept out of politics and politics out of public libraries'[4] and maintain that 'it is important that librarians be politically active' and that the librarian's profile must be characterized by specific qualities such as that of an 'agent for change'.[5]

One suspects that the debate is mainly about an overtly political role for the library service because the part played by the public library in the provision of free access to information, ideas and works of imagination is not normally disputed. Although there are some exceptions to this professional rule,[6] most would argue that by providing such access the library helps strengthen a political system that requires citizens to make intelligent and informed decisions. There is assumed to be a direct relationship between the political process and the information needs of citizens. Social progress is seen to depend on access to information and the democratic premise is to be found in many, indeed most, of the public statements of purpose provided by public library authorities.

PUBLIC LIBRARIES AND DEMOCRACY

One of the earliest of such pronouncements is that provided in 1852 by the Trustees of the Boston Public Library. They maintained that:

> Reading ought to be furnished to all as a matter of public policy and duty; ... For it has been rightly judged that – under political, social and religious institutions like ours – it is of paramount importance that the means of general information should be so diffused that the largest possible number of persons should be induced to read and understand questions going down to the very foundations of social order, which are constantly presenting themselves, and which we, as a people, are constantly required to decide and do decide, either ignorantly or wisely.[7]

Much more recently, and with an international perspective, the UNESCO Public Library Manifesto,[8] in a paragraph headed 'The public library in support of democracy', states that: 'Freedom, prosperity and the positive development of society and individuals benefit from the ability of independent well informed citizens to exercise their democratic rights and responsibilities. Their constructive participation depends on satisfactory education as well as free and unlimited access to universal knowledge, thought and culture'.

Such views have not gone entirely unchallenged. Simeon Strunsky in *No mean city*, for example, observed that 'people who want to understand democracy should spend less time in the library with Aristotle and more time on the buses and in the subway.'[9] Despite such pronouncements, it is now almost part of the conventional professional wisdom that the public library has a role to play in developing an informed and educated democracy. Members of the profession believe that the public library service serves to extend citizenship by providing access to the ideas, information and works of imagination that make involvement in social and community life possible. For instance, the City Librarian of Copenhagen has recently called for 'the library to be a cornerstone in the endeavour to sustain the country's democratic development',[10] while a Scandinavian colleague has observed that it is 'the political dimension that gives our job that extra touch'.[11]

The recently published Department of National Heritage (DNH) public library review refers to public libraries' 'contingency value', whereby the library acts as a type of insurance policy for citizens who may need to use it at some time in their lives. The Review gives some examples of such use: 'A planning application may affect their properties and put their interests in jeopardy; a new government policy may make an impact on their families ... they can visit the public library and elicit information and guidance on events, remedies and possible courses of action'.[12] While the DNH document tends not to use the word 'politics', the examples given above are about helping people influence political events.

Outside the profession, two political scientists, Newton and Karran,[13] have argued that the very presence of a public library service has resulted in a more politically aware population. They are of the view that the children of middle- and upper-class parents 'have made use of public libraries and other cultural facilities, and have become a new and more articulate political force for further expansion of state services': justification, perhaps, for the fears of those nineteenth century Tories who feared that the introduction of public libraries would lead to 'unhealthy agitation'.

Public libraries as political instruments

At times, the public library has been seen and used as a political instrument for political and social change, although it is doubtful whether many British librarians ever reached the level of political activism to be found in America in the 1960s when 'hundreds of . . . librarians and library school students became involved in championing socially related change in librarianship'.[14] Of course, it could be argued that these librarians were concerned about social rather than political change, although for many the issues were closely linked. In Britain, organizations such as Librarians for Social Change saw public libraries as part of 'the revolution'. In a 1977 publication, it declared 'Education and the raising of political consciousness is the keystone in the struggle for revolution . . . and it is up to public libraries to provide the means for such education'.[15]

This statement seems to owe something to the view in the former Soviet Union where:

> Lenin put forward and grounded the principle of partisanship of libraries, of their active participation in carrying out socialist transformation, criticised the bourgeois assertions on the non–political, non-Party character of library work in a class society. After the victory of the October Revolution Lenin repeatedly stressed the indissoluble link of library organisation with the policy of the Party and the government and with tasks of building socialism and communism.[16]

During the Cold War it is also reported that the *Soviet encyclopaedia* claimed that the purpose of the public library was to produce good Communist citizens.[17]

In Nazi Germany, Stieg reports that 'Politicization was something to be recognized, accepted, and advocated. Franz Schriewer, a leading librarian of the time, was forthright: "The public library is a political library today, which word is to be understood in its breadth; that is, the public library is to be oriented to the Volk and state".'[18] She goes on to say, 'Suddenly the public library was a political institution in a totalitarian state dedicated to the creation of an unthinking, chauvinistic population'. As one historian has observed, 'Hitler needed the willing co-operation of professionals for his broad ideological imperatives to be translated into action and policy'.[19] That this applied to librarians is demonstrated by Stieg 's comment that 'Political reliability had, in fact, become a professional prerequisite . . . as the list of evidence required for admission to library school shows'.[20]

Closer to home, and from a very different political perspective, Muddiman and Black are of the opinion that 'in the mid eighties . . . a moderate number of local authorities had begun to recognise the radical potential of public libraries as an agency of social change'.[21] Documents from a number of sources lend some support to this argument. For instance, in Manchester, positive stock selection policies were 'implemented to remove from the library shelves material which depicts people of particular races in a derogatory or incorrect way, and attempts made to select material for all libraries in the city which will actively assist the development of mutual understanding between races'.[22]

From the same period, a Sheffield District Labour Party manifesto stated:

> The economic and political strategy of central government would attempt to weaken the ability of many thousands of Sheffield people – in and out of work– to resist its broader policies: our aim must be to actively provide the information needs of people seeking to resist. We make no apologies for responding in a political manner with our libraries and museums policies, for in the current climate a political response is the only way to ensure the existence of these services for future generations of Sheffield people. The educational and information resources of these services will, therefore, be increasingly directed at the campaign to defend and improve all local authority services.[23]

However, despite the existence of such policies, the overtly political British public library was, and is, the exception rather than the rule.

SOCIAL CHANGE AND THE ROLE OF THE PUBLIC LIBRARY

That having been said, it is clear that 'when information is . . . exposed as an important power tool . . . a role for the public library emerges dramatically different from its generally passive and socially uninvolved past'.[24] The materials stocked in libraries can contribute to the process of social change. This need not be restricted to factual material. Poetry and literature can provide a means by which people obtain greater insight into the issues of the day. Public libraries have the ability to empower people through the strength of the ideas to be found in the material they hold and organize.

The library service can help users in ways that go well beyond the walls of a library building, even when that library is behind the walls of a prison. Those who have seen that excellent film 'The Shawshank redemption' will have seen a fictional representation of this, but a Sheffield PhD student obtained the following confirmation of that idea from an interview held with a Prison Education Coordinator in a real-life prison:

> I would see part of the function of the library as empowering people to take responsibility for their own life – if many of these men had been doing that, they would not be here in the first place. So part of addressing offending behaviour is helping people take responsibility . . . Actually being able to deal with . . . questions themselves is one of the ways in which people become able to function when they get outside. The more library staff can do to normalise a man the better – so they should stock everything they can.[25]

In the wider society, effective access to information and ideas is increasingly important in a world where the ordinary citizen is confronted and confused by a vast number of important issues that she or he needs to understand and evaluate. Public library collections can reflect every recorded point of view or shadow of opinion. Compared with the stock of the average library, the range of material on any given subject presented by the electronic media is shallow and narrow. As one distinguished observer of contemporary Britain has written:

> The media are the mirror for the economic and social disintegration of the country. The focus of the newspapers, notably the tabloids, has narrowed to a right-wing populism that pays scant attention to accuracy, the brew leavened by sexual titillation and obsessional royal family watching. The power to form opinion has been accompanied by a more careless attitude to the way such power is exercised.[26]

There are then serious disadvantages in relying only on the mass media as a source of information. In addition, it has been estimated that the number of words contained in a half-hour television news bulletin could quite easily be put on just one page of a broadsheet newspaper. How much more about an issue can be contained in the collection of a good public library.

As the Comedia report reminded us, 'the idea of citizenship should not simply be conceived in national terms, given the increasing importance of our duties and responsibilities as citizens of the European community'.[27] Public libraries have taken up this challenge. The European Commission is using public libraries to disseminate information about its work. A relay network has been established involving public library authorities. This does, however, raise interesting questions about the dividing line between providing information and promulgating a political idea. It is a specific example of a more general problem which has been faced by information workers in both local and national government.

Free access or charging?

The role of the public library in helping the democratic system has implications for the arguments for and against charging users. Central to the public library's political purpose is the fact that it makes information, ideas and works of imagination available to all, regardless of their ability to pay. The introduction of direct charges on those who use public libraries will restrict such availability and increase the gap between the information haves and have nots. Writers such as White and Norton have attempted to justify charging the user on the basis of statistics and the language of the market. White called his book *The public library in the 1980s*,[28] and its arguments remain rooted in that discredited and dreary decade, while Norton demonstrates that market values are not always in tune with those of democracy when he asks: 'Is protection of the disadvantaged a function of government as a regulatory body and is this incompatible with the drive towards a commercial competitiveness in a market society?'[29]

In a civilized society, the protection of the disadvantaged has to be a function of government, and the public library is a means by which society reduces the inequalities in access to the wealth of information and ideas, inequalities that are often reflected in educational opportunity, housing conditions, social status and life chances. The public library service is highly relevant to the aim of evening out these critical inequalities and can help people who are subject to them, to find their way round the bureaucratic system so they can influence the decisions that can affect their lives.

Moreover, as the recent DNH public library review demonstrates, the condition of free access continues to be supported by the public and the professional librarians. The review recommends that 'the principle of free and equal access to library materials should be extended when conditions allow' and makes 'a case for allowing uncharged access to those Internet or World Wide Web sources that are essentially "free", that is available at no more than the cost of local calls to telecommunication nodes'.[30] This, in fact, should be a minimum requirement at a time when success is often linked with the ability to use computers and access the superhighways of the information world. Without such access there is a very real danger that the gap will widen between the rich and the poor, the educated and uneducated, the black and the white. As Frankena and Frankena have observed, technical expertise has become 'a crucial political resource in controversies because access to knowledge and the resulting ability to question the data and information used to legitimate decisions is an essential basis for power and influence'.[31] The public library could be an important agency to help people acquire the technical expertise and gain confidence in the use of the new technology. Roszak has argued that the public library is the best place for information technology because of its tradition of providing democratic access.[32]

Technology and the library

Anybody can visit and make use of a public library, but it is highly unlikely that electronic newspapers and expensive electronic equipment will be widely available in the slum houses of the inner city or the cardboard homes of the dispossessed thrown on to the streets by political processes that they don't understand. The public library could help to reduce such inequality by becoming an integral part of an information infrastructure that takes the information superhighway to rural lanes and the crowded backstreets of the inner city, something that will not happen if the development of information technology (IT) is left to market forces alone.

The Danish Government has recognized this in its consideration of the Info Society 2000. Policy 17 in this document states that 'Even in the future – when electronic publications will be taking over the role of magazines and books – libraries must maintain a major intermediary function as providers of public information to all citizens and must help the public to navigate through the increasing flood of information'.[33] If the public library service is to be one of the agents to produced informed citizens, it will need to provide effective and equal access to word, image and sound.

Peter Young, the Executive Director of the US National Commission on Libraries and Information Science (NCLIS), has said that 'libraries provide more than computers, conduits, and content; libraries provide the context for answering questions and navigating Internet and the intellectual output of the human race. Interactive networks change political, economic and social processes . . . '.[34]

Some claim that by early in the next century, lack of access to the technology will in fact prevent people from taking part in the democratic process. The advocates of hyper-democracy foresee a time when people will vote by modem. The dangers inherent in a populist electronic plebiscite or a virtual Downing Street appear not to trouble such futurists. Such simplistic ideas are perhaps seen at their best or worst in the computer conservatism of Newt Gingrich.

In fact, despite the high-minded claims of the industry, the new communications technology, like much of the old communications technology, will not be over-concerned with increasing human knowledge but with entertainment, and entertainment of the most trivial kind. As one American commentator has put it 'All the cables will lead back to an enormous, leaking landfill of vicarious crap. Incredible sums of money will be made from this'. He concludes:

> every propagandist for the zillion channel environment talks piously about 'education'. Whenever an . . . entrepreneur invokes education in this context it behooves [sic] the citizen to smell a rat. Education is, or ought to be, about reality, and the dark star that lurks out there in cyberspace has less to do with reality than with the infinite replication of simulacrums, a hugely overscaled way . . . of amusing ourselves to death.[35]

Even if it is accepted that that is a slightly exaggerated analysis, it does point out the need for an alternative agent of communication that is less concerned with making incredible sums of money. Certainly, where the communications and telecommunications media are part of a commercial concern their ultimate objective is profit and this can and does limit the range of ideas and the type of information that is communicated. As we have seen, there are considerable profits to be made from the commercialization of IT and, indeed, broadcasting by terrestrial means. Profits most often are obtained on the basis of the amount of advertising revenue obtained. Programmes, increasingly thought of as products, therefore have to attract large audiences. It is therefore relatively rare for stations, such as those owned by Rupert Murdoch, to carry anything that is controversial, experimental or only likely to appeal to minority tastes. In addition, while it might do something to curb the expansion of Mr Murdoch's empire, the recent government announcement on cross-media ownership will do little to increase the range of material on offer. It is highly unlikely that, by letting Carlton television get bigger or the *Daily mail* run television stations, the new rules will add much to Britain's cultural life.

There is one profitable niche market which 'as all in the entertainment industry know but none will admit, will be pornography. Strap on your helmet and enter the wonderworld of virtual S&M'.[36] Alternatively, or perhaps additionally, people can opt for the comparatively low-tech provision of the 'adult channel' or the chat lines which bring the privatized British Telecom 49p a minute. The size of the audience or the cost of access has little to do with the quality of the programme.

Without the pressure to deliver large audiences to advertisers, public libraries, like public service broadcasters, are, if left alone by government, in a far stronger position to present material that will extend, excite, challenge or even annoy. Such a service provides a vital political purpose in that it will enable people to view issues from different perspectives and take greater control of their own lives. It has, however, been difficult for the public library service to achieve all of this, especially at a time when the ideas of public ownership and collective action are being challenged.

COMMERCIALIZATION AND THE LOSS OF PURPOSE

Certainly, in the 1980s some British public librarians, like many other public servants, seemed to lose their way. Many in the profession appeared to shift to the Right in order to make use of the prevailing winds of political change. There was a less than strategic withdrawal from the idealism that had been a feature of many services in the 1960s and 1970s. Too many in the profession became converts to the idea of market forces and took on board the consumerist approach advocated by the Thatcher government. This was specifically, and officially, outlined in the Green Paper,[37] and more aggressively stated in the work of the Adam Smith Institute.[38]

A mixture of the new managerialism and political imperatives has led to the commercialization of library services. The results of this were often seen in stock selection policies that were more concerned with the quantity of issues than the quality of material on offer. John Stuart Mill, who knew something about political purpose, described the dangers of such an approach in his *Utilitarianism*:

> Men lose their high aspirations as they lose their intellectual tastes, because they have no time or opportunity for indulging them; and they addict themselves to inferior pleasures not because they deliberately prefer them but because they are either the only ones to which they have access or the only ones which they are any longer capable of enjoying.[39]

History has shown that literature and the other arts can sometimes bring about social and political change. This can occasionally be direct, as was the case with BBC television's 'Cathy come home', but more often it is by providing people with insights into the lives of other people and/or by communicating across the barriers of race, class and age. Public libraries can, of course, do this directly by displays and publications that introduce their public to different cultures and different views on issues of the day. Beatie, the working-class woman in Arnold Wesker's *Roots*, recognized the importance of challenging people through the arts and literature. Her final speech should be taken to heart by those librarians who seek to patronize their readers by 'giving them what they want':

> 'Blust,' they say, 'if they don't make no effort why should we bother'. So you know who come along? The slop singers and the pop writers and the film makers and women's magazines and the Sunday papers and the picture strip love stories – that's who come along and you don't have to make no effort for them, it come easy, 'We know where the money lie.' they say, 'hell we do! The workers 've got it so let's give them what they want. If they want slop songs and film idols we'll give 'em that then. If they want words

of one syllable, we'll give 'em that then. If they want the third rate, *blust!* We'll give 'em *that* then. Anything's good enough for them 'cos they don't ask for no more!' The whole stinkin' commercial world insults us and we don't care a damn . . . [40]

In fact, it was not just the British librarians who lost their sense of political purpose. In Scandinavia, Audunson feels that 'the aggressive conservative wave of the eighties seem to have produced lasting ideological effects within all political camps'.[41] An American analysis of democratic ideals and the American public library also found that, 'in their conscious attempts to copy and compete with the mass communications industry for customers . . . librarians are promoting the very conformity and sameness that they, as symbols of our highest political ideals, should be fighting against.'[42] In very much the same tone, Chu reports that some of the public libraries in China now 'ignore their fundamental aims while excessively concentrating on economic income alone'.[43] The tension between the traditional and commercial culture in Polish libraries was also examined by Kolodziejska in her paper to the IFLA Conference. In this she asked, 'whether under the new cultural situation there will be a place for the public library'.[44] This may be a too pessimistic conclusion at least in the British context where the 1990s have seen some librarians develop a much more positive approach to purchasing and promoting good quality material.

Moreover, at the macrolevel, as Will Hutton has pointed out in his brilliant critique of the state of our nation, 'The political difficulty for the zealous neo-liberal crusaders against 'serfdom' is that the welfare state is deeply popular and entrenched'.[45] This was borne out by the results of the user survey carried out as part of the DNH Public Library review.[46] This showed quite clearly that the public did not want private companies to run public libraries and that they were not in favour of some of the entrepreneurial activities put to them by the consultants. At the time this contribution is being written, there is a smell of death about the 1980s' philosophy and even the City, or so we are told, is preparing for a return to a more civilized and compassionate culture.

That having been said, it is still on the political agenda of the right to redefine the way people relate to public institutions. Protagonists of the New Right have recognized that 'Change is partly effected through changing the way that people talk about and think about what they do'. As a result, 'the rhetoric of the market has developed very strongly in the public service. Talk of "customers", "business plans" . . . is common. The danger of the translation of political issues and relationships into the language of the market is that we become separated from our responsibilities, and political debate becomes more difficult'.[47]

This can be seen in the language used to describe the people who use our public library services. In a very real way, what we call them communicates a great deal about our attitudes towards them. David Marquand recently explained how 'the Thatcher and Major governments have redefined the citizen as customer, society as supermarket and the state as a kind of Securicor. Those who can, shop; those who can't beg. Inside the supermarket anything goes. On the streets huddle the excluded'.[48] As Hutton explains, 'the importance of customers is that they spend; the capacity to be a citizen depends upon spending power, without which citizenship disappears'.[49] Thus such consumerist language and the world it represents makes it that much more difficult for the public library to fulfil its political role so that every citizen is able equally to take part in the decision-making process, whether that be in the workplace, the local community or the state.

The present writer believes that the time has long since come to do away with what David Edgar has called the 'C word'.[50] However, it is recognized that such has been the debasement of our professional language that it is now widely used. A project being undertaken jointly at Sheffield and Loughborough Universities has revealed that in the region of 50% of authorities use the word, with the remainder using a variation on the theme of borrower, reader or user.[51]

There are, though, some interesting divisions of opinion. In one authority, our researcher was told by an elected member, 'We will not use the term customer, it smacks too much of buying a pound of sugar over the counter'. In another, a councillor claimed that the customer concept had enabled them to 'move the service forward on a business footing, prior to the use of the word customer, things were much too wishy washy.' One might be forgiven for thinking that this is part of the management-speak rhetoric that has caused some users responding to the DNH review to have such a false perception of the reality of the state of the library service. For while Gerald Kaufmann is of the opinion that, 'if you think services will magically improve because you use the word customer you are living in cloud cuckoo land',[52] most users interviewed for the DNH survey felt that the public library had improved over the past five years and would continue to improve over the next five.[53] The political implications, indeed dangers, of such a finding will not be lost on the readers of this paper.

INTELLECTUAL FREEDOM AND COLLECTION DEVELOPMENT

As indicated earlier, there are also political implications in what librarians decide to include or not to include in their collections. The library literature has, over the years, suggested that intellectual freedom is essential to a democratic society. In the United States, this concept is defined by the ALA Office for Intellectual Freedom as the 'right and freedom to express one's beliefs or ideas' and the 'right of unrestricted access to all information and ideas'.[54] Oboler argues that no censorship can be justified within a democracy and that censorship is in fact the antithesis of democracy.[55] However, the question of what is censorship within the context of the public library has been the subject of much debate. Jones, for example, has argued that labelling is a form of post-selection censorship, from which 'injustice and ignorance' results.[56] A less extreme position is taken by Leigh, who views censorship as the rejection of a book by the library authority after pressure from either the librarian, the library board or the public who may believe the text to be too obscene, radical, critical or subversive.[57] In a recent study, 'political reasons for justifying either access or restrictions on access to material were used most often in the contexts of race and gender'. A librarian interviewed as part of this work argued that what is not made available through choice and a structured approach is not censorship because this material is available to people through all kinds of different means. To this respondent, 'censorship means, essentially state suppression of information or it means suppression of information by powerful interest groups.'[58]

The issues of censorship and intellectual freedom are too complex to be reduced to some of the knee-jerk reactions that have been applied in the past by some writers, the present author included, in the library literature. If it is the role of the public library to offer individuals and communities a range of materials that will extend rather than limit the growth of citizenship, public librarians will have to be prepared to make value judgments. Indeed, it is their responsibility to do so. It is difficult to see how members of a profession that claims to be concerned with social responsibility and the development of an educated democracy can not make such judgments.

In recent years, market economics and the current fashion on the Left and the Right to attack professionals or any other group willing and able to make a judgment means that public librarians are in danger of not fulfilling their democratic role and political purpose. Across the Atlantic they now talk of the 'dumbing of America' and it is interesting to note that at the same time as Hollywood has deified the moronic and Talk Radio and the Internet recycle racist, homophobic and other assorted prejudices, that country has taken a frightening shift to the Right. This is a 'coincidence' to be drawn to the attention of those on the Left who make accusations of elitism.

It is without any sense of pleasure that it is recorded that the previous paragraph was written some time before the bombing in Oklahoma City, but there can be little doubt that in America the First Amendment has permitted a torrent of hatred to spread across the nation's airwaves and the new information technology. 'Shock jocks' such as Rush Limbaugh, Oliver North and

G. Gordon Liddy 'the long-ago Watergate convict whose contribution to free speech, post Oklahoma was to explain to his audience how best to kill federal agents',[59] have left an impression that violence is acceptable. As *The economist* said in its comment on the American tragedy, 'Playing with fire is not the same as playing with bombs. But more people are now going to point to the perils'.[60] They are perils that the public library service must not ignore.

Neutrality or engagement?

Nearly a quarter of a century ago, Sanford Berman addressed what he called 'the value problem' for public librarians and asked:

> Were our profession magically transmuted in time and space to Germany of the 1930s, would it be 'neutral' about Yellow Stars, Blitz-kriegs, KZs, book burning, forced labour, organization-banning, Gypsy guinea pigs, etc.? Would these events and practices not be regarded as anathema to humane values, to uninhibited scholarship, learning and dialogue, to the very well being of our clientele and colleagues?[61]

In her study, Cole found that 'political justifications for restricting access to material were applied when discussing holocaust revisionist material'. She quotes one respondent at length:

> There isn't any justification for having it in the sense that it's not substantial historically, it's not properly researched, it's been disproved many times over, it has a purely political, i.e. anti-Semitic and racist justification so you couldn't say people need to be aware of it because you cannot study the development of twentieth century Europe with this, it's pure and simple political propaganda I think, and inaccurate.[62]

This is a point of view that is supported by academic and professional studies.[63, 64]

Today, as we see the manifestation of dark forces in the United States, Europe and elsewhere, we must again ask if, in the name of intellectual freedom, our public libraries should promote and defend materials that perpetuate paranoia and attitudes that will stunt the intellectual and political growth of individuals and communities. The answer is not easy, especially when faced with Stieg's observation that 'Rejecting neutrality was one aspect of the most striking change the National Socialist revolution brought to librarianship'.[65]

On reflection, this merely reinforces the need to make value judgments and ensure that the public library promotes the kind of society that encourages an enlightened, thinking and broad-minded population. In the moving, mind-expanding interview that he gave just before his death, Dennis Potter recalled the world of television that he and Melvyn Bragg had entered in the early

1960s. He observed:

> I'm not saying that world wasn't paternalistic, and I'm not saying it can be preserved as it was, and I'm not saying there mustn't be change, but that world was based on a set of assumptions that are now almost derisible, laughable. Like in politics, certain statements become derisible. We're destroying ourselves by not making those statements.[66]

His words are equally applicable to the world of public libraries. By making statements and providing access to material of high quality, the public library can carry out a very significant political role and help to even out the inequalities in our society. The reverse is also true, as Garceau warned American librarians nearly half a century ago. On the basis of his research into *The public library in the political process*, he observed:

> the emphasis on easy reading for the masses begs the question of the library's purpose. The answer, that the public must be given what it wants, has been too readily accepted by librarians for them to command the public respect accorded to learning. In the equation of politics the policy chosen may well be a source of weakness not of strength.[67]

Quality and choice

In discussing the political role of the public library, one becomes aware of a series of paradoxes. For instance, as we have seen, the political purpose of the public library reflects the tension between the democratic ideal and the professional desire for the library to provide material of a high quality. This has been a subject of some debate since the days of the American Library Association's Public Library Inquiry. This divided American librarians regarding the role of the public library in a democratic society. One side supported the view of the library as an instrument to promote an educated and informed citizenry while the other equated democracy with giving people what they want or public choice.

The paradox is that while democracy demands an intelligent and informed electorate, anti-intellectualism and ignorance are also part of a democratic society. Should people have the right not to know? Thomas Jefferson is reputed to have said, 'If a nation expects to be ignorant and free in a state of civilization, it expects what never was and never will be'.[68] Such ignorance, as recent history shows, can disadvantage society at large and we would argue that if the public library is to help citizens participate in and run their society then it has a duty to liberate people from ignorance and provide access to the best, however that is to be defined.

That is to say, it should provide people with the skills to make a political judgment and with the ability to enable them to assess the evidence that is put before them by politicians and self-serving media moguls. Such a view can lead to the accusation of elitism, but is this a greater danger than paternalism or a pandering to popularization that itself often promotes prejudice and bigotry? – prejudice and bigotry which in the past led to Belsen and in the present to the dead children of Oklahoma City. To paraphrase a Dutch colleague 'In short the purpose of libraries is to urge the citizens to do good and avoid doing evil.'[69]

In a recent book, Trevor Haywood identifies a further 'relentless unfolding paradox – that people now need more information to help them understand their world and multiple forms of entertainment to help them escape it'.[70] We have dealt with the entertainment issue elsewhere, but the idea that by providing access to information public libraries will always aid the democratic process needs to be questioned. To some extent it will depend on who organises and controls the information that the library provides. This issue was identified by Raymond Williams in his reworking of the Lasswell formula for the study of communications. Williams suggested that we rephrase the Lasswell question to read, 'who says, what, how, to whom, with what effect *and for what purpose?* This would at least direct our attention to the interests and agencies of communication, which the orthodox question excludes' (emphasis added).[71]

CONTRADICTORY FUNCTIONS AND ROLES

There is also a contradiction in the fact that public libraries are, at the same time, agents of free communication and also formal institutions of the national or local state. Thus there will be times that serving one function will disadvantage another. The problems faced by librarians in totalitarian regimes have already been outlined, but at the local level there are examples from both Left- and Right-wing councils where the views of the elected members have been in apparent conflict with the professional requirement for free expression and free access to information. The public library, in addition to sustaining the political process, can also be vulnerable to it.

It can, of course, be argued that the public library serves both the capitalist ideology of individualism and the collectivist notions of community. Reading is often a very private activity and can certainly be said to support the Thatcherite notion of 'enlightened self-interest' but at the same time the public library is increasingly seen as an agent for social and community development or 'enlightened citizenship', as the American Library Association called it in its 1947 National Plan.[72] Thus, while the UNESCO public library manifesto talks about the development of society and individuals, the New Right maintains 'There is no such thing as society . . . There are individual men and women, and there are families. And no government can do anything except through people and people must look to themselves first.'[73] In Britain, John Major's big idea, The Citizen's Charter, as the position of the apostrophe demonstrates, is much more about the individual than any collective notion of citizenship.

That having been said, the word 'public' in public library is in itself a political statement and a reflection of political purpose. It essentially exemplifies the benefits of collective action. As the Comedia report indicated, 'The library is based on the principle of borrowing from a common resource that is greater than any individual or family could afford or accommodate.' It brings the argument up-to-date saying that 'the high cost of CD Roms ... takes the library back to one of its original purposes, to buy for collective use items that individuals are unlikely to afford'.[74]

Research has shown that some members of the Labour Party believe their political ideology to be absolutely in line with the provision of public library services.[75] The former Labour leader Michael Foot has described public libraries as 'socialism in action' while a Labour councillor stated, 'It is important to me as a Socialist that as many people as possible should have as much access to as much good material as can possibly be provided'. For another, 'public access and equal access ' was a principle of socialist thinking'.[76]

We need to be aware that there appears to be some difference between the rhetoric of some professional pronouncements and the reality of public library use. As we have seen in a market-driven public library service fiction is no longer regarded as the nuisance it was in the nineteenth century,[77] but there are still observable differences between the realities of user demand and the more academic view of public library purpose.

Research in this country and elsewhere has shown that, for most people, the public library is first thought of as a source of reading materials. This led the right wing Adam Smith Institute to dismiss the public library as a source of information. Its simplistic judgment was that, 'while the ambitious librarian may like to look on him or herself as part of a vital information industry, the bulk of the customers use the service as a publicly funded provider of free romantic fiction'.[78] This conclusion ignores the significance of reading in the creation of a literate society and the way that it can transform the lives of people. Moreover, it is not supported by most of the other research in the field. The DNH review, on the basis of its own and other investigations, concluded that:

> library users ... seek out a wide range of material, not merely the superficial. According to students of reading habits people borrow fiction mainly for recreational purposes. However, there is a body of research that reinforces the common sense view that borrowers of fiction also derive other worthwhile benefits from their reading, in particular the factual content of novels often helps to inform readers.[79]

CONCLUSION

It is true that the users of the public library rarely mention specifically its political or democratic purpose. However, they do see it as an important agency for enlightening children, as a place for study and a point of access to knowledge and culture from every part of the world, as a source of information on the local community, and as a place where they can find the resources and skills to enable them to obtain information on vital issues of the day.[80] These and the other core functions, identified by the DNH public library review, do in fact reflect many of the political issues discussed above. Likewise, in the United States, while the public library does not appear to be a major source of information, it is highly regarded as an institution and approved of 'because it provides free access to books and information and learning, which have positive connotations in our society'.[81]

Of course, in their day-to-day lives most people do not perceive themselves as constantly searching for information, and many would argue that they are bombarded with too much information already or, in the words of Andre Brink, 'the problem is . . . the babble of too many voices'.[82] An important role, therefore, for the public library is to help people obtain information that is relevant to their circumstances and enables them to have more control over their lives: in short, to provide information that relates to political power.

Political power takes many forms and the political purpose of the public library is often defined by the decisions taken by national and local governments. As we have seen, this can be used to promulgate directly the ideologies of those in power. More often, the public library is expected to aid the democratic process by providing access to a range of opinions, promoting free expression and providing information to help people cope with the issues they face in their everyday lives. In some circumstances the library is expected to promote equality of access by providing for needs and making special efforts to satisfy the requirements of the disadvantaged.

At the heart of the public library movement is the idea of a just information society, a society that guarantees the disadvantaged, as well as the advantaged, access to information, ideas and works of imagination. It is a service that provides people with the opportunity to play a more effective part in their society and to improve their own situation and that of their children. Public librarians can claim, on the basis of their own experience and independent research in the field, that they have an important part to play in promoting the values of a democratic society. They can help to democratize knowledge and that is a significant political function. It remains to be seen if, at a time when 'our society is . . . being shaken by profound changes and great uncertainty',[83] the profession is willing and able to perform it in the years to come.

REFERENCES

1   Potter, D., *Seeing the blossom. Two interviews and a lecture*, London, Faber and Faber, 1994, 14

2   Budge, H. D. , The public library service, *In:* Rose, B. (ed.), *The councillor's work*, London, Charles Knight, 1971, 83–7

3   Office of Arts and Libraries, *Press Notice OAL/53*, 18 September 1986.

4   Shavit, D., *The politics of public librarianship*, Westport, Conn. Greenwood Press, 1986 (New Directions in Information Management, No. 12).

5   Do Amamal, S. S., 'Library services for social development some considerations', *IFLA journal*, **21** (1) 1995, 19– 25.

6   See, for example, Adam Smith Institute, *Ex libris*, London, ASI, 1986.

7   Quoted in Bundy, A., Preface to Hazell, A. (ed.), *Access and equity. Challenges in public librarianship*, Adelaide, Auslib Press, 1992, i–v.

8   UNESCO Public Library Manifesto 1994, *IFLA public library news. Newsletter of the section of public libraries*, **12**, January 1995.

9   Strunsky, S., *No mean city*, New York, E. P. Dutton, 1944, Ch .2.

10   Quoted in Koefoed, I., *A cornerstone in the democratic development*, Paper delivered at the 14th Anglo-Scandinavian Public Libraries Conference, Viborg, Denmark, 1994.

11   Lunden, I., *A friend in need – is a friend indeed*, Paper delivered at the 14th Anglo-Scandinavian Public Libraries Conference, Viborg, Denmark, 1994.

12   Aslib, *Review of the public library service in England and Wales for the Department of National Heritage. Final report*, London, Aslib, 1995, 155.

13   Newton, K. and Karran, T. J., *The politics of local expenditure*. Basingstoke, Macmillan, 1985, 56.

14   Bundy, M. L. and Stielow, F. J., *Activism in American librarianship*, New York, Greenwood, 1987, 1.

15   O'Kelly, J., *The political role of public libraries*, Brighton, John L. Noyce, 1977.

16   *Lenin and library organisation*, Moscow, Progress Publishers, 1983, 10.

17   Quoted in Hafner, A. W. and Sterling Folker, J., 'Democratic ideals and the American public library', *In:* Hafner, A. W. (ed.), *Democracy and the public library*, Westport, Conn., Greenwood Press, 1993, 9–43.

18   Stieg, M., *Public libraries in Nazi Germany*, Tuscaloosa, The University of Alabama Press, 1992, 21.

19   Kershaw, I., 'Herr Hitler man of the volk', *The Guardian*, 22 April 1995, 21.

20   Stieg, M., *Public libraries in Nazi Germany*, Tuscaloosa, The University of Alabama Press, 1992, 181.

21   Muddiman, D. and Black, A., *The public library policy and purpose*, Bournes Green Comedia, 1993 (Comedia Working Papers. The future of public library services, Working paper 9).

22   City of Manchester Cultural Services, 'Services to ethnic minorities', Mimeographed document, undated.

23   Sheffield District Labour Party, *1984 Manifesto*.

24   Bundy, M. L., 'The social relevancy of library education: an accounting', *In:*

Bundy, M. L. and Stielow, F. J., *Activism in American librarianship*, New York, Greenwood, 1987, 83–97.

25 This quote from a prison education officer was included in a working paper prepared as part of Tony Stevens' Doctoral studies at The Department of Information Studies, The University of Sheffield.

26 Hutton, W., *The state we're in*, London, Jonathan Cape, 1995, 9.

27 Comedia, *Borrowed time? The future of public libraries in the UK*, Bournes Green, Comedia, 1993, 39–40.

28 White, L., *The public library in the 1980s*, Massachusetts, Lexington Brooks, 1983.

29 Norton, B., *Charging for library and information services*, London, Library Association Publishing, 1988, 12 (Viewpoints in LIS 1).

30 Aslib, *Review of the public library service in England and Wales for the Department of National Heritage. Final report*, London, Aslib, 1995, 27.

31 Frankena, F. and Frankena, J., 'The politics of expertise and the role of the librarian', *Behavioural and social science librarian*, Fall/Winter, 1986, 39.

32 Roszak, T., *The cult of information*, Cambridge, Lutterworth Press, 1986.

33 *From vision to action. Info-society 2000. Statement to Parliament on 'Info-Society 2000' and IT Political Action Plan 1995*, Denmark, Ministry of Research and Information Technology, 1995, 39.

34 Tullis, S. E., Summation of Peter Young's remarks to Federal Depository Conference (Public Libraries and the Internet/NII) provided to multiple recipients of list, GOVDOC 14 April 1995.

35 Hughes, R., 'Take this revolution . . . ', *Time*, Special Issue, Spring, 1995, 70–1.

36 *Ibid*.

37 Office of Arts and Libraries, *Financing our public service: four subjects for debate*, Cmnd 324, London, HMSO, 1988.

38 Adam Smith Institute, *Ex libris*, London, ASI, 1986.

39 Mill, J. S., *Utilitarianism. Liberty and representative government*, London, J. M. Dent & Sons, 1948.

40 Wesker, A., 'Roots', *In*: Wesker. A., *The Wesker trilogy*, Harmondsworth, Penguin Books, 1967, 147–8.

41 Audunson, R., *Public library management in a changing political environment: the quest for institutional leadership*, paper presented at 14th Anglo-Scandinavian Public Libraries Conference. Viborg Denmark, 1994.

42. Hafner, A. W. and Sterling Folker, J., 'Democratic ideals and the American public library', *In*: Hafner, A. W. (ed.), *Democracy and the public library*, Westport, Conn., Greenwood Press, 1993, 9–43.

43 Chu, J., 'Self development of public libraries in China. The current situation and some problems', *Library review*, **43** (8), 1994, 40–4.

44 Kolodziejska, J., *Five years of freedom in culture in the Polish experience* paper presented at the IFLA General Conference, Havana 020–READ-4-E, 1994.

45 Hutton, W., *The state we're in*, London, Jonathan Cape, 1995, 196.

46 Aslib, *Review of the public library service in England and Wales for the Department of National Heritage. Final report*, London, Aslib, 1995, 211–25.

47   Walsh, K., *Public services and market mechanisms*, Basingstoke, Macmillan,1995, 252–3.

48   Marquand, D., 'Labour's new model army', *The Guardian*, 26 May 1993, 18.

49   Hutton, W., *The state we're in*, London, Jonathan Cape, 1995, 218.

50   Edgar, D., 'Are you being served?', *Marxism today*, 28 May 1991, 28.

51   Sheffield and Loughborough Universities currently have a joint research project looking at Quality Management and Public Libraries.

52   Kaufmann, G., speaking in a House of Commons debate on the Citizen's Charter 13 February 1995.

53   Aslib, *Review of the public library service in England and Wales for the Department of National Heritage. Final report*, London, Aslib, 1995, 133–7.

54   American Library Association, Office for Intellectual Freedom, *Intellectual freedom manual*, Chicago, American Library Association, 1974.

55   Oboler, E. M., *Defending intellectual freedom: the library and the censor*, Connecticut, Greenwood Press, 1980.

56   Jones, F. M., *Defusing censorship. The librarian's guide to handling censorship conflicts*, Phoenix, Oryx, 1983.

57   Quoted in Serebnick, J., 'Self censorship by librarians: an analysis of check-list based research', *Drexel library quarterly*, **18** (1), 1982, 35–56.

58   Cole, N., *Intellectual freedom and the public library; professional and public perceptions*, unpublished dissertation, The University of Sheffield, 1994. Some of the literature used in the preparation of the present paper was drawn to my attention by this dissertation.

59   Young, H., 'Middle America's loud voice of hate', *The Guardian*, 23 May 1995, 13.

60   'American survey. The politics of blame', *The Economist*, **335** (7912), 29 April 1995, 59–60.

61   Berman, S., 'Let it all hang out', *Library journal*, 15 June 1971, 2054–8.

62   Cole, N., *Intellectual freedom and the public library; professional and public perceptions*, unpublished dissertation, The University of Sheffield, 1994.

63   Ceserani, D., 'Bad and dangerous', *New statesman and society*, 10 July 1992, 19–20.

64   Katz, J., 'Revisionist history in the library: to facilitate access or not to facilitate access?', *Canadian library journal*, **48** (5), 1991, 319–24.

65   Stieg, M., *Public libraries in Nazi Germany*, Tuscaloosa, The University of Alabama Press, 1992, 21.

66   Potter, D., *Seeing the blossom. Two interviews and a lecture*, London, Faber and Faber, 1994, 15.

67   Garceau, O., *The public library in the political process,*. New York, Columbia University Press, 1949, 116.

68   Quoted in Dougherty, R. M., 'The opportunity to empower: ALA, children, and reading', *American libraries*, February 1991, 176–9.

69   Emerek, L., 'The future of public libraries', *In:* Verwer, R. *et al* (eds.), *The future of librarianship. Proceedings of the 2nd international Budapest symposium, January 1994*, Amsterdam, Hogeschool van Amsterdam, 1994, 97–102.

70   Haywood, T., *Info-rich info-poor. Access and exchange in the global information society,*

London, Bowker Saur, 1995, 181.

71 Williams, R., *Television, technology and cultural form*, London, Fontana/Collins, 1974.

72 Joeckel, C. B., Winslow, A. and Martin, L., *National plan for public library service*, Chicago, American Library Association, 1948, 16.

73 Thatcher, M., *The Downing Street years*, London, Harper Collins, 1993, 626. (The author refers to an interview she gave to 'a woman's magazine'.)

74 Comedia, *Borrowed time? The future of public libraries in the UK*, Bournes Green, Comedia, 1993, 56.

75 Usherwood, B., *Public library politics*, London, Library Association Publishing, 1993.

76 Quoted in Usherwood B., *Public library politics*, London, Library Association, 1993, 104–5.

77 Sturges, P. and Barr, A., ' "The fiction nuisance" in nineteenth century British public libraries', *Journal of librarianship and information science*, **24** (1), 1992, 23–2.

78 Adam Smith Institute, *Ex libris*, London, ASI, 1986.

79 Aslib, *Review of the public library service in England and Wales for the Department of National Heritage. Final report*, London, Aslib, 1995, 126.

80 *Ibid*, 11–12, 169–72.

81 Hafner, A. W. and Sterling Folker, J., 'Democratic ideals and the American public library', In: Hafner, A. W. (ed.), *Democracy and the public library*, Westport, Conn., Greenwood Press, 1993, 9–43.

82 Brink, A., 'A tough life in a free regime', *The Guardian*, 21 August 1993, 25.

83 Aslib, *Review of the public library service in England and Wales for the Department of National Heritage. Final report*, London, Aslib, 1995, 43.

AUTHOR'S NOTE

I also wish to acknowledge the following work which drew my attention to some relevant literature: Rogers, J., *Will a Freedom of Information Act make Britain a more democratic society?* (unpublished dissertation), The University of Sheffield, 1993.

❖ Index